Contents

THE NEW
Teaching Elementary Science

SECOND EDITION

WHO'S
AFRAID
OF
SPIDERS?

THE NEW
Teaching Elementary Science

SECOND EDITION

WHO'S
AFRAID
OF
SPIDERS?

Selma Wassermann
and J.W. George Ivany

TEACHERS COLLEGE PRESS

Teachers College
Columbia University
New York and London

Published by Teachers College Press, 1234 Amsterdam Avenue, New York, NY 10027

Library of Congress Cataloging-in-Publication Data

Wassermann, Selma.
    The new teaching elementary science : who's afraid of spiders? /
Selma Wassermann, J.W. George Ivany.—2nd ed.
      p.   cm.
    Rev. ed. of: Teaching elementary science. 1st ed. 1988.
    Includes bibliographical references and index.
    ISBN 0-8077-3512-4 (pbk)
    1. Science—Study and teaching (Elementary)   I. Ivany, J. W.
George, 1938–   . II. Wassermann, Selma. Teaching elementary
science. III. Title.
LB1585.W29   1996
372.3'5044—dc20   95-41119

ISBN 0-8077-3512-4 (paper)

Printed on acid-free paper

Manufactured in the United States of America

03 02 01 00 99 98 97 96   8 7 6 5 4 3 2 1

Preface

In the brief six year period since the first edition of *Teaching Elementary Science: Who's Afraid of Spiders?* was published, science and technology have taken a giant leap into the future. The original manuscript was written on an electric typewriter. That machine, considered state-of-the-art at the time, is now buried in the attic, like some dinosaur relic of a prehistoric time.

The universities at which we teach are moving to implement the "virtual university" that involves the use of information/computer technology, including telelearning for the advancement of educational effectiveness. The virtual university concept will make use of teleconferencing and the more interactive forms of computer-aided learning that will extend instruction far beyond face-to-face classrooms. The mind-boggling information superhighway allows for instant information access to topics that are encyclopaedic in range. E-mail and FAX have taken over "snail mail" as more preferred means of instant communication. No waiting, no stamps to lick.

When Alvin Toffler wrote in 1970 that the pace of change was accelerating, many of us had difficulty appreciating his admonitions. Now, 1970 seems like ancient history. We are today, as Toffler warned, in an "abrupt collision with the future."

While life all around us is moving at e-mail speed, quality science teaching in elementary classrooms marches forward in painful half-steps, like snail mail. The American Association for the Advancement of Science (AAAS) document, *Science for All Americans*, published in 1990, reports that

> A cascade of recent studies has made it abundantly clear that by both national standards and world norms, U.S. education is failing too many students. . . . The nation has not acted decisively enough in preparing young people . . . for a world that continues to change radically in response to the rapid growth of scientific knowledge and technological power. (p. 3)

Clearly, not enough attention has been focused on the quality of instruction in science in the elementary schools. What's more, the preparation of elementary teachers is still found wanting in the areas of science and technology, leaving many teachers at a loss in bridging the gap between the theoretical constructs offered in university classes, and the application of effective strategies that promote scientific literacy in young learners.

It was our hope that the first edition of *Teaching Elementary Science* would provide a resource for classroom teachers to develop students' knowledge, attitudes, and skills that would prepare them to become more scientifically literate. By articulating a clear theoretical framework, coupled with accessible teaching strategies, we hoped that teachers who felt unprepared for and intimidated by teaching science would be helped to cross the bridge to more effective, more satisfying, more joyful science teaching experiences. Virtually all of the feedback we have had from both preservice and inservice teachers in the last seven years has suggested that those hopes were not unfounded. Teachers and prospective teachers have told us that this text has helped them to understand better how science might be more effectively taught, and it has provided them with tools and resources that allow them to translate these understandings into classroom practice. Wherever we have met with teachers who have used this book, they have told us the same story: "These teaching strategies work! Children love this way of learning science! I'm losing my own fears and learning to love science teaching!"

In writing this new edition, we have kept much of the "stuff" that has demonstrably worked for teachers thus far: the emphasis on investigative play, or "sciencing" as a way for children to think about and do science that builds conceptual understanding about scientific phenomena; the focus on "debriefing," the classroom discussion that helps children make connections and promotes scientific literacy; the extensive collection of resources and activities that are easily applicable to classroom use. We have, however, made some important changes—additions that we hope will make the book even more useful. The recent work done by the AAAS, with its emphasis on the development of "scientific literacy," has been articulated with our own vision of sciencing. Current literature and research in science education, cooperative group work, and constructivism are now explicit reference points for what we have proposed. The use of portfolios in student assessment has also been incorporated into the chapter on evaluation. The identification of the "big ideas"—those important science concepts that are being examined and investigated in each activity—have been identified for all 60 activities. There is an added emphasis on the technology side of science, since it is in this area that major breakthroughs have occurred in the past dozen years. Helping children to become more scientifically literate is now explicitly identified as a key goal. By adding these new dimensions to the text, we hope that we will have increased its value and its effectiveness for teachers and teacher educators.

There is still more work that we, as educators, need to do to satisfy the demands and expectations of a radically changing and increasingly complex world. But we still very much believe that *Teaching Elementary Science: Who's Afraid of Spiders?* in its new and updated edition offers teachers useful information and practical help to take giant steps toward more effective science teaching.

Many significant contributions made to the first edition continue to enrich what we have done here. To Drs. John Wormsbecker and Stewart Martin, and to all the teachers and children in the Vancouver classrooms where the original research was carried out; to Heather Hamilton, Marti Edwards, and Susan Sheremeta, whose classroom work contributed to the development of the instructional model; to members of the research team, Neil and Maureen McAllister, Pat Holborn, Fiona Crofton, Rob Henderson and Harold McAllister; to Dennis Smith for his drawings; to Christ Hildreth and Linda Hof, for the live-action photographs—our heartfelt thanks once again.

In putting this new edition together, several people have made singular and valuable contributions to our thinking and to the writing of the text. Allan MacKinnon and Wendy Lim, our colleagues at Simon Fraser University, reviewed the manuscript and made suggestions that helped extensively in our reconceptualization of the changes that were made. Marge Sato looked after details of xeroxing the manuscripts and was ever faithful in making the extensive arrangements required for two "at-distance" colleagues to meet. Ronna Lee Stefan spent hours in the library to review new references and put together an updated bibliography for our use. Jack Wassermann, with his keen editorial eye, refined the list of big ideas for Chapter 4 and kept us on the mark with respect to clarity and scientific accuracy. Susan Liddicoat, our esteemed and excellent editor, once again sheparded this work from draft to book. To all, our gratitude and affection.

THE NEW
Teaching Elementary Science

SECOND EDITION

WHO'S
AFRAID
OF
SPIDERS?

chapter

1

Teachers, Children, and Science: Theoretical Perspectives

THIS BOOK IS FOR TEACHERS

In recent years science has been singled out as a much neglected area in the elementary school curriculum. From kindergarten through sixth grade, science education is perceived as "in deficit" with respect to its scope, its confusion of purpose, and the inadequacy of methods of instruction. Elementary school consultants complain that science materials, purchased to complement classroom texts, are left to gather dust in hallway closets; that emphasis in classroom teaching is on the collected wisdom of an assortment of science texts, the content of which has been substantially watered down to meet various objections of the most vocal local interest groups; that in some classrooms, science teaching is virtually nonexistent. The charge has been made that students are graduating from school as scientific illiterates.[1]

No doubt some of the charges are extreme. Yet many of them strike home. Look into these classrooms. In one, Sean, a bright fifth grade boy, is describing an aspect of the evolutionary process by stating that "the feet of fish turned into fins—which took about a hundred years." In another, Sally fills out a science worksheet, answering such questions as "The sea is made of *salt* water." In a third, when Neil tells his teacher that his "experiment" did not lead to the "correct" results, the teacher tells him to do it again so that it will.

It is much too easy to blame teachers for such deficiencies. After all, haven't teachers been made the scapegoats for virtually every societal malaise? If children are not learning, isn't it the fault of teachers everywhere? It is far easier to assign blame to teachers than it is to identify and come to terms with the profound, complex, and multidimensional factors at the roots of the problems.

This book is on the side of teachers. We have made the assumption that most teachers are in the profession for one important reason: to help children grow and learn. We also assume that teachers work very hard at their jobs and that most of them teach to the very best of their abilities. We carry these assumptions several steps further. We believe that teachers *want* to teach science effectively but that they are handicapped by inadequate preparation in professional coursework and insufficient background of experience with science. One cannot teach what one does not know. Ideas *about* teaching science are not so easily translated into classroom practices. As a consequence, many teachers are fearful of the subject. Science is too full of unknowns. Electric current sizzles. Bunsen burners are potential fire hazards. Spiders and other creepers are yucky. It's much safer to keep these things at arm's length, to stay within the clearly defined and protected domains of textbook exercises and pencil-and-paper worksheets.

There are other reasons. In the last recent history of educational reform, when "back to basics" became the educational cause célèbre, such revisionist policies took a heavy toll in their neglect of science (and other "nonbasics") in favor of excessive emphasis on phonic, spelling, and arithmetic drills. Science became a curriculum stepchild, implicitly cast out of the front lineup of what was educationally valued.

Curriculum is very much like the weather in London. If you wait a little while, conditions are bound to change. Now, once again, science is at the forefront of our thinking.[2] What's more, this very recent concern combines with widespread attention to the development of pupils' thinking skills. Given these shifts in our current educational priorities, is it possible that we may provide some help to teachers who deeply and genuinely share our concerns about the improvement of their classroom science programs? Is it possible that we can make clear the kinds of teaching methods that will result in pupils' learning science, with a full appreciation of this extraordinarily rich and exciting field of study? Is it possible that we can help teachers overcome some of their entrenched fears about science, tempt them into taking some initial steps, and see them through the development of a successful classroom program? We certainly hope so—for these are our goals in writing the new edition of this book.

PERSPECTIVES ON SCIENCE AND SCIENCING

Scenario A: Teaching Science

The teacher stands at a table on which she has set a magnet and a small collection of objects—some metal, some wood, some plastic. The children are seated around the table, watching and listening as she explains.

TEACHER: *(holding up the magnet)* What is this thing I'm holding?

STUDENTS: *(in chorus)* A magnet.

TEACHER: Yes. It's just like the one in the picture in your book. Remember we were reading about magnets? Now what is going to happen if I bring the magnet close to these things, like this? *(She lowers the magnet toward a metal ball and the ball "jumps" toward the approaching magnet and sticks fast.)*

STUDENTS: *(talking all at once and some shouting)* It will stick. It attracts things.

TEACHER: *(managing the behavior)* Now, you know the rules. One at a time, please. Yes, Martin.

MARTIN: The magnet sticks to the ball because it's metal, but it won't stick on the wood and stuff.

TEACHER: That's right. Martin is right. Remember how we read in the book that magnets attract some things? We call them "magnetic." Metals are often magnetic. That's why the ball is attracted. But let's see what happens with the wood. What do you think is going to happen?

STUDENTS: *(in chorus)* Nothing.

TEACHER: See—you are right. Nothing happens! Wood is not magnetic. Here *(she holds out the single magnet),* some of you try these other objects.

STUDENTS: *(There is some noticeable movement within the group and some talking together, while several students take turns moving the magnet around among the objects. After a few moments the teacher stops the activity.)*

TEACHER: I'll tell you what we are going to do. Let's make a list of all the objects and place them in two columns. We'll label the first column "Magnetic." *(She writes "Magnetic" on the chalkboard.)* We'll label the second column "Nonmagnetic." *(She writes this too.)*

The activity concludes as the teacher elicits from the students the names of the objects that belong in each column.

Scenario B: Learning Sciencing

A group of six children are working together around a table on which the following materials are found: a bag of ice cubes, newspapers, a ruler, balance scales, several plastic dishes and other containers, a small digital clock, a hammer, scissors, nails, and a dish of coarse salt. The teacher's goal for this activity is to provide opportunities for the pupils to carry out investigations that will promote increased awareness of the properties of ice, under several variable conditions. She observes what the pupils are doing from a discreet distance. Sonia and Mark have placed three ice cubes on the balance scale.

SONIA: *(to Mark)* Weigh them. Tell me how much they weigh. I'll write it down.

PHILLIP: *(Dips an ice cube into the dish of coarse salt and sets it down on another dish.)* I'm going to see how long it takes this to melt. *(He records the time.) (Heather and Angela have wrapped some ice cubes in newspaper. Heather hits the wrapped ice with the hammer.)*

ANGELA: *(Opens the paper and finds the ice is crushed.)* Look at this. Let's see how long this takes to melt. *(They note and record the time.)*

WALTER: *(observing Heather and Angela)* It's going to melt faster, you know. It melts faster when it is crushed.

ANGELA: *(to Walter)* Let's see if it does. Here, I'll put these four ice cubes in this dish, and I'll put the crushed ice in this dish. Then we can see which goes faster. You may be right, Walter. I think you could be right.

HEATHER: Look at this. There's little drops of water already around the crushed ice, but there's hardly any water in the ice cube dish.

WALTER: If you put it on the heater, you'd really get some melting.

The children continue with their self-initiated investigations for about 20 minutes, until the teacher calls for a cleanup. Notes of their investigations are gathered while the table is cleared and the materials are put away. The teacher calls the group together, and they come to her with their notes. Using teaching-for-thinking questioning strategies, she will work with the students to help them extract meanings from their investigative play experiences. She begins by asking them to tell her about the observations they have made about the ice cubes.

Science Versus Sciencing

To know science is not merely to learn the words, the names of science. It is not merely to know that water boils at 212°F or that Mercury is the planet closest to the sun. It is not merely to know that spiders are not insects or that bees make honey. It is not merely to know the names of parts of a flower or that the human heart has four chambers and pumps blood. Although emphasis on the names of science has been a preoccupation of science teaching, it is only the merest fragment of what real science is actually about. Lewis Thomas, in his book *The Youngest Science,* writes this about science:

> Making guesses at what might lie ahead, when the new facts have arrived, is the workday business of science, but it is never the precise, surefooted enterprise that it sometimes claims credit for being. Accurate prediction is the accepted measure of successful research, the ultimate reward for the investigator. Convention has it that prediction comes in two sequential epiphanies: first the scientist predicts what the experiment says about future experiments—his, or someone else's. It has the sound of an intellectually flawless acrobatic act. The mind stands still for a moment, leaps out into midair at precisely the millisecond when a trapeze from the other side is hanging at the extremity of its arc, zips down, out and up again, lets go and flies into a triple somersault, then catches a second trapeze timed for that moment and floats to a platform amid deafening applause. There is no margin for error. Success depends not so much on the eye or the grasp, certainly not on the imagination, only on the predictable certainty of the release bars to be caught. Clockwork.
>
> It doesn't actually work this way, and if scientists thought it did, nothing would get done. There would be only a mound of bone-shattered scholars being carried off on stretchers.
>
> In real life, research [in science] is dependent on the human capacity for making predictions that are *wrong* and on the even more human gift for bouncing back to try again. This is the way the work goes. The predictions, especially the really important ones that turn out from time to time to be correct, *are pure guesses. Error is the mode.* . . . To err doesn't really mean getting things wrong; it means "to be in motion." In order to get anything right, we are obliged first to get a great many things wrong.[3]

"Science," the way it has often been taught, emphasizes what is *known*—the naming and the labeling of certain bits and pieces of information. Such an approach is unidimensional, moving from what is already known into the heads (and, it is hoped, minds) of the pupils. For example, magnets attract metal objects; the sea is made of salt water; air exerts 14.7 pounds of pressure per square inch; mammals are warm-blooded animals. This picture of science teaching is that of a body of knowledge, well delineated and utterly without equivocation, from which all the profound implications of hypothesizing, of tentatively held concepts, of experimentation, have been extinguished. There is no margin for error; answers are either right or wrong. We carry on pseudo investigations to "find" what has already been found. If a pupil has done an "experiment" that doesn't provide the expected results, she is admonished to try it again until it does. The prevailing attitude is *not* to err; we are in fact penalized for it. The most important goal in teaching science is to know the "facts." The concern is with product.

"Sciencing" by contrast, begins with a different attitude about both the content of what is being taught and the context in which it is taught and learned. It is not by chance that the term *sciencing* appears in the present participle form, making it sound as if it is in motion. Sciencing is being in motion; it describes a generative process, the basis of which is inquiry, exploration, examination—all "in-motion" activities. Sciencing is a creative act, and as an act of creation it is by nature messy. It involves manipulation of data—trying things that do not work and "bouncing back to try again." The essence of sciencing is on playing with variables: Will this work? Maybe it will. I'll set up the test and see what happens. Say, it's not working. I wonder what will happen if I try this instead?

Sciencing involves making predictions, setting up an experimental design in which hypotheses are tested, gathering data, making observations, examining results, and evaluating their validity. In sciencing, the emphasis is on finding out. We don't look for the answers we already know.[4]

In the landmark work on the reform and restructuring of science education generated under the auspices of the American Association for the Advancement of Science, the authors make clear that the acquisition of scientific knowledge does not necessarily lead to an understanding of how science works. In teaching science, "emphasis should overwhelmingly be on gaining experience with natural and social phenomena and on enjoying science." It is by "gaining lots of experience *doing* science, becoming more sophisticated in conducting investigations and explaining their findings" that children can accumulate those concrete experiences that enable them to reflect on the process.[5]

Sciencing calls upon the ability to use several higher-order thinking skills: observing; comparing; suggesting and testing hypotheses; gathering and classifying data; interpreting and evaluating results.[6] We would like to suggest that science plus thinking equals sciencing.

As the content and the context of science and sciencing are different, so are the observable results. When children learn only science, they might leave school with a collection of names and labels, some of which may even be correct. But without the added dimension of thinking, without being actively engaged in the process of sciencing, they will not be able to apply principles to new situations, interpret data intelligently, observe accurately, test hypotheses, evaluate data, or even more important, learn what all scientists must know in order to be successful: how to fail and keep trying.

From work in sciencing, on the other hand, we expect that pupils will become competent to chart unexplored terrain. We expect that they will become experienced as investigators—learning to think, to take cognitive risks, to predict and test, to evaluate wisely and thoughtfully—and through the process gain and use scientific knowledge more effectively. It is through the process of sciencing that we may hope to expect the breakthroughs that vastly enhance the quality of our lives on this planet and that will allow us to understand in fuller measure the extraordinary demands of living in a scientifically and technologically driven world.

Implications for Classroom Practice: The Play-Debrief-Replay Instructional Model

What does all of this mean for the elementary school teacher? How are these ideas (to which many teachers already subscribe) to be translated into the day-to-day operation of the classroom? In this book we offer an instructional model that encompasses the principles of sciencing in a way that is practicable even for teachers with a limited background in science. Through this model, we expect that the noble goals of producing scientifically literate pupils may more readily occur.

The instructional model of teaching science, which we call Play-Debrief-Replay, is a constructivist approach to learning, rooted in the principles of sciencing. "People have to construct their own meanings regardless of how clearly teachers or books tell them things. Mostly a person does this by connecting new information and concepts to what he or she already believes."[7] As a curriculum model, it is not complicated, nor is it difficult to implement. It does not require massive expenditures of funds; nor does it require a sophisticated background in physics, chemistry, or biology. The data we have gathered suggest that effectively implemented, this model can both broaden pupils' knowledge base and develop their skills as scientific inquirers.

The Play-Debrief-Replay model resulted from our work with classroom teachers in Project Science-Thinking.[8] Twenty teachers tested instructional strategies in which the principles of an effective sciencing program could be carried out. As we observed and worked with them in their classrooms, we were able to develop and refine the instructional model. We are the first to admit that this particular approach is not the only way to develop

pupils' skills in science; other plans and science programs also bear serious consideration.[9] We nevertheless offer ours as one approach that may be effectively used to promote the scientific literacy we all say we want for children.

Play is the first stage of the sciencing experience. It is during this stage that the teacher creates the conditions in which scientific understandings may grow. During the Play stage, pupils carry out investigative play in cooperative learning groups with materials provided. Investigative play is in fact the equivalent of scientific investigation.

During Play, students are actively involved in learning, in which they manipulate experimental variables; generate hypotheses; conduct tests; observe, gather, classify, and record data; examine assumptions; and evaluate findings. During Play, children also reflect on their investigations and make decisions about worth and value, about what should be done and why.

Play provides the tangible, sensory experiences on which children's scientific concepts are built. Through play, they "grow in their ability to understand abstract concepts, manipulate symbols, reason logically and generalize,"[10] while at the same time acquire important information. During play, children conduct their own inquiries; the teacher refrains from directing their investigations. If the teacher does intervene, it is primarily to facilitate the children's own inquiries.

When Play is concluded (this period may vary from 15 to 30 minutes), the teacher calls the group together for the Debriefing session. The term *Debriefing* is used to describe how the teacher (or group leader) assists the group in reflecting on their experiences to help them construct meanings from those experiences. During Debriefing, the teacher elicits from the pupils what they have observed during their investigations. This is done through the use of reflective questioning strategies, which promote pupils' thinking about their observations and relate their findings to science concepts.[11] Such questioning strategies enable pupils to reconsider what they have observed, to reflect on data gathered and conclusions drawn, and to think more analytically about new hypotheses to be tested. Effectively done, Debriefing enables students to use their observations to heighten conceptual awareness, to construct meanings, and to extract scientific principles underlying their investigations. Effectively done, Debriefing also lays the groundwork for carrying out subsequent inquiries with the same materials.

At the next sciencing opportunity, the pupils Replay with the same materials. Sometimes, investigations already carried out will be repeated, promoting healthy respect for replicating results. Often the reflective questions posed during the Debriefing session will stimulate new explorations. "Students cannot learn to think critically, analyze information, communicate scientific ideas, make logical arguments, work as part of a team, and acquire other desirable skills unless they are permitted and encouraged to do these things over and over in many contexts."[12] The sciencing process of Play-Debrief-Replay is cyclic—very much like what is seen in actual laboratories with real scientists at work. Only the materials that pupils use are more rudimentary.

The process allows students to create meanings, to construct knowledge based upon understandings of phenomena observed through investigation,[13] which are further refined and shaped in the examination of ideas during Debriefing. This process permits the learner to discard persistently held, naive theories formed through earlier experience (i.e., the earth is flat), and replace them with more sophisticated and intelligent constructs.

In the remainder of this chapter, the principles on which the Play-Debrief-Replay instructional model is based are made more explicit. They should help teachers come to terms with what we believe are some prior questions regarding classroom implementation of this model—for example, questions of congruence between what is being proposed and a teacher's belief system about pupils and how they learn, about the role of play in school, about the development of thinking skills, about the content and context of teaching science. A teacher will not choose an instructional model that is discrepant with that teacher's beliefs about these dimensions of teaching, no matter how good the plan, and we think it is of utmost importance for teachers to begin by examining the "goodness of fit" between what is being proposed here and individually held beliefs. If a teacher's beliefs are congruent with the principles, the matters of classroom implementation may be addressed. Chapters 2, 3, and 4 are devoted to making the implementation of this instructional model as explicit and potentially helpful as possible.

In the final chapter, Chapter 5, we raise in advance some of the "yesbuts"—the kinds of questions teachers are likely to ask as they consider some of the problems involved in implementation. We hope that through such a discussion, we can alleviate some anxieties, identify some misconceptions and assumptions, and provide yet additional information with respect to classroom practices.

We do not guarantee that successful implementation will result in teachers' all-out love for spiders. We do not expect the spider to become the national class pet. But based on our work with many teachers, we can ensure that the Play-Debrief-Replay approach to sciencing can generate an enthusiasm for the subject that is considerable in both students and teachers and promote the kind of growing and learning in science that we all value in our classrooms.

PERSPECTIVES ON CHILDREN

Scenes from the Classroom

The children are sitting on the carpet, studying a series of photographs depicting scenes from birth to old age. The teacher says, "Tell me what you see."

CHARLES: I see him here, where he's a baby. Here's where he's a little boy playing and going to school. Here's where she's growing up and getting married and here's when she's a grandma.

DONALD: Uh-uh, Charles. You can't say that. You can't say, "Here's where *he's a* little boy and here's where *she's* getting married"! When you're *born* a boy, you *die* a boy.

Some of the others nod in vigorous agreement, except for Fancy, who shakes her head from side to side.

TEACHER: Tell me, Fancy, what do you think? You seem to have another idea.
FANCY: Well, that's not right, you know. If you want to change, you can.
TEACHER: *(ever so gently)* And how would you do that, Fancy?
FANCY: Well, you just go to the doctor and *(thumps her chest)* tell him to change your stuff!

There are no biological creatures more wonderful than young children. A living, breathing set of paradoxes, they are at once both in the present and in the future; they are full of sweet innocence yet crafty as old con artists, outrageously silly yet deadly serious, short on experience and unequivocal about what they know, gently loving and demonically mischievous, fiercely independent yet afraid of monsters, unselfconscious yet needing adult approval. They are vigorous, demanding, excessive, frustrating, and exhausting—but never boring. What's more, their capacity to be frank is disconcerting: "Say, Mrs. Meyer, how come you've got those little hairs growing out of your nose?"

If you can keep up with the pace, it is a gift to teach young children, for they will bestow on you their greatest treasures—their most intimate secrets, their hearts' desires, the depths of their feelings—as older children are less able to do, their innocence having been traded for experience. In the primary years, children's curiosity to know is unbounded, and their zest for learning seems limitless. Often this ceaseless quest to know takes the form of an endless run of questions: "How come?" "But why?" "How?" "Where?" "What will happen?"—the questions that try our souls. Yet this fervor for learning is the greatest capital of the primary teacher. To harness this energy and to convert it into productive and significant learning without diminishing its intensity or spirit—ay, there's the rub.

The intermediate-grade teacher has other capital. Older children have a greater capacity to understand. "Don't disturb us unless it is an emergency" is a clear directive that needs no extensive explanation. Their vocabulary base is large, and the range of their experience greater. They have seen the Grand Canyon and can speak knowledgeably of its depth. While they are wise in their years—for example, they know there is no Santa Claus—they still cling to idealistic hopes of what a superhero can do in righting the world's wrongs.

They have learned much more to curb their impulses; they begin to see relationships between means and ends, between action and consequence. They have even learned some social graces. A 6–year-old sibling, offering his teacher a Christmas gift and saying, "This handkerchief is for you, but don't blow your nose in it because it cost two dollars" will get a punch in the arm for such a serious social gaffe. Older children are learning responsibility—to clean up their rooms, to help with the chores, to bicycle to the store to fetch another quart of milk—but they have not learned to love it. They covet their independence fiercely but despise the means by which it is attained.

The older elementary child is a many-splendored gift. Personal identities and values have become more solidly formed: "I have my rights," Steven insists, stomping his feet, to let us know that he is disgusted at being taken advantage of. Older elementary children are much more wary in their acceptance of adults; you must work to win their affection and respect. But having won their hearts, they are exceedingly loyal, unremittingly generous. "My teacher" is the arbiter of the highest court, and "My teacher says so," the final word at the dinner table.

Most intermediate grade children are action-oriented and would rather be participants than observers. Participation strengthens their sense of "can do" and their egos, and there are few things that they won't try at least once. Logic is both their strength and the chink in their armor; they will use it to their advantage in reasoning yet must also allow it as a way of confronting their outrageous demands. These intermediate years are the last of the precious years of childhood, before self-consciousness sets in, like hardening of the arteries, by gonads run amok. Teachers who are lucky enough to work with children at this age level will find them frustrating and fascinating; the greatest challenge is to protect and cultivate their individuality while at the same time bringing each into full membership with his or her social group.

Children Today

Several dozen scholarly tomes over the past 30 years have dealt in depth with the developmental history of children. Each informs us in detail about their physical capabilities, their physical limitations, their social-emotional development, their intellectual expertise, the range and extent of their individual differences in each of these developmental areas, and how these differences profoundly influence children's abilities and their styles of learning.[14] However, more recent writings point to some new and alarming trends in the development of today's child. Such works as Neil Postman's *The Disappearance of Childhood*, David Elkind's *The Hurried Child*, Marie Winn's *Children Without Childhood*, Vance Packard's *Our Endangered Children*, Valerie Suransky's *The Erosion of Childhood*, Alex Kotlowitz's *There Are No Children Here*, Joshua Meyrowitz's *No Sense of Place: The Impact of Electronic Media on Social Behavior*, and Sylvia Ashton Warner's *Spearpoint* urge us to examine the effects of today's culture on the developmental stages of childhood.[15] Each of these authors writes about major observable changes in the behavior of children, seen as early as the primary years, which may signal, in Postman's phrase, "the disappearance of childhood." If these data tell us anything at all, it may be that teachers are facing greater challenges than ever before in their struggle to protect the natural growth and development of the children in their classes.

Implications for Teaching

To consider a curriculum plan without first considering to what extent that plan reflects our knowledge of children may be asking for trouble. Successful curriculum building is very much tied in with what we know about children and how they learn. The more we know and the more perceptively we know, the better are we able to conceptualize, to organize, to gather the appropriate materials, to deliver the curriculum experience. The dozen principles we include in this discussion represent what we have extracted from the literature on children and how they learn. They are also closely tied to the principles of effective teaching and learning described in Chapter 13, "Effective Learning and Teaching," in *Science for All Americans*.[16] They are presented here to establish the developmental guidelines that inform our instructional model. The list is not exhaustive, but the principles included here are at the very bedrock of our own beliefs about the effective and healthful growing and learning of today's elementary school children.

   We suggest that readers of this text begin their own studies in curriculum implementation by first asking, "To what extent do I believe this?" with respect to each of the principles identified. Such self-examination would, first of all, enable each of you to become clearer about where you stand with respect to each of the beliefs. You would also become strengthened in the affirmation of personally held beliefs. Such examination might also prevent you from "signing on" to a science program that would be, in its philosophical core, very different from your own philosophical base. When this beliefs-identification process can occur for teachers, it paves the way toward classroom practices that are more in harmony with each teacher's educational values and reduces the tension that is likely to arise out of the discord of a clash of beliefs.

Principles of Child Development

1. *Every child is different.* Therefore, a curriculum plan for a science program must provide for individual differences in learning capabilities and learning styles. A curriculum plan that treats all children as one child makes it virtually impossible for many children to learn successfully. [To what extent do you believe this? To what extent is this belief in evidence in your classroom practice?]
2. *Each child brings the sum total of his or her life experience to each learning task.* Therefore, children whose life experiences have been rich need a curriculum that is rich in order to sustain and challenge their interest. Children whose life experiences have been meager and restrictive are even more in need of a curriculum that is rich and full in order to compensate for the deficits. [To what extent do you believe this? To what extent is this belief in evidence in your classroom practice?]
3. *Children are naturally gregarious. They thrive in a socially active environment.* Therefore, curriculum experiences must provide for extensive social interaction among children. Through these social interactions language learning is enhanced, problem-solving and decision-making skills are exercised, and personal responsibility grows.

Curriculum experiences that insist on silence, enforce isolation, and forbid social interaction are counterproductive to normal growth. [To what extent do you believe this? To what extent is this belief in evidence in your classroom practice?]

4. *Each child has a distinctly different and unique concept of self as a person and as a learner.* Therefore, a curriculum in science must ensure that each child is enabled and no child diminished in the process of learning. Learning experiences that instill fear and feelings of failure militate against productive and significant learning. [To what extent do you believe this? To what extent is this belief in evidence in your classroom practice?]

5. *Most elementary-age children are action-oriented and require firsthand experiences to gather data and form concepts.* Therefore, a curriculum in science must be founded in active, experiential learning if conceptual understanding is to grow. Curriculum experiences that require children primarily to sit still and listen are physically and psychologically inappropriate to learning science. [To what extent do you believe this? To what extent is this belief in evidence in your classroom practice?]

6. *Gender differences do not influence children's ability to love science.* Therefore, a curriculum must provide equal opportunity for boys and girls to have happy, successful, and productive experiences with science learning. A science curriculum that favors boys' involvement contributes to the diminishing of girls' abilities and attitudes toward science. [To what extent do you believe this? To what extent is this belief in evidence in your classroom practice?]

7. *Most elementary-age children, while largely dependent in many ways, want and need to function on their own power. Such autonomous functioning is imperative in their growth toward psychological health and feelings of empowerment.* Therefore, curriculum experiences must encourage growth toward personal autonomy and independent functioning. Children learn to be independent by practicing independence; they learn responsibility by practicing being responsible. A curriculum that fosters and perpetuates children's dependency disables and diminishes their capabilities and their self-esteem. [To what extent do you believe this? To what extent is this belief in evidence in your classroom practice?]

8. *Children have a great need to understand their world, to make sense of what is happening around them. They tend to interpret new data in terms of what they already know.* Therefore, curriculum experiences in science can provide many opportunities for children to broaden their understanding, by observing, touching, smelling, listening, and testing their ideas to see what works. Such curriculum experiences broaden a child's experiential base and contribute to the formation of conceptual frameworks into which new data may be integrated. A science curriculum that bypasses the experiential aspects of learning and relies primarily on pencil-and-paper tasks emphasizing the accumulation of miscellaneous information impoverishes scientific experience; it also presents a distorted view of what science actually is. [To what extent do you believe this? To what extent is this belief in evidence in your classroom practice?]

9. *Most children in today's world have fewer multisensory experiences. A great deal of children's time is spent with electronic media—television, computer games, Nintendo.*

Therefore, a science curriculum should provide extensive opportunities for children to experience directly and to carry on investigations with a variety of primary media. Curriculum experiences that are largely two-dimensional and rely heavily on technological media contribute to the increased sensory deprivation of children. [To what extent do you believe this? To what extent is this belief in evidence in your classroom practice?]

10. *Many children are expressing deep concerns and fears about war, violence, death, and the uncertainty of the future.* Therefore, a science curriculum can be seen as a means of using knowledge and human resources to improve world conditions. It can provide children with a sense of control over their lives and their future. [To what extent do you believe this? To what extent is this belief in evidence in your classroom practice?]

11. *Children need to be respected and intellectually challenged if they are to grow up developmentally sound.* Therefore, a curriculum plan for science should preserve and protect the dignity of each child, as well as stimulate children's interest and enthusiasm for science and thinking. Curriculum experiences that diminish children and extinguish their natural curiosity for wonder and for scientific experimentation damage children for all time. [To what extent do you believe this? To what extent is this belief in evidence in your classroom practice?]

12. *Children learn sciencing and thinking by doing sciencing and thinking.* Therefore, curriculum experiences must provide many opportunities for children to engage actively in sciencing and thinking. Learning *about* science and allowing the teacher to do most of the thinking is inadequate to do the job. [To what extent do you believe this? To what extent is this belief in evidence in your classroom practice?]

PERSPECTIVES ON PLAY

> We all learn by experience, but some of us have to go to summer school.
>
> PETER DE VRIES

The pendulum of educational reform movements switches us back and forth between extreme positions on the curriculum spectrum as often as we let it. In education, as in no other profession, these switches are largely initiated by public outcry, and in education, as in no other profession, defensive reactions on the part of school personnel trigger the switches. Consequently, classroom activities are vulnerable to the whims and caprices of those whose voices are the loudest and who have the greatest vested interests.

What saves us from complete and total chaos is the insistence of many of us on the use of educational research to inform educational change. And though our research methodology may be far from perfect and in some instances the data may be inconclusive or even contradictory, the process of using the best available data to inform our educational decisions is heartening.

The role of play in children's learning has received more than its share of pushes and pulls. In an earlier era, influenced by the work of John Dewey, play was viewed as "children's work" and recognized as an important medium in children's learning.[17] Play was a natural condition in the primary grades; in the later elementary years, "activity programs" made extensive use of hands-on experiences in the language arts, social studies, math, and science curricula. When public outcry over *Sputnik* forced a major pendulum swing, play and "activity programs" became suspect, and teachers were encouraged to stop "wasting children's time" and to *teach* more and at earlier stages of life. Out went the sandbox and the blocks as frivolous, and teachers in the middle grades who insisted on experiential play as a basis for learning did so at their own peril. Copious workbook exercises and other sitting-down pencil-and-paper tasks became the established order of the day.

Pulled once more by a newly emerging view of these seatwork activities as "mindless and crippling,"[18] the curriculum pendulum swung wide, and play was once again sanctioned and affirmed as imperative for the healthful growth and developmental learning of children. Hardly had we gotten the sandbox back in place when the back-to-basics advocates cast play in a villainous and hedonistic role. We found ourselves once more wrestling with demands of "direct instruction," "formal teaching," increased "time on task," and extended school days to "cover" more and more subject matter—all of which was to be tested and examined with a rigorous battery of short-answer, information-based standardized tests, classifying the children like eggs: jumbo, large, medium, small, and cracked.

Fortunately for teachers who have been knocked back and forth by public opinion enough times to make their sandboxes spin, we may now call on some hard empirical evidence to support the importance of play for enhancing children's learning. In examining the relationship between the role of play and the problem-solving capabilities of children, Jerome Bruner, Harvard's distinguished cognitive psychologist, reported his research findings:

> The group of children who had the opportunity to engage in previous free play with creative materials were better prepared to solve the subsequent problems that experimenters presented to them than were the groups of children who were (a) allowed to handle, but not play with the materials; (b) were only shown the principles underlying the solutions by an adult.[19]

Although research data are not likely to change the opinions of those whose minds have already been made up, they may at least provide some ammunition for teachers who have held fast to their belief in the importance of play in children's learning.

Additional data to support the importance of creative play in the socio-psychological development of young children came from the work of Sylvia Ashton-Warner, whose book *Teacher* became a classic in early childhood education. In it, she described the need for play as imperative not only in fostering children's creativity but also in reducing destructive impulses:

> I cannot disassociate the activity in an infant room from peace and war. So often I have seen the destructive vent, beneath an onslaught of creativity, dry up under my eyes. Especially with the warlike Maori five-year-olds who pass through my hands in hundreds, arriving with no other thought in their heads other than to take, break, fight and be first. With no opportunity for creativity they may well develop, as they did in the past, with fighting as their ideal of life. Yet all this can be expelled through the creative vent, and the more violent the boy, the more I see that he creates, and when he kicks the others with his big boots, treads on fingers on the mat, hits another over the head with a piece of wood or throws a stone, I put clay in his hands, or chalk. He can create bombs if he likes or draw my house in flame, but it is the creative vent that is widening all the time and the destructive one atrophying. . . . With all this in mind, I try to bring as many facets of teaching into the creative vent as possible. And that's just what organic teaching is; all subjects in the creative vent.[20]

It was the British infant school movement that opened our eyes to the dynamic interface of children's play and the promotion of inquiry-type learning, collapsing the traditional view of work and play as separate entities in the cognitive development of children and enabling us to see how a curriculum might be organized around such ideas.[21]

Featherstone was among the first to note that this work-play environment, where children were free to conduct experiments and continuous inquiries, was conducive to promoting higher-order thinking capabilities.[22] In the British infant school, teachers use the work-play context to engage children in the tasks of observing, comparing, suggesting hypotheses, testing ideas, solving problems, making decisions, evaluating procedures—providing many opportunities for the children to develop skill in these higher-order mental functions.

Play is, of course, the main avenue of creativity and imagination, "one of the most highly valued of human qualities,"[23] its role in the intellectual, social, personal, and physical development of children supported by abundant research.[24] According to Einstein, creativity is far more consequential than knowledge in furthering the significant advances of humankind. The creation of new ideas does not come from minds trained to follow doggedly what is already known. Creation comes from tinkering and playing around, from which new forms emerge, like the geodesic dome, the dymaxion car, the theory of relativity, the Fallingwater House at Bear Run, and the first airplane of Orville and Wilbur Wright. "If I don't play with it, how can I understand it?" Richard Feynman, Nobel Laureate in Physics, remarked of his work on the motion of mass particles that ultimately led to the Nobel Prize.[25]

In earlier days, imaginative play was one of the foremost activities of children. If not in school, it was evident in the make-believe world of sand-castle building; of "good guys and bad guys" scenarios; in dress-up plays in the basement or the backyard; in paper dolls and doll houses and firefighters' hats. As children, we learned to be dreamers, and in our dreams flourished the images that shaped our lives. Of leaves we created fairy costumes; of dolls we created queens; of stories in books, we imagined fantastic pretend worlds as real as any we knew.

Children today have far fewer opportunities to live in the life of the mind. "In the place of traditional childhood games that were still popular a generation ago, in the place of fantasy and make-believe play . . . today's children have substituted television"[26] as well as Nintendo and other computer games. In kindergarten, children may prefer "creative daydreaming" to coloring stenciled pumpkins orange, but the teacher, to be held accountable, is already preparing them for the arduous work of first grade with more and more trickle-down pencil-and-paper activities. With such limited opportunity to tap a child's creative imagination, and with such a counterproductive set of forces in motion, what kinds of adults are today's children likely to become? And what kind of world are they likely to create? "Scientists, mathematicians, and engineers prize the creative use of imagination. The science classroom ought to be a place where creativity and invention—as qualities distinct from academic excellence—are recognized and encouraged."[27]

Today's children play computer games in the amusement arcade instead of stickball in the sandlot. They choose computer camp for holiday fun, and they ask for Power Macs for Christmas. If TV is contributing to the "disappearance of childhood," how will the computer age affect the creative vents of children? Is it possible that today's children may be more urgently in need of play activities than ever before?[28]

Implications for Classroom Practice

The data about play in relationship to children's healthful development and academic learning have important implications for the classroom teacher. They suggest classroom practices that need our most thoughtful consideration. Here are some principles emerging from the literature and research that point to action:

- Research data provide evidence of the importance of play in children's cognitive development.
- Exploratory-investigative play activities enable children to grow to a fuller, richer understanding of their world.
- Exploratory-investigative play experiences promote children's problem-solving capabilities and give children practice in decision making.
- Creative play promotes the healthful psychosocial development of children.
- Creative play encourages the development of fantasy and imagination, the primary sources of innovation and invention.

Translated into classroom practices, these principles underscore the need for increased emphasis on play—on children's active involvement with a variety of media—as being at the very core of their learning in science in the elementary grades.[29]

PERSPECTIVES ON TEACHING FOR THINKING

MYLORA: What did you learn in school today, Nelson?
NELSON: We're not learning anything, Mylora. We're just developing cognitive skills.

The children sit quietly with impeccable good manners around the table. They are well groomed in their designer jeans and expensive haircuts. But their stylish appearance does not divert from the apprehension in their eyes. The teacher removes a card from a large box of thinking activities and offers it for their study.

"How do you suppose pigeons can be trained to deliver messages?"

They are clearly stumped, and there is a long, pregnant silence, after which Sharon timidly queries, "Could you tell us what you mean?"

The teacher repeats the question, unwilling to play into their transparent ruse of soliciting clues to "the answer." The repeated question again draws silence. Finally, Des mumbles, "We didn't study birds yet."

Kevin, a little more bold, tentatively offers, "A pigeon trainer?" He forms his answer as a question to protect himself from the possibility of having gotten it "wrong."[30]

These elegant, finely coiffed, stylish children are having a great deal of trouble thinking for themselves. Within the parameters of their standard grade 4 curriculum, they are considered the "good" students. And observably, they are quite good at performing the hundreds of school exercises that require single, correct answers. However, when it comes to a task that calls for imagination, for suggesting hypotheses, for connecting means with ends, for taking some cognitive risks, for extending their thinking into new territory, they flounder and fail.

How does this occur? How can it happen that bright young minds become so narrowed in their functioning that creative thinking and intelligent problem solving are tasks quite beyond their comfortable reach? Why is it that in spite of all our affirmations about the importance of higher-order thinking, it is the least exercised skill in many of today's classrooms?[31]

There Is Thinking and There Is *Thinking*

Higher-order thinking means the ability to function in certain more sophisticated mental tasks. Like learning other skills, these higher-order thinking skills need to be developed through frequent practice. Without adequate practice, cognitive or any other type of skills do not have sufficient opportunity to grow and develop. When teachers provide a lot of practice in lower-level mental operations like arithmetic calculations, spelling drills, and fill-in exercises, pupils learn to become expert at these more rudimentary tasks. Unfortunately for us, ability to perform these lower-level skills does not transfer to the higher-level tasks of *thinking*. A person practicing typing does not automatically transfer typing skills to writing a literary masterpiece. Pupils practicing memorization of facts cannot transfer this expertise to creative problem solving. If you want to learn to be a writer, you have got to practice writing. If you want to become a successful problem solver, you have got to have a lot of experience doing problem solving.[32]

In his seminal text *Teaching for Thinking: Theory, Strategies, and Activities for the Classroom,* Louis Raths's presentation of a theory of thinking helps us to understand how these ideas are applied in the classroom. Children who have had limited opportunity to exercise their thinking skills in the higher mental operations show this deficit in certain observable behavioral patterns, such as extreme impulsiveness (moving into action before thinking about what is to be done); very dogmatic behavior (insisting one's idea is right even in the presence of contradictory evidence); rigidity in their ideas (the inability to move from the more comfortable systems into new frameworks); an inability to connect means with ends; an inability to comprehend ("I don't get it!"); an inability to take the next step, remaining dependent on the teacher for direction ("I'm stuck. What shall I do now?"); and a lack of confidence in their ability to put forth new ideas. When these behaviors are seen as consistent patterns in our pupils, we may begin to hypothesize that they have occurred as a result of insufficient opportunity to think. These children have had too much practice with the lower-order mental tasks of remembering and recalling—tasks that require single, "right" answers and depend on the storage and retrieval of information. They have had too little practice in processing information, in applying principles to new situations, in creating and imagining, in making decisions, and in analyzing consequences of those decisions.[33]

Raths's theory goes on to explain how children who receive practice in the higher-order functions learn to give up their counterproductive thinking-related behavioral patterns. Raths's ideas have been tested in more than a dozen empirical studies, at almost every grade level from primary through secondary school, and the supporting evidence is very substantial.[34]

What, then, does a teacher have to do to join that group of teachers who have learned to put an emphasis on thinking in their classrooms? What must a teacher do to diminish those counterproductive thinking-related behaviors and work instead to help pupils develop into more autonomous, more creative, more self-initiating people, who have increased confidence in their ability to think for themselves?

Teaching for Thinking and Classroom Practice

To help students grow as thinkers, it is necessary that teachers (a) use more curriculum materials that call for higher-level thought and (b) emphasize the kinds of teacher-pupil interactions that require students to exercise those higher-level mental functions.[35] What's more, the use of such materials and such interactions must play a major role in the life of the classroom. If teaching for thinking is a truly valued educational goal, these teaching materials and instructional strategies must be woven into the entire fabric of the curriculum. It is inadequate that they be left to casual inclusion or to fill the time on an empty Friday afternoon.

Instructional Materials   John Goodlad, in his study of schooling, examined a large assortment of textbooks and other instructional materials and quizzes used by teachers.[36] These curriculum materials, gathered from over 1000 classrooms across the United States, revealed an overemphasis on activities that "require low-level cognitive responses." In other words, instructional materials that rely primarily on memorization and recall of information play the most dominant role in what the teacher is teaching and in what the pupils are learning. It should come as no great surprise that children have become very expert at low-level cognitive functioning, since they are practicing these skills day after day, in class after class.

Overthrowing the reigning curriculum materials monarchy is, like the difference between canned soup and homemade, neither difficult nor complicated; it is merely a matter of knowing how. Converting lower-level tasks into activities that are more intellectually challenging is the teacher's first job, and that begins with knowing the difference between the two.

Lower-level activities require pupils to come up with single correct answers. These tasks may involve recall of information, arithmetic calculation, or selecting an answer from among a list of given alternatives. In working on lower-level activities, thought is directed toward coming up with the one answer that will be considered correct by the teacher. Intellectually challenging activities, by contrast, are concerned with promoting the process of analysis and reflection. Intellectually challenging activities are open-ended and allow for many different answers that are appropriate and acceptable.

For example, in a lower-level activity, pupils may be required to calculate the distance a letter travels from Chicago to Vancouver. In a more intellectually challenging activity, pupils may be asked to develop hypotheses to explain why it had taken two weeks for an airmail letter mailed from Chicago to arrive in Vancouver. In this task, the focus is on examining many possible alternative explanations. No single "correct" answer is sought.

Completing ten math examples, practicing spelling words, and selecting the correct word to complete a sentence are some examples of lower-level activities. Comparing squid and oysters, observing the swing of a pendulum, hypothesizing about how a pencil sharpener works, and inventing a new toy are examples of more intellectually challenging activities. A more detailed description of how to develop intellectually challenging activities for an elementary school sciencing program is found in Chapter 4.

Words of caution: We are not suggesting here that teachers should never require students to work at activities that require "right" answers. What we are suggesting is that if the goals of teaching for thinking are to be realized, such activities must not play the dominant role in the classroom but must instead take a back seat to activities that concentrate on developing the higher-level mental functions.

Teacher-Student Interactions   Goodlad's study of schools also shed light on the ways in which teachers question and respond to their pupils. In most classrooms he found very little emphasis on teacher-student interactions altogether. In fact, teachers were found to do most of the talking, with teacher-student interactions playing a minor role. However, even within this minor role, the interactions showed emphasis on questions that ask pupils to recall specific information and aim at having students come up with the specific answers the teacher seeks.[37]

> TEACHER: What's the name of the animal that has a pouch?
> PUPIL: Kangaroo.
> TEACHER: Right.
> OTHER PUPIL: What about the koala?
> TEACHER: That's right, but for now we are only going to consider the kangaroo.

It is not wrong for teachers to expect children to know that kangaroos have pouches. Yet when this type of interaction is the staple of the children's cognitive diet, opportunities for children's thinking are seriously reduced. Thinking is restricted to the level of dealing with "inert ideas—ideas that are merely received into the mind without being utilized or tested or thrown into fresh combinations."[38]

Teaching-for-thinking interactions require the teacher's use of questions and responses that call for students to reflect on their ideas, to make deeper analyses of their ideas, and to take cognitive risks in extending their thinking into new realms of inquiry.[39] An interactive dialogue that follows this approach might look like this:

TEACHER: Tell me what you see in this picture.

FRANK: Houses.

TEACHER: Say a little more about that, Frank.

FRANK: Well, there are two kinds of houses. One is made of wood, it looks like. And the other is made of concrete, it looks like.

TEACHER: You are saying that one house looks like it is made of wood and the other house looks like it is made of concrete. That suggests that you are not certain.

FRANK: I'm pretty sure. But you can't be positive, you know. Pictures can be misleading.

TEACHER: It's hard to tell for sure. I see. Thank you, Frank. Does anyone have any other observations to make about the houses?

ANN: It looks like one house is where one family might live. The other house looks like many families might live there.

TEACHER: What clues in the photograph suggest that one is a single-family residence, while the other is a multiple-family dwelling?

ANN: Well, for one thing, the building on the left is larger. Much larger. If just one family lived there, it would have to be a pretty big family. *(She laughs.)*

TEACHER: So the size of the building suggests that it would be suitable for many families.

ANN: Uh-huh.

TEACHER: Are there other observations that you'd care to make?

JOANNE: It looks to me as if this house *(points)* is in a city somewhere. The other *(points)* looks as if it is in the country.

TEACHER: You are making comparisons about where the houses might be located.

JOANNE: Yes. I can't see this house *(points)* in the country.

TEACHER: It's not likely that you'd find a house like that in the country.

JOANNE: Yeah.

TEACHER: Do you have some ideas to explain why such a house might not be easily found in the country?

JOANNE: Well, for one thing, there's a lot more land to build in the country. That house is a city house—where you have a little space, and you have to build close together to use the space you have.

TEACHER: So your hypothesis is concerned with the amount of space needed for building. I see. Thank you, Joanne. Does anyone have some other hypotheses that either support or contradict Joanne's idea?

An interactive dialogue that would be more restrictive of children's thinking might look like this:

TEACHER: Tell me what you see in the picture.

ROB: Houses.

TEACHER: How many houses do you see?

MICKEY: Two. There are two houses.

TEACHER: What do you notice about the house on the left *(points to the multiple-family dwelling)?*

AARON: It's bigger than the other one.

TEACHER: What do you mean by bigger?

AARON: Well, it's taller, and fatter *(laughs)*.

TEACHER: What else does it mean when a house is bigger?

MARK: Well, it takes up more space.

TEACHER: Does anyone have another answer?

KIM: It's got many more rooms.

TEACHER: Speak up, Kim. Let's all hear your answer.

KIM: More rooms.

TEACHER: Put your idea in a whole sentence, Kim.

KIM: It's got more rooms.

TEACHER: Well, what does that mean?

PATSY: More people can live in it.

TEACHER: Very good, Patsy. That's exactly right. More people can live in this house, as you can see from the size of it. It's called a multiple-family dwelling—that means that it can accommodate several families—whereas the house on the right side of the page can accommodate only one family.

JACKIE: I don't know. There's a house that size on my block and several families live in it.

TEACHER: That's different. It's still a single-family residence, Jackie.

There are, unfortunately, no shortcuts to unlearning one style of questioning and responding to pupils and learning a different style in its place. An entirely different attitude and set of expectations is called for, as well as an entirely different repertoire of verbal responses. The ways to accomplish this are not difficult, but they do require practice over time, beginning with an undistorted examination of current interactive functioning and a step-by-step movement toward new response patterns. For those who would embark on such a course of action, a program of self-help materials is included in Chapter 3.

Implications for Classroom Practice

- Learning to think intelligently, like learning to read intelligently, requires substantial time on task. Teachers who want their students to become thinkers must provide them with substantial time on task in higher-order mental functioning. Children do not become skillful at these higher-order operations as a by-product of learning to add, spell, or remember facts.
- When teachers give children intellectually challenging curriculum tasks, rather than lower-level activities, they are giving children opportunities to practice higher-order mental functioning. Intellectually challenging activities should receive more classroom emphasis than lower-level activities if children are to develop habits of mind. Activities that stress single "correct" answers should take the back seat to more intellectually challenging tasks.
- A teacher's classroom interactions may work to promote pupil inquiry and give pupils more practice in being reflective. Teacher-student interactions should call for pupils to reflect, analyze, hypothesize, give examples, and process information. Interactions that stay at the level of asking pupils to recall factual information and "lead" pupils to the "right" answers are actually limiting to the higher-order processes.
- Teachers who wish to emphasize teaching for thinking in their classrooms need to begin by examining closely the curriculum materials and the classroom interactions currently in use. It would be helpful for teachers to calculate the percentage of time pupils spend on lower-level activities, compared to the time spent on intellectually challenging tasks. Teachers might also install a tape recorder in the classroom and listen to the amount and kind of teacher talk in any given 30-minute instructional period.
- When teachers work to emphasize teaching for thinking in their classroom practices, children's "thinking-related behaviors" diminish, and they grow in their ability to function independently and maturely. Teachers who wish to assess the progress of children as thinkers may do so through the close and systematic observation of children's behavior. Behavioral measures adapted from the text *Teaching for Thinking: Theory, Strategies and Activities for the Classroom*[40] have been provided for this purpose in the appendix.

Teachers who wish to embark on a course of action learning to become teachers of thinkers may begin by examining their teaching practices closely and by using the materials provided in this text to grow and change. As in learning any new skills, the success of this growth process is largely dependent on teachers' willingness to commit themselves to study, to practice, and to the critical analysis of their classroom performance. As in learning other new skills, growth toward mastery takes energy, commitment, self-confidence, and time.

PERSPECTIVES FROM THE CLASSROOM

Main Street splits Bay City into two zones, like east and west L.A., with rites of passage just as formidable. In the western zone, the large, stately homes and the tree-lined streets speak of Old World and old money. Once you cross the mainline, traveling east, the symbols of affluence dissipate. In Bay City, the west is orderly, Scots-Presbyterian, and white; the east is multihued and redolent of garlic and coriander. If the west is the power pocket of the city, the east is its heart.

Marti E. teaches at the Fifty-ninth Avenue School, deep in the eastern zone. It is an old school, with none of the accouterments of contemporary design—no rambling suburban clusters, no green lawns, no softening of the effect of institutionality. Just your basic red brick, three-story building, straight out of the 1930s. Marti, a veteran teacher, was the last to join the school staff, and she found that her classroom had become the "dumping ground" for other teachers who availed themselves of the chance to unload their unwanted kids on the newcomer. As Marti embarked on her teaching program, she certainly did not have the deck stacked in her favor.

Although the pupils were far from the intellectual elite of the school, and although Marti had more than her share of children with "behavior problems," she was nevertheless committed in her belief that given the "right" conditions, these children, too, could grow and learn. Starting from square one just made the job that much more difficult.

In the first few months, Marti emphasized interpersonal functioning and helped the children learn to work productively with each other in small cooperative learning groups. It was not easy. But her behavioral standards were clear and consistent, her discipline never punitive and always fair. Underlying all of her work was the calm and clear communication of her caring, her warmth, her respect for the dignity of each of the children, her explicit belief in their ability to grow and learn. Inch by painful inch, the children learned to work responsibly, productively, and skillfully. In this climate Marti embarked on her sciencing program. Her approach emphasized investigative play—active hands-on manipulation of a variety of science materials, cooperative groupwork, intellectually challenging science activities, and classroom interactions emphasizing higher-order questions and responses.

Midway into the school year, classroom routines had been successfully established, and the children's abilities to work together responsibly, in small groups, were clearly observable. Though the children's behavior had initially been troublesome, there was little evidence of extreme behavioral difficulties. In fact, the children's engagement in their sciencing activities was energetic and productive, their experimentation with the materials imaginative and spirited. It was a matter of some surprise to visitors that children coming from home environments that were largely unsophisticated in terms of educational backgrounds and aspirations gave themselves so enthusiastically to their inquiries. To expect less of any children is to do them a vast disservice.

Marti announces the beginning of the afternoon's sciencing program and organizes the approach to the work centers. There are five work centers operating today, and each will accommodate a group of five children. Each group of five will have a chance to work in three different centers this afternoon. At the end of the sciencing period, all the groups will move to the carpeted area for a debriefing session. In the days following this debriefing, sciencing at these centers will continue, for as many sessions as interest in the activities of the center is sustained.

These are today's work centers:

1. *Siphoning.* Center contains two buckets, plastic tubing in varied lengths and diameters, and water.
2. *Magnets.* Center contains bar and horseshoe magnets, iron filings, and a variety of metal and nonmetal objects.
3. *Floaters and sinkers.* Center contains two plastic tubs filled with water and a variety of objects including pieces of wood, modeling clay, plastic bottles and cups, sponges, chestnuts, toothbrushes, pieces of styrofoam, and a funnel.
4. *Sound.* Center contains tuning forks, buckets of water, rocks, string, elastic bands, and bottles.
5. *Observing.* Center contains a large, hairy spider in a glass jar and some magnifiers.

After the groups of children have moved into their work centers, each group begins work by deciding on the procedures to be used during their inquiries. These arrangements are discussed and decisions made without adult supervision. When the procedures have been clarified, the group's sciencing activity begins. In all the centers, emphasis is on investigative play in cooperative learning groups, and although activities may include observing photos and pencil-and-paper thinking activities, most of the activities involve children's active engagement with the tasks. As a part of each activity there is a requirement that children record the observations they have made during their exploration and manipulation of the materials. At the end of each group's activity in the center, all pupils participate in the cleanup, making the area ready for the next group's entry.

A visitor to the classroom observes the five centers in dynamic operation, and the room is filled with the noise of scientific explorations under way. The teacher moves from group to group observing the children's activities, but she intervenes only occasionally, sometimes simply to reflect what is occurring. She generally does not raise challenging questions at this time, for they are likely to redirect the children's thinking away from their own sciencing explorations and toward the teacher's view of how the inquiry should proceed. It is important to note that Marti's responses to the children's investigations are neither judgmental ("Oh, isn't that good!") nor directive or leading ("Why don't you try it this way and see what happens?"). They are instead reassuring ("Well, the water has spilled, but I'm sure you will find ways to clean it up"), affirming ("Yes, I can see how you have worked that out"), and reflective ("I can see you've got the water moving out from the higher bucket into the lower bucket").

If we were to observe the activity in one center closely, we see the amalgam of children's science explorations and play emerging as one activity: sciencing. Five children working at the floaters-and-sinkers center are placing objects into the water in both tubs. Discussion ensues over the plastic lid, which at first floats, then sinks. The children remove the lid from the water and place it in again several times to see if the floating-sinking pattern persists. More discussion ensues over how this particular item is to be recorded. Each item is subject several times to a similar "floating-sinking test." The objects are then classified: all the "sinkers" into tub 1 and all the "floaters" into tub 2. Sam and Harpreet are in consultation over the recording of the items. On the recording sheet, Harpreet writes *clay, toothbrush, and eraser* in the "Sinkers" column. Sam writes *Styrofoam, bottle, and sponge* in the "Floaters" column. Edward, Raj, and Mei are continuing their manipulation of the materials. They start to build constructions with the objects in tub 2 to determine how many floating objects can be piled on top of each other and still remain floating. This problem is not made explicit, but it appears to be implicitly understood as the working problem, and inquiries continue. Edward then begins to manipulate the modeling clay in tub 1 and shapes it into a bowl. He reinserts it into the tub and it sinks. He takes it out and continues to reshape it, testing it in the water each time until it has a shape that floats. "Hey," he exclaims to the others, "look at this. When you put the modeling clay into this shape, it floats." In science language, Edward has tested a hypothesis, gathering data from several field trials, each of which was unsuccessful. He continued and found that his hypothesis was eventually supported. The other children observe the floating clay bowl, and some of them begin to test other shapes. Sam flattens the modeling clay into a large pancake shape and watches it sink to the bottom of tub 2. What is occurring in this sinking-and-floating center is scientific experimentation in microcosm: observing, predicting, testing and retesting of hypotheses, gathering of data, the manipulation of experimental variables, the rechecking of data, the recording of data, the consultation among peers. Through these hands-on explorations, conceptual frameworks grow.

Sciencing along similar lines is occurring in each of the other centers as well, as children construct meanings, incorporating new ideas into their conceptual frameworks, making connections, and thereby making better sense of their worlds.[41] In none of the centers does the teacher redirect children's thinking away from their own self-initiated inquiries.

When the hands-on, investigative Play is concluded for the day, the children gather in a group on the carpet for Debriefing. It is now time for the teacher to ask the children about their explorations and to use this discussion as a vehicle for promoting deeper reflection and analysis of what was observed. Marti's use of questioning and responding strategies encourages students to express their thoughts in a climate of safety. She asks them to examine their ideas from a variety of perspectives. The debriefing works to solidify some of the findings of the sciencing inquiries, to raise new questions, to raise doubts about potential theories, and to invite possibilities for further experimentation. In the spirit of scientific inquiry, no single "correct" answers are sought, nor does the teacher attempt to "get the students to learn a specific concept." It is rather the process of examination of phenomena observed during Play that is given emphasis, so that children may extract meaning from their experiences. Implicitly, the children are encouraged to tolerate ambiguity, to entertain tentative judgments, and to examine alternate hypotheses.

In the sciencing inquiries of the days that follow, children may choose to repeat some of the experiments that they or others have done. Or they may choose to begin new explorations that flow from the discussions in the debriefing session. In this brief scenario lies the potential for the construction of a model for teaching science, integrating the dimensions of science, play, and the cognitive development of children. We call this Play-Debrief-Replay constructivist model *sciencing*.

The Play-Debrief-Replay Instructional Model

The Play-Debrief-Replay instructional model is grounded in the belief that investigative play in learning science is a major contributor to children's cognitive growth and to the development of their conceptual understanding of science. Data from studies of children's play suggest that not only are conceptual understandings promoted but also that this occurs much more substantially through play than through direct systematic instruction.[42] Play, moreover, invites and encourages creativity and invention, builds self-initiative, and provides for recurring practice of skills. It has been observed that children's play with science materials closely resembles the creative activities of scientists at work in their laboratories; studying science as a way of knowing.[43]

In the sciencing program, children's play with science materials may reflect work in physics, chemistry, biology, geology, zoology, mathematics, or combinations of these subjects. The teacher sets out the equipment with which inquiries are to be made. This is usually done with some articulated goals for conceptual development in mind. Some ground rules set the behavioral standards and expectations. A specific time interval is allotted for the sciencing explorations. Although materials and content may vary, certain conditions are maintained:

First, play with science materials is generally carried out in small cooperative learning groups. The teacher is the best judge of how many and which children make up a successful working group.

Second, when the children are at play, behavioral standards are explicit. The teacher ensures that behavioral expectations for productive group work are met. The procedures for ensuring socially acceptable behaviors are never punitive or demeaning to the self-concept of any child. (More about how this is done is found in Chapter 2.)

Third, when children are involved in investigative play, the teacher is cautious about intervening in ways that might lead the pupils away from their own inquiries and into realms that are subtly dictated by the teacher's concerns. The data gathered in Project Science-Thinking indicated that when teachers intervened in students' group work, pupils abandoned their own investigations in favor of what they thought the teacher wanted them to do or ceased investigation because they were unable to respond to a teacher's poorly timed challenging questions.[44] Interventions that seem to facilitate pupils' investigative play include reflective responses ("Yes, I can see you've tried many ways to put that together"), reassuring responses ("You seem to be having a hard time figuring it out, but I think you will find a way"), and affirming responses ("You really worked hard to figure that out!"). Interventions that seemed counterproductive to investigative play included responses that challenged too early in the process ("Why do you suppose that worked?"), responses that led the investigation into a certain direction subtly commanded by the teacher ("Why don't you try mixing the oil and the water and see what happens?"), and responses that rewarded the children's efforts, either positively or negatively ("That wasn't a very smart thing to do, Hugo" or "Look at the way Hugo has classified his rocks. Now that's a really good idea!").

A more appropriate time for the teacher to help pupils dig more deeply into the various aspects of their sciencing explorations follows the play activities. In the debriefing sessions following Play, the teacher promotes analysis of the phenomena observed, stimulates conceptual awareness, promotes healthy skepticism, excites imagination, challenges ideas, and asks for data to support developing theories. This is done by making it safe for every child to volunteer ideas without fear of rejection, by welcoming and appreciating children's contributions, by showing keen and genuine interest in all discoveries. Analyses are encouraged through the use of questions: "What are the supporting data?" "How was that discovery made?" "How did you figure that out?" "Why do you suppose that particular strategy worked?" "How might you account for that?"

In the discussion, new hypotheses emerge, discoveries are examined and explored. But no closure is brought to the debriefing session, and the inquiries are left "suspended" so that there is increased motivation for the children to continue the explorations in Replay.

During Debriefing, emphasis is on extracting meaning from the investigative play. When the teacher calls the children to this discussion, once again ground rules for appropriate and acceptable group behavior are made explicit. Debriefing sessions are generally held immediately after Play. The following guidelines are suggested for more effective discussion:

- All ideas volunteered by the children are accepted and acceptable. In order for the teacher to make it safe for the children to express their thoughts, no child's statement is counted as "wrong" or "right," "good" or "bad."
- The teacher's interactions work to promote further examination of the ideas presented, that is, to help a child to "process" an idea. This is done by reflective responses and questions that require the children to examine particular dimensions of their ideas.
- To promote additional inquiry about the sciencing explorations, the teacher uses questions and responses that allow for further cognitive processing of the child's ideas. The teacher avoids seeking answers or leading pupils to "learn" specific pieces of information.
- When teachers "talk too much" or try to articulate the children's ideas for them, children's opportunities to think for themselves are diminished. Thinking is best encouraged by giving children opportunities to articulate their own ideas.
- An important part of learning science is learning the development of a healthy respect for ambiguity. That is why the teacher avoids bringing closure to the debriefing sessions. When closure is brought, the need for further inquiry ceases. Without closure, children's motivation to explore and discover on their own is maintained.[45]

Replay follows Debriefing, generally over the next days. Replay may involve repetition of the acts until skills are mastered; it may be a time when tests are replicated and confirmed or when new hypotheses are tested. The entire process is cyclic and terminates when the teacher or the students implicitly or explicitly concur that certain materials no

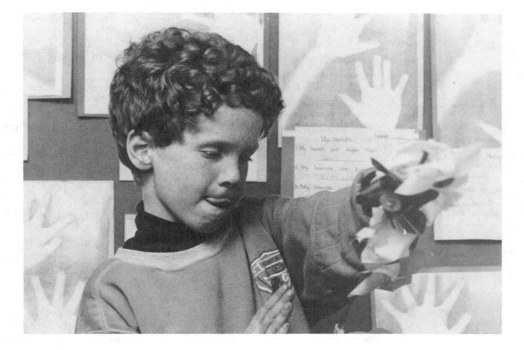

longer have interest for them. It is then time to collapse that center and create new sciencing opportunities.

CONCLUSION

This chapter has been devoted to extensive discussion of the theoretical and philosophical frameworks of the Play-Debrief-Replay model of learning science. An attempt has been made to draw together the dimensions of what we know about children and how they learn, about current thinking in teaching and learning in science, about the role of play in children's learning, about the emphasis on thinking in the curriculum, and to fuse all these elements into a whole cloth, a coherent instructional model that will result in the kinds of learning outcomes we all want for all children.

In the chapters that follow, we include explicit help for teachers who share our enthusiasms about the possibilities of sciencing and who are interested in moving some of these ideas into their classroom practices. By making classroom applications specific and concrete, we hope that we can help teachers bridge the gap between the ideas and the day-to-day life of the classroom, thus ensuring potential success for every teacher in sciencing.

NOTES

1. Deborah C. Fort, "Science Shy, Science Savvy, Science Smart," *Phi Delta Kappan*, 74 (1993), 674–683.

2. American Association for the Advancement of Science, *Benchmarks for Science Literacy* (New York: Oxford University Press, 1993), pp. 4–5.

3. Lewis Thomas, *The Youngest Science* (New York: Viking, 1983), pp. 81–82.

4. J. W. George Ivany, *Today's Science* (Chicago: Science Research Associates, 1975); Alfred DeVito, *Creative Wellsprings for Science Teaching* (West Lafayette, IN: Creative Venturing, 1984).

5. AAAS, *Benchmarks*, pp. 4–5.

6. Louis E. Raths, Selma Wassermann, Arthur Jonas, and Arnold Rothstein, *Teaching for Thinking: Theory, Strategies, and Activities for the Classroom* (New York: Teachers College Press, 1986).

7. American Association for the Advancement of Science, *Science for All Americans* (New York: Oxford University Press, 1990), p. 198.

8. Project Science-Thinking was a two-year field study carried out by the authors of this text with 20 classroom teachers in 12 elementary schools in British Columbia. The objectives of the study were (a) to develop and implement a training program to retrain practicing teachers in the principles and instructional strategies of sciencing and teaching for thinking and (b) to observe and assess pupil learning outcomes related to the implementation of such practices.

9. See particularly Mary Budd Rowe, *Teaching Science as Continuous Inquiry* (New York: McGraw Hill, 1973); Arthur Carin and Robert B. Sund, *Teaching Science Through Discovery* (Columbus, OH: Merrill, 1985); Lazar Goldberg, *Children and Science* (New York: Scribner, 1970); Glenn O. Blough and Julius Schwartz, *Elementary Science and How to Teach It* (New York: Holt, Rinehart and Winston, 1984); The Elementary Science Study (ESS), Classroom materials organized into units intended to provoke questions and explorations in topical areas (New York: McGraw Hill/Webster, 1967–1971); Science Curriculum Improvement Study (SCIS), Classroom materials based on systems concepts (Washington, DC: National Science Foundation, 1978); Teaching Elementary Science series, Curriculum units for science studies emphasizing topical themes (London: Nuffield Foundation and the Social Science Research Council, 1973); Bonnie Shapiro, *What Children Bring to Light: A Constructivist Perspective on Children's Learning in Science* (New York: Teachers College Press, 1994); Robert M. Hazen and James Trefil, *Science Matters: Achieving Scientific Literacy* (New York: Doubleday, 1990).

10. AAAS, *Science for All Americans*, p. 199.

11. Selma Wassermann, *Asking the Right Question: The Essence of Teaching* (Bloomington, IN: Phi Delta Kappa, 1992).

12. AAAS, *Science for All Americans*, p. 199.

13. Shapiro, *What Children Bring to Light*, p. 5.

14. See, for example, Alison Clarke-Stewart, Susan Friedman, and Joanne Koch, *Child Development: A Topical Approach* (New York: Wiley, 1985); Urie Bronfenbrenner, *The Ecology of Human Development* (Cambridge, MA: Harvard University Press, 1979); Paul S. Kaplan, *A Child's Odyssey: Child and Adolescent Development* (St. Paul, MN: West, 1986); Julius Segal and Herbert Yahraes, *A Child's Journey: Forces That Shape the Lives of Our Young* (New York: McGraw Hill, 1978); David Wood, *How Children Think and Learn* (Oxford, England: Blackwell, 1983).

15. Neil Postman, *The Disappearance of Childhood* (New York: Dell/Delacorte Press, 1982); David

Elkind, *The Hurried Child* (Boston: Allyn & Bacon, 1982); Marie Winn, *Children Without Childhood* (New York: Pantheon, 1983); Vance Packard, *Our Endangered Children* (Boston: Little Brown, 1983); Valerie Suransky, *The Erosion of Childhood* (Chicago: University of Chicago Press, 1982); Alex Kotlowitz, *There Are No Children Here* (New York: Doubleday, 1991); Joshua Meyrowitz, *No Sense of Place: The Impact of Electronic Media on Social Behavior* (New York: Oxford University Press, 1985); Sylvia Ashton-Warner, *Spearpoint* (New York: Knopf, 1972).

16. AAAS, *Science for All Americans*, pp. 197–207.
17. John Dewey, *On Education* (Chicago: University of Chicago Press, 1964).
18. Charles Silberman, *Crisis in the Classroom* (New York: Random House, 1973), pp. 10–11.
19. Kathy Sylva, Jerome S. Bruner, and Paul Genova, "The Role of Play in the Problem-Solving of Children Three to Five Years Old," in Jerome S. Bruner, Alison Jolly, and Kathy Sylva, *Play—Its Role in Development and Evolution* (London: Penguin, 1974), p. 256.
20. Sylvia Ashton-Warner, *Teacher* (New York: Simon & Schuster, 1963), pp. 93–94.
21. Mary Brown and Norman Precious, *The Integrated Day in the Primary School* (London: Ward Lock, 1970); John Blackie, *Inside the Primary School* (New York: Schocken Books, 1971); Gertrude Cooper, *The Place of Play in an Infant School and Junior School* (London: National Froebel Foundation, 1966).
22. Joseph Featherstone, *Schools Where Children Learn* (New York: Liveright, 1971).
23. Jacob Getzels and Philip Jackson, *Creativity and Intelligence* (New York: Wiley, 1962), p. vii.
24. James E. Johnson, James F. Christie, and Thomas D. Yawkey, *Play & Early Childhood Development* (New York: Harper Collins, 1987).
25. Richard P. Feynman, *Surely You're Joking Mr. Feynman*! (New York: W. W. Norton, 1985), p. 157.
26. Marie Winn, *Children Without Childhood* (New York: Pantheon, 1983), p. 75.
27. AAAS, *Science for All Americans*, 1990, p. 204.
28. "Playful Interaction," position paper of the National Association for the Education of Young Children. Washington, DC, 1986; Judy Spitler McKee, ed., *Play: Working Partner of Growth* (Washington, DC: Association for Childhood Education International, 1986); Joe. L. Frost and Sylvia Sunderlin, eds., *When Children Play* (Washington, DC: Association for Childhood Education International, 1985); P. F. Wilkinson, ed., *In Celebration of Play* (New York: St. Martin's Press, 1980); Frost, "Children in a Changing Society." *Childhood Education*, 63 (1986), 242–249; Fergus P. Hughes, *Children, Play and Development* (Boston: Allyn & Bacon, 1991); Janet R. Mayles, *Just Playing? The Role and Status of Play in Early Childhood* (Philadelphia: The Open University Press, 1989).
29. Bruner et al., *Play*; Brian Sutton-Smith, ed., *Play and Learning* (New York: Gardner, 1979); McKee, *Play*; D. J. Pepler and K. H. Rubin, eds., "The Play of Children: Current Theory and Research," *Contributions to Human Development*, 6 (1982), 64–78; B. Vandenberg, "Play, Problem-solving and Creativity," in K. H. Rubin, ed., *Children's Play* (San Francisco: Jossey-Bass, 1980); G. G. Fein, ed., *The Play of Children: Theory and Research* (Washington, DC: National Association for the Education of Young Children, 1986); R. E. Herron and Brian Sutton-Smith, eds., *Child's Play* (New York: Wiley, 1971).
30. Raths et al., *Teaching for Thinking*, p. x.
31. Howard Gardner, *The Unschooled Mind* (New York: Basic Books, 1991).
32. AAAS, *Science for All Americans*, p. 199.
33. Raths et al., *Teaching for Thinking*, pp. 24–30.
34. Ruth Berken, "A Study of the Relationships of Certain Behaviors of Children to the Teaching of Thinking in Grades Five and Six in Selected Schools in West Side Manhattan," unpublished

doctoral dissertation, New York University, 1963; Roger Cartwright, "An Account of the Development and Application of a Resource Unit Stressing Thinking for a Course: ETA 2: Values, Teaching and Planning," unpublished doctoral dissertation, New York University, 1961; Arthur Jonas, "A Study of the Relationship of Certain Behaviors of Children to Emotional Needs, Values and Thinking: Grade 4," unpublished doctoral dissertation, New York University, 1960; Ernest Machnits, "A Study of the Relationship of Certain Behaviors of Children to Emotional Needs, Values, and Thinking: Grade 3," unpublished doctoral dissertation, New York University, 1960; Donald Martin, "A Study of the Relationship of Certain Behaviors of Children to Emotional Needs, Values and Thinking: Grade 5," unpublished doctoral dissertation, New York University, 1960; Arnold Rothstein, "An Experiment in Developing Critical Thinking," unpublished doctoral dissertation, New York University, 1960; Selma Wassermann, "A Study of the Changes in Thinking-related Behaviors in a Selected Group of Sixth Grade Children in the Presence of Selected Materials and Techniques," unpublished doctoral dissertation, New York University, 1962; Ira Leroy Stern, "The Preseverance or Lack of It of Specified Behaviors Among Children in Selected Elementary Schools in Nassau County," unpublished doctoral dissertation, New York University, 1963.

35. Raths et al., *Teaching for Thinking.*
36. John Goodlad, *A Place Called School* (New York: McGraw-Hill, 1984), pp. 197–245.
37. *Ibid*, pp. 229–232.
38. Alfred North Whitehead, *Aims of Education and Other Essays* (New York: New American Library, 1929), p. 13.
39. Wassermann, *Asking the Right Question.*
40. Raths et al., *Teaching for Thinking*, pp. 206–209.
41. AAAS, *Science for All Americans*, p. 199.
42. Bruner et al., *Play*: "Playful Interaction."
43. AAAS, *Benchmarks*, 1993, p. 3.
44. Selma Wassermann and J. W. George Ivany, Project Science-Thinking (see note 8).
45. Ways to translate these conditions into classroom practices are given in Chapters 2, 3, and 4.

chapter

2

Organizing
the Science
Program

This afternoon a group of 12 student teachers are heading out to Nelson School to observe Heather's sciencing program. Heather's grade 3 and 4 classroom offers a rich opportunity to see the Play-Debrief-Replay instructional plan in a state-of-the-art program. The late April day has turned warm and fair, a welcome change from the rain in beautiful downtown Vancouver.

Today four centers are in operation, and as the student teachers quietly slip into the room, the children, deeply engaged, pay little mind to the large influx of adults. Except for an occasional "hi," the children continue with their investigative play. Annabella's group is at work making observations of worms in a "wormarium." They are discussing their observations and making decisions about what they will record. Seema's group is at the bubble center making bubbles, using several different implements and comparing the results. A plastic sheet covers the carpet at this center, so the children don't have to be overly cautious about water dripping on the floor. Tara's group is working with mirrors, and the mirror center contains several small, flat hand mirrors, a piece of reflective metal, a large full-size mirror, a magnifying shaving mirror, and another, more obviously curved mirror. Peter's group is at the pendulum center. Three pendulums with different bobs and different lengths of string are being observed and compared. The children are also planning to make their own pendulums.

When cleanup is announced, the groups tidy each center and get it ready for the next group's use. All this cleanup and changing of centers is carried out with a minimum of fuss and with the efficiency born of considerable practice and experience. It is a short afternoon, and after the second round of sciencing activities, Heather calls the groups together for Debriefing. She asks the children about their observations, and she asks about ideas to be shared. The children respond to her requests for their observations, and she encourages them to formulate hypotheses and theories that flow from their explorations with the materials. The children participate enthusiastically, hands waving eagerly to share their observations, yet there is considerate attention for each speaker. Heather's responses keep the inquiries open. They do not bring closure or lead pupils to learn specific facts. Through her questions she helps the children extract meaning from their investigative play experiences ("Hmm, I wonder why that happened." "Do you have any ideas about it?" "Would that happen again if you tried it on another day?" "I wonder how you could figure that out?") as well as develop an increased understanding of scientific phenomena. Debriefing also opens the doors to further inquiry.

The student teachers who are observing Debriefing later inquire, "How do you get the program working so smoothly?"

Developing, organizing, and managing a sciencing program is the key to its effective operation. And while there is no single, correct way to do this, we'd like to offer some guidelines, based on teachers' classroom experiences, that may be helpful in getting it going.

CHILDREN WORKING IN GROUPS: A QUESTION OF THE TEACHER'S BELIEFS

In any classroom it is the teacher who creates the program, and each teacher makes choices, from among alternatives, about what is to be learned and how the learning experiences will be organized. The teacher also decides on the amount of time given to subjects and on the level of active involvement of the pupils, as well as on the extent of teacher control or domination of the learning experience. All of these decisions are made by the teacher—and in spite of budgetary considerations, administrative pressure, school board policy, and parental concerns, it is the classroom teacher who ultimately makes the bottom-line decisions that bring shape to the curriculum and create the conditions under which learning will occur.

The curriculum and the learning conditions that a teacher creates are, to a very major extent, a reflection of that teacher's beliefs about education, about teaching and learning, and about children. What you believe about your pupils makes a lot of difference to the way you teach. It is not what you *say* you believe that is the shaping force. It is rather the beliefs *inside* you that leak out into your classroom practices. You may say, for example, that you are for a democratically organized classroom, but your *actions* may betray that belief.

A key factor in developing and organizing a sciencing program is the teacher's deep belief in the importance of children's working cooperatively in small groups. This means that the classroom is perceived not as a place of profound silence where pupils sit quietly and listen and watch the teacher doing the work but as a place where the children do the work—talking, discussing, debating, arguing, laughing, moving about the room, finding the materials they need. It is also a place where children spill water, knock over paint, break the bubble pipe, tear plastic sheets, and have all the other "accidents" that occur when people work with materials. You can't make an omelet without breaking eggs. It is a room in which children's busyness and the noise connected with normal, healthy productivity are the order of the day. In short, such a classroom reveals all the benefits and by-products of children's doing the work.

Before considering a sciencing program for your own classroom, we think it is imperative that you begin by giving yourself a "beliefs test" to tap into those beliefs that will inevitably shape your classroom practices. If you believe in the kind of science program that is rooted in pupil inquiry, in pupils' working cooperatively in groups, and in the promotion of pupils' higher-order thinking skills, a program in which pupils are given much control over their learning, this book is likely to be of value for you. If your perception of teaching and learning is shaped by beliefs that insist on the teacher's being at center stage and in full control of pupil learning—a quiet, orderly classroom in which children are listening to the teacher giving the lesson—it is likely that another approach to teaching science will be more appropriate than what is offered here.

Beliefs Test

*(An informal, nonstandardized, not altogether empirically valid way
of identifying some of your deeply held beliefs)*

Spend a few moments reflecting on each of the belief statements. Then consider the extent to which you hold that belief, using the following ratings:

1 = agree strongly   2 = tend to agree   3 = uncertain
4 = tend to disagree   5 = disagree strongly

1. There is a fixed body of knowledge to be learned in science at each grade level. _____

2. Pupils must master this body of knowledge in science before they can go on to study the material of the next grade. _____

3. For pupils to learn science properly, they must be taught it in a systematic way. _____

4. A teacher needs to follow a tight schedule in order to cover the prescribed content of science. _____

5. Learning science occurs best in a quiet and orderly classroom where the children are sitting still and listening to the teacher. _____

6. Competition is good for children; it spurs learning in science. _____

7. Noise and movement in the classroom diminish opportunities for learning. _____

8. The best way to find out what pupils have learned in science is to give them quizzes on which they can show if they know the right answers. _____

9. The teacher must do a lot of telling and showing in order to get pupils to understand. _____

10. A teacher must instruct each pupil until he or she understands the lesson fully. _____

11. You cannot expect elementary pupils to behave responsibly in unsupervised group activities. _____

12. Teaching science is primarily concerned with getting children to learn the right answers about scientific phenomena. _____

13. Students have to learn a certain amount of factual material before they can think. _____

Scoring

Add up your total score. If it is 50 or higher, go directly to the next section. If your score falls between 30 and 49, reread Chapter 1 and take the Beliefs Test again. If your score falls between 13 and 29, read another science book; this approach to teaching science is not for you.

PREPARING PUPILS FOR SCIENCING

When training to become a chef, one of the first things you learn is the importance of preparation. Regardless of the culinary undertaking, the recipe is first carefully studied and understood. Then all ingredients are measured and laid out and all cooking implements prepared and made accessible. The chef in training starts out by setting up the conditions that will make the process as problem-free as possible. Croissant making is chore enough without the added complication of having to search for the rolling pin at a crucial moment or finding that the butter is insufficiently soft or suddenly realizing that you have run short of eggs.

A program that is new to the children depends very largely for its success on the teacher's preparation. This preparation begins with the teacher's careful study and understanding of the instructional plan. Then, procedures, behavioral expectations, goals—all these need to be "out on the table" for the children to see. In this way, much difficulty can be avoided.

We are suggesting that the teacher begin by becoming familiar with the instructional plan. This can be accomplished by reading this text and understanding what the sciencing program entails and how it may be organized and implemented.

Second, the teacher will want to ensure that materials for creating investigative play centers are gathered and available in the classroom and that workspace for the program is available. The third step is to prepare the children for the program. It is recommended that this be done in two stages: first, by explaining to the children the kind of program it is, the way it is going to function, and the behavioral expectations; second, by providing guidance and supervision, including immediate intervention in the event of on-the-spot difficulties that arise. The initial orientation stage of informing and explaining is intended to make clear to the children the nature of the experience and the procedures to be followed. The second aspect of the orientation, guidance, recognizes that children may require a slow and careful weaning away from their dependence on teacher direction toward more independent, self-disciplined functioning. In this second stage, the teacher's supervisory role gradually tapers off as the children grow toward independent functioning. This tapering-off process may take between two and five months, depending on the previous experiences of the children, and the teacher should allow for that considerable amount of learning time.

Suggestions for Orientation

1. Talk to the children about the program. Tell them what Sciencing means; about the materials they will be using; about their working in groups. Allow them sufficient opportunity to raise questions about their concerns.

2. Communicate your own enthusiasm for the program and for science.

3. Communicate your confidence in the children's ability to undertake the program.

4. Be explicit about the behavior you expect—about the need for cooperation, for sharing, for working together harmoniously.

5. Identify procedures for handling problems that may arise.

6. Be explicit about the way materials are to be cared for.

7. Be explicit about cleanup procedures and about how and where materials are to be stored.

8. Invite the children's ideas and suggestions for making the working procedures more effective.

9. Where children are to have choices about who works in what center, make the procedures for making such choices explicit.

10. Where recording of observations is to be done, make procedures clear and explicit.

11. Undertake a "trial run" with four or five groups working at four or five centers. Have the children participate in an evaluation of the trial run. Ask for their suggestions and ideas for improving procedures.

12. In the first weeks of the program, elicit the children's participation in an evaluation of the experience directly after each sciencing period.

13. Supervise the children's work closely at first. Taper off the close supervision slowly, as you observe children's increased ability to work together on their own initiative.

There will eventually come a time in your classroom, a magic moment, when you will be able to step back and see at a glance that all the children are productively engaged in sciencing, that there is no need for you to intervene with guidance and direction, that the interpersonal relationships of the children are cooperative and not combative. Exhale, relax, and congratulate yourself. Your sciencing program is at last functioning as you dreamed it might.

GATHERING THE MATERIALS

There is virtually no limit to the extent and type of material that can be put into a classroom in the building of a successful sciencing program. While the scope of materi-

als can be vast, it is certainly not essential to gather everything at once. Good sciencing programs can operate with carefully selected materials. The intrepid teacher can add to the basic list whatever seems attractive as an extension of sciencing activities.

The following list contains suggestions as to what might be considered potentially valuable for constructive and creative investigative play. Materials marked with an asterisk (*) represent, to a close approximation, what is needed for most of the sciencing activities in Chapter 4.

Materials for a Sciencing Program

Key

Where items are likely to be found:

1. Somewhere in the school
2. High school science or industrial arts department
3. Junk stores, secondhand stores, flea markets, garage sales, etc.
4. Five-and-tens, supermarkets, drugstores
5. Hardware stores
6. Restaurant supply stores
7. Toy stores
8. Garden stores, pet stores
9. Possible donations from parents
10. By beachcombing, scrounging, rummaging, and using other artful strategies known only to teachers

Materials

absorbent cotton (4)
air pump* (2, 4)
alcohol (4)
aluminum foil* (4)
ammonia (4)
animals (small): mice, lizards, hamsters, guinea pigs, chicks, gerbils, fish, turtles, etc.* (8, 9)
apple juice (4)
atomizer (10)
baby carriage wheels* (9, 10)
baking soda* (4, 9)
balance scales* (1, 2, 3, 4, 5)
ball bearings* (2, 5)
balloons* (4)
ballpoint pens* (1)
balls* (4, 9)

barometer* (2, 5)
basins* (1, 3, 9, 10)
bathroom scale* (3, 9)
batteries* (2, 5)
beans* (4, 8)
bedsheets* (9, 10)
bells* (1, 2)
binoculars* (3, 9)
birdseed* (4, 8)
block and tackle (2, 5)
blocks* (1)
blotting paper* (1, 2)
bobs* (1, 2)
bones* (2, 4, 10)
bottles* (3, 9, 10)
bowls (3, 9)
boxes* (9, 10)

brace and bits (5)
bricks* (3, 5, 9)
bubble pipes* (4, 7)
bulbs (electric light)* (4, 5)
bulgur* (4, 9)
buttons (3, 4)
buzzer* (1, 2, 5)
calipers* (2)
camera* (3, 9, 10)
candles* (4)
can opener* (4)
cans* (9)
carbon paper (1)
cardboard tubes* (9)
cement (5)
chalk* (1)
cheesecloth* (4, 6)
chisels* (5)
chopsticks* (6, 9)
clay (1)
clinical thermometer* (4)
clocks* (2, 3)
clothesline* (4, 5)
clothespins (wooden)* (3, 5)
colander* (3, 4, 9)
collecting trays* (2, 6)
comb* (4)
compass (magnetic)* (1)
compasses (measuring)* (1)
concrete blocks* (5)
cooking thermometer* (4)
corks* (5, 6)
cornstarch* (4)
crayons* (1)
detergent (liquid) (4, 9)
doweling* (5)
drums* (1, 2)
dry cells* (2, 5)
dry ice (5)
earthworms* (2, 10)
egg cartons (9, 10)
eggs* (4)
egg whisk (mechanical)* (3, 9)
electrical appliances (for taking

apart): toasters, coffee pots, irons,
mixers, radios, etc. (3, 9, 10)
electric fans (3, 9)
electric motors (toy)* (3, 7)
electric push buttons, lamps, and
sockets* (5)
eraser* (1, 4)
extension cords (new)* (5)
extension cords (old) (3, 9)
eyedropper* (4, 9)
eyeshades* (4)
fabrics of all kinds* (3, 9, 10)
feathers* (10)
felt pens* (1)
fertilizers (8)
filmstrip projector* (1)
fired clay tiles* (3, 5, 9)
fish weights* (5)
flashlights* (4, 5)
flour* (4, 9)
flowerpots* (8, 9)
flowers* (4, 8)
fly wheel* (2)
foam rubber* (3)
food coloring* (4, 9)
foods* (4, 9, 10)
forceps* (2)
fruits* (4, 9)
funnels* (4, 6)
fur* (3, 9)
fuses (burned out) (9, 10)
geometric shapes (1)
glass (for making slides) (2)
glass (plate)* (1, 2, 3)
glass beads (3, 5)
glass cutters (5)
glasses (drinking)* (1, 3, 4)
glass jars* (1, 3, 4)
glass tubing (2, 5)
glue and paste* (1)
glycerine* (4)
graph paper* (1)
gravel (10)
gyroscopes* (2)

harmonica* (7)
hay or straw (10)
height measure (1)
holograms (2)
honey* (4)
hourglass* (2)
ice-cream sticks* (2)
ice cubes* (1, 4)
instant coffee powder* (4)
insulated copper wire* (5)
iodine (4)
iron filings* (1, 2, 5)
jacks (automobile)* (2, 3)
jars (gallon)* (3, 9)
jugs (gallon)* (3, 9)
kaleidoscope (7, 9)
kazoos (1, 2)
knives* (1, 3, 4)
lamp* (1, 3, 10)
lamp chimneys (5)
laths (2)
leather* (3, 9, 10)
leaves (10)
legumes (dry)* (4, 9)
lenses of all kinds* (2, 3)
light bulbs (burned out) (9, 10)
limewater (8)
logs* (10)
machines (for taking apart): adding machines, typewriters, calculators, pencil sharpeners, clocks, telephones, etc.* (3, 9, 10)
magnetic wire* (2, 5)
magnets of all shapes and sizes* (1)
magnifying glasses* (1)
mallets* (1, 2)
maps (2, 4, 7)
marbles* (7)
marking pens* (1)
measuring cups* (1, 3, 4)
measuring implements: yardsticks, meter sticks, tape measure* (1)
medicine dropper* (2, 4, 10)

metals (all kinds and weights)* (2, 5, 10)
metal scraps* (10)
metal sheeting* (5, 10)
metal wire* (5, 10)
meteorological equipment (2)
microscopes* (1)
milk powder (dry)* (4)
"minibeasties": spiders, ants, caterpillars, worms, etc.* (2, 8)
mirrors* (4, 5)
modeling clay (1)
model windmill* (2)
molds (forms) (2, 10)
motors* (2, 3, 9)
mousetraps* (5)
muffin tins (3, 4, 5, 9)
nails of all sizes* (4, 5)
needles* (4)
newspaper* (1, 9)
newsprint* (1)
nuts and bolts* (5)
overhead projector* (1)
pails* (1, 3, 9)
paper: posterboard, tissue, waxed, bond, etc.* (1)
paper clips* (1)
paper cups* (1, 4)
paper punch* (1)
paper towels* (1)
paraffin (5)
peanuts* (4)
peas* (4)
pebbles (10)
pencil sharpener* (1)
pendulum frame (2)
pendulums* (2)
picture collections* (1)
pillows* (3, 9, 10)
Ping-Pong balls* (4, 7)
pins* (1)
pinwheel* (7)
pipe cleaners (4)
pitcher* (4, 9)

plants (3, 9)
plaster of Paris (5)
plastic bags* (4)
plastic cake containers (4, 6)
plastic cups* (3)
plastic dishes* (3, 4, 9)
plastic sheeting* (4, 5)
plastic tubing* (8)
plastic tubs, buckets, basins* (1)
playing cards* (4, 9)
poster paints* (1)
potatoes* (4, 9)
potting soil* (4, 8)
printing ink (1, 4)
prisms* (2, 5)
protractor* (1)
pulleys, double and single* (2, 5)
rheostats (2, 5)
ribbon (4, 9)
rice* (4, 9)
rocks* (10)
rock salt (5, 9)
room thermometer* (1, 3, 9)
rope* (5, 9)
rubber bands* (1)
rubber suction cups* (2, 3, 5)
rulers* (1)
salt (4)
sand* (1, 10)
sandpaper* (1)
saws* (5)
scissors* (1)
scrap lumber* (10)
screen* (1)
screws of all sizes* (5)
sealing wax (5)
seeds* (8, 9)
seesaw balance on a fulcrum* (1, 2, 5)
shells* (10)
skeletons* (2)
skins (animal)* (2, 10)
Slinky (5, 7)
snail shells* (4)
soap flakes* (4)

soldering iron* (2, 3, 9)
spinning tops* (7)
sponges* (1)
spools (3, 9, 10)
spoons, graded sizes* (4)
sprayers* (8)
springs (5)
spring scales, kitchen scales, scales
with weights* (2)
squid (frozen)* (4)
stapler* (1)
staple remover* (1)
staples* (1)
star charts (2, 7)
steel wool* (4)
stethescope* (2, 7)
sticks* (4, 10)
stones* (10)
stopwatch* (5)
straws* (1)
string* (1)
Styrofoam chips* (4)
sugar* (4)
sunlamp (3, 9)
switches* (2, 5)
syringes* (2, 4)
tape* (1)
tape measures* (1, 4, 5)
tape recorder* (1)
tapes (music)* (1)
teapot (3, 9, 10)
tea strainers* (3, 9, 10)
telegraph key* (2, 5)
telegraph set* (2)
telescope* (2, 7)
test tubes (2)
thermometers* (1, 2, 4)
thread, string, twine* (1)
thumbtacks* (1)
timer (egg)* (6)
timer (10-second)* (5)
tin cans* (9, 10)
tissue paper, all colors* (1)
toilet plunger* (3, 5, 10)

toilet roll centers* (9, 10)
tongue depressors* (4)
tools: hammers, pliers, screwdrivers, drill, saws* (1)
toothpicks* (4)
toys: cars, airplanes, furniture, utensils (3, 9)
transistor radio (3, 9)
transparent flexible tubing of various diameters* (3, 5, 8, 9)
trays (1)
tree parts: bark, leaves, twigs, branches, driftwood* (10)
triangles* (1, 2)
trundle wheel (1, 2)
tuning forks* (1, 2)
turntable (3, 9)
umbrellas* (9)
unglazed clay tiles* (3, 5, 9, 10)
vacuum cleaner (3, 9)
vegetables* (4)
vinegar (4)
vise (2, 5)

washers (5)
watch (wind-up)* (4)
watch (with sweep second hand)* (4)
water containers* (3, 9)
watering can (3, 5, 8)
waxed paper* (4)
wedge* (1, 2)
weights* (3, 5, 9)
wheels of all sizes* (3, 9, 10)
whistles* (1, 7)
wire* (1, 2, 5)
wire cutters* (2, 3, 5)
wooden balls, various sizes* (1, 4, 7)
wooden beads (3, 4)
wood of different types: scraps, bamboo, balsa, peg board, etc.* (9, 10)
wood shavings (10)
"wormarium"* (2, 8)
X-acto knife* (1)
xylophone* (1, 2)
yeast (cakes)* (4)
yeast (dried)* (4)
yo-yos* (7)

MAKING ROOM FOR SCIENCING

I found an old, wrecked rowboat and hauled it into my class . . . a rowboat for science! The kids and I are sanding and painting it this week. They love it and I think it's pretty neat too.

BEV C., GRADE 6
PRINCE RUPERT, BRITISH COLUMBIA

In classrooms where most curriculum activities occur in "learning centers," there would normally be one or two sciencing centers that would function along with math centers, language activity centers, social studies centers, and a variety of other theme-work or investigative centers that are created, evolve, and collapse in response to children's interests and curriculum guidelines. Should teachers wish to explore such a learning-centers approach to curriculum implementation, we recommend texts by Virgil Howes; David Johnson, Roger Johnson, and colleagues; and Selma Wassermann (especially for the primary grades).[1]

The approach that we are taking in this text pursues a more specific curriculum path, that of the creation of investigative play centers to promote inquiry and higher-order thinking skills in the area of science. We have put aside consideration of other subject areas, choosing instead to give our full concentration to science—although the Play-Debrief-Replay approach that we advocate here is as applicable to other subject areas as it is to science.[2]

We have envisioned elementary classrooms that may be operating under one of several types of organizational plans and in which investigative play in science can be "parachuted in" with a minimum of difficulty, no matter how instruction in other areas of the curriculum has been organized. There must, however, be enough room for sciencing.

There should, of course, be storage space to contain the materials needed in the new investigative play centers. Plastic bins are ideal for larger equipment and are generally found in most schools in many sizes and colors. Failing these, cardboard boxes from the supermarket can be used as is or painted and decorated by the children. A supply of large plastic garbage bags will come in handy to line cardboard boxes, in case damp materials are to be stored. Smaller pieces of equipment may be stored in shoeboxes, in plastic 5-gallon ice-cream buckets, cottage cheese containers, and other plastic food containers. A restaurant supply store may offer plastic storage containers in many sizes and shapes at great bargain prices. Parents may welcome opportunities to unload some of their excess plastic storage containers and donate them to the room.

Wherever the large storage bins are kept, they should be easily accessible so that the getting and putting away of sciencing materials is hassle-free. If the space in your classroom is already overcommitted, consider unloading rarely used textbooks or equipment into longer-term storage areas, possibly outside the classroom, making more room for sciencing.

In creating the sciencing workspace, consider using project tables, several children's desks grouped together, or even the floor—all can be protected and used as working space. The workspace should easily accommodate an entire working group (up to five children) without the children having to push their way into the space. Vinyl or plastic sheeting can be quickly laid down over the floor or carpeted areas to protect against spills and mess and can be easily cleaned and picked up after use. The important consideration in creating sciencing workspace is to make the entry into the sciencing activities and the creation of the centers as trouble-free as possible. If it is going to take 30 minutes of the teacher's time just to set up the room each day, the likelihood is great that such a time expenditure will be too costly and eventually the teacher's enthusiasm for sciencing will be eroded away by mere logistic difficulties. Creating adequate workspace is one of the major challenges of the program, and most teachers find ways to do this successfully. If space arrangement is not your particular forte, you might wish to bring in a fellow teacher to act as consultant in brainstorming some practicable and attractive workspace options.

There should be easy access to supplies that will be in constant use—water, paper towels, newspapers, scissors, measuring equipment, string, assorted paper, pens, pencils, chalk, jars, and the like. Children ought to know where to find these supplies without having to ask the teacher each time and should be made responsible for their care and storage.

In making room for sciencing, one extreme alternative is to keep the materials and workspace "in a suitcase"—like a traveling road show—and to open the case and re-create the context each time there is a sciencing period. This may occur in a classroom where space is tight and where other important activities vie for that space. When a teacher has considerable space options, another alternative is to keep sciencing materials and workspace open and in constant readiness. Between these two extremes, the imaginative teacher will find a solution that will cheerfully and successfully serve the sciencing program.

It should be emphasized once more that the children need to play a role in caring for the workspace and the sciencing materials and that they should be helped to learn to do this thoughtfully and responsibly. When children are expected to exercise care, when they learn to accept responsibility, they are being helped toward mature, independent, and thoughtful behavior that in turn encourages their personal involvement in the sciencing program.

CHOOSING THE RIGHT APPROACH
TO AN ELEMENTARY SCIENCING PROGRAM

Starting a new program can be very exciting. It can also be very intimidating. There are lots of risks to be taken, lots of new roads to travel, lots of unexpected events in the journey. Sometimes the path to innovation can have so many obstacles that progress is thwarted. Sometimes there are so many problems to deal with that the task of creating a new program becomes overwhelming.

Potential stumbling blocks can be overcome and sometimes avoided altogether when the teacher carefully selects an approach that feels right. That means that the approach selected should (a) feel reasonable, given the teacher's expectations; (b) be consonant with the teacher's level of security; (c) be compatible with other curriculum demands; (d) be acceptable without great conflict with the administration; (e) be appropriate to the physical space available; and (f) create a minimum of stress and a maximum potential for success. Given the variations of these conditions for each teacher, we offer several alternative approaches to beginning a sciencing program and suggest that teachers select one that corresponds most closely to individual teaching concerns.

Approach 1: Tread Softly and Carry a Big Balloon.

a. Choose a sciencing activity that feels "safe"—one for which you can obtain the materials easily and one that incurs a minimum of mess. (See the suggestions in Chapter 4.) Let's say that you have chosen pendulums. Make five pendulums.

Create five working groups.

Position the pendulums in strategic places in the classroom so that there are, in effect, five investigative play pendulum centers and so that five working groups may work at these centers without getting in one another's way.

b. Give explicit instructions to the pupils about carrying out their investigative play in the pendulums center. (See the suggestions in Chapter 4 for developing activity cards for the center.) Allow about 10 minutes for this sciencing activity. Instruct the groups to work together and, if it is feasible, to record their observations. Be explicit about your behavioral expectations for group work, care of materials, and cleanup.

c. Move around the room, from group to group, observing what the children are doing during their investigative play. Be responsive to what is happening. Be available to deal immediately with behavior management if needed. Otherwise, do not direct the children's inquiries.

d. At the end of the Play period, gather the children together and ask them to talk about their observations. Make it safe for all children to share their ideas by avoiding judgmental responses. Use reflective responses to help children think about their statements. (See Chapter 3 for specific help with questioning and responding strategies.) Limit this Debriefing to about 10 minutes.

e. At the end of Debriefing, evaluate the events of the sciencing experience with the children. What did they like about it? What were some things that went wrong? What might be helpful to do the next time to make it work more smoothly?

f. The next day, follow up the sciencing activity with a Replay of pendulums. This might be done with single pendulums again, or with a double-pendulum activity, in which each group observes two pendulums, each with a different length of string and a bob of a different weight. After the Replay, follow procedures *b* through *e* of this approach. Consider reconstituting some groups if you perceive that a particular group has experienced serious interpersonal conflicts.

Approach 2: Tread Gently and Carry a Big Bucket.

a. Choose two sciencing activities that feel "safe" for you—activities that you would not consider to be high risk. (See the suggestions in Chapter 4.)

b. Obtain the materials needed and set up six investigative play centers—three for each of the activities. Use the suggestions in Chapter 4 for developing activity cards to focus the investigative play in the centers.

c. Allow each group to have one turn at each of the two centers during the investigative play period. Allow no less than 10 minutes for each sciencing activity.

d. Instruct the children to carry out explorations using the materials in the center. Ask them to make observations of what is happening as the materials are used. As an option, ask them to record their observations.

e. Move around the room during the investigative play period and observe what the children are doing. Be responsive. Be available to deal immediately with behavior management as needed. Otherwise, do not direct the children's inquiries.

f. After each activity, instruct the children to clean up at their centers and make them ready for the next group. (If the sciencing period is concluded for the day, instruct the children to clean up and put all materials away.) Allow sufficient time for cleaning up and provide help during the cleanup as needed.

g. Debrief the sciencing activities by gathering the children together and asking them to tell what they have observed. Make it safe for all children to share their ideas by avoiding judgmental responses. Use reflective responses to help children think about their statements. (See Chapter 3 for specific help with this procedure.) Limit the Debriefing to about 10 minutes.

h. At the end of Debriefing, evaluate the events of the sciencing experience with the children. What did they like about it? What were some things that went wrong? What might be helpful to remember to do the next time?

i. Ask the children if they want to continue with their investigative play in these same centers. Get an idea of how "fresh" and how appealing each center is for the children. If interest is high, maintain Replay activities using the very same centers. If interest in a center is waning, collapse the center and create a new one. If the children have been recording their observations, it might be an added source of interest to mount these notes on a science bulletin board.

We put some rocks in the bucket of water. It turned a different color.
    To float a rock we can put a plastic bag under the rock. We choosed two rocks and they were different because they were not the same color or size

We made spoons out of tin foil and then we put salt in the spoon and we put the spoon on top of the flame and the water disappeared but the salt dident.

Me and Amerjeet put the eyedropper in the beaker. We put the balloon on the beaker. When me and Amerjeet prest the balloon the eyedropper went down and bubbles came out. We had lots of fun at the Divers

At center 6 I was pushing down on the eyedropper when some of the air went out of the balloon and the eyedropper went right down and I put a new balloon on and pushed and stopped pushing and it came up. I was feeling like if there was gravity in the balloon.

Approach 3: Tread Firmly and Carry a Big Squid.

a. Choose three different sciencing activities from among those presented in Chapter 4. Choose at least one activity that is of higher risk for you—perhaps one from the "Wet, Wetter, Wettest" group or one from the "Who's Afraid of Spiders?" group. (How about siphoning? Aaaaarrrgggghhhh! Well, what about spiders, then?)

b. Organize the investigative play period so that each group may participate in at least two different sciencing centers that day.
c. Follow the procedures as in approach 2, steps *b* through *i*.

d. Observe the children's work in the "higher-risk" center. Think about why it was higher risk for you. If children's responses to that center were troublesome, think of ways in which the trouble might be avoided or eliminated. *Do not abandon the center until you have really given yourself a very good chance to get it working successfully.*

Approach 4: Tread Strongly and Carry a Giant Python.

a. Choose five different sciencing activities and set each one up with the materials needed to carry out successful investigative play.

b. Include at least one activity that is a higher-risk activity for you.

c. Follow the procedures as in approach 3, steps *b* through *d.*

Approach 5: March to Your Own Drummer.

Use combinations of approaches 1 through 4, or create your own set of procedures incorporating the principles outlined in them.

Guidelines and Ground Rules

Whichever approach you choose, use the following guidelines to help you in implementing it successfully.

- Begin with a clear idea of how you will group the children so that behavioral difficulties may be avoided and successful group functioning is encouraged. You may have to experiment with grouping arrangements before you find strategies that are most successful. Give yourself the time and the opportunities for these trial runs, and don't expect that you should be successful in the first trial.[3]
- Make sure you have relatively easy access to the materials you need for the centers you have chosen. If you begin with elaborate plans to acquire hard-to-get materials, your efforts may be soon frustrated, and your enthusiasm may soon evaporate.
- Try to spot the problems that arise and plan to deal with them in the early stages of the program. Problems may come from unwieldy group arrangements, from children's inability to work responsibly in groups, from lack of space, from inappropriate organization—from many different sources. Organizing a classroom for effective learning is a highly complex and creative task under the best of circumstances. Undertaking an innovative program increases the potential for things to go awry. Taking a diagnostic and problem-solving approach can be helpful, but be sure you institute corrective procedures in advance of your becoming disenchanted with the

program. In some classes it takes a good deal of time for children to grow toward responsible group behavior.

- Communicate to the children your own enthusiasm about beginning this new sciencing program. Children are very much influenced by what teachers think. If you show your own enthusiasm about sciencing to them, they are likely to respond enthusiastically.

- Try to avoid communicating your own anxieties or frustrations to the children. If children perceive that you are worried about their ability to undertake this work successfully, your expectations may translate into pupils' poor performance. Conversely, high expectations of what children can do will likely yield richer and more productive results.[4]

- Be a thoughtful, sensitive observer. Assess what is happening in a diagnostic way, and use this feedback to keep building and improving the program. The most inventive and successful professionals use "reflection in action" as a means for examining existing situations, diagnosing weaknesses and strengths, and creating strategies that will lead to improved practice.[5] The teacher who is a reflective practitioner can keep the classroom dynamic and be consistently responsive to instructional improvement.

- Ask the children if they are enjoying the activities. If they are not, try to determine what might account for this. Under normal circumstances, most children will respond favorably to sciencing. If they do not, it may be very helpful to discover the reasons for their disinterest or lack of enjoyment and to address their concerns directly. The best way of finding out and of dealing with children's concerns is in the postsciencing evaluative sessions, described in this chapter.

It is also important to recall some of the ground rules for sciencing.

- Children's investigative play in the centers is self-initiated. Teachers' interventions during investigative play should avoid telling the children what to investigate.
- Investigative play is not intended to lead pupils to learn specific facts.
- Behavioral standards for children working with science equipment and in small groups are explicit and consistent. Good behavioral management is never punitive or hurtful to a child's dignity and pride.
- The teacher avoids judging, rewarding, acclaiming, and condemning children's ideas and their investigative play.
- The emphasis is on inquiry, exploration, and promoting a higher tolerance for *uncertainty*. Remember Lewis Thomas: Sciencing is learning to *err* and to bounce back to try again.
- Love for science and increased expertise in sciencing occurs after many, many happy and productive experiences. Good results do not come about after only a week of classroom trials. Give your program the time it needs to grow into a successful classroom experience. This may take as long as three to four months, depending largely on the "entry behaviors" of your pupils and the extent of practice experience you are willing to provide in sciencing.

It has been our experience that over time, many teachers who free themselves from their original dependence on textbook teaching and workbook exercises can move to the creation of their own original, successful sciencing programs. When that occurs, we believe that they are preparing children to learn science in the best ways possible.

TEACHERS HELPING TEACHERS

Teaching is a lonely job. Throughout the developing years of the modern school system, schools have been organized around teacher separation rather than teacher collaboration. Teachers perform their professional functions in single cells, isolated from both the critical appraisal and the critical acclaim of their colleagues. When a teacher has demonstrated an extraordinary accomplishment in this solitary cell, there are only the children to see it. Regrettably, they rarely have the sophistication to understand and appreciate its artistry. No colleagues witness the event, murmur words of praise and admiration, and feed that teacher's sense of collegial acceptance and self-esteem. Children may appreciate superlative teaching, but that is hardly the same as collegial acclaim.

Teacher isolation is not only bad for the ego. It also makes it virtually impossible to bring about the quality of professional growth that results from collaborative professional teamwork. Physicians working together in a health care facility are expected to plan together, to discuss diagnoses, medical procedures, alternate therapies, disease etiology, and the various ramifications of the illness and the care of each patient. Implicit in such teamwork is the close critical scrutiny of each individual's work on that team. But it also means mutual support in understanding and dealing with the complex and multifaceted problems of medical caregiving. It is quite likely that such critical scrutiny and cooperative teamwork, combined with the psychological support that comes from working in a team, have played a major role in virtually every significant medical breakthrough, from coronary bypass surgery to organ transplants to in vitro human fertilization. It is impossible to conceive of such medical innovation resulting from doctors practicing in separate cells, in isolation from one another's professional input and support.

A new classroom program is certainly not as fraught with life-and-death consequence as open-heart surgery; yet for the teacher on the threshold of innovation, the anticipated problems may be just as awesome. To face innovation alone may be a choice born of unexplored options, a decision by default of teachers' historical isolation. Yet surely there are alternatives. A teacher must have one or two colleagues in the same school with whom to form a working partnership. Such a cooperative liaison could have substantial payoffs: the development of an emotional support system, a means for brainstorming and identifying courses of action for problems related to innovative practices, the building of a caring and intelligent interpersonal feedback system, all to heighten critical awareness of individual classroom functioning. It is important for teachers to work with committed, concerned teammates in curriculum development. The support they provide each other helps each to keep growing and learning in the potentially turbulent seas of innovation until they establish the confidence they need to carry the task through. Teachers helping teachers are an important "natural" resource in virtually every school, and we suggest that such a resource be fully exploited for increased success in professional development.

EVALUATING PUPIL GROWTH

In these days of increased emphasis on standardized tests as measures of pupil learning, it may not be a popular move to recommend against such procedures for evaluation of learning in sciencing. Yet we choose to do so, and our choice is based on what we believe to be the best means of evaluating pupils' growth for this program. It should be noted that we are not alone in holding such ideas; they are shared by other professionals who are also concerned with keeping alive children's capacity to be excited about science and their natural wonder and joy in finding out about the world around us.[6]

The procedures for evaluating pupil gains in any program must be consistent with the articulated goals of that program if the goals are to be realized. Evaluation practices have a funny way of taking over and shaping all the educational experiences of a school. No matter what we *say* we want (goal statements), the procedures we choose to evaluate with implicitly dictate the kinds of learning outcomes we are going to get in actual practice. It's what to *do* that delivers the outcomes, not what we say. That is why evaluation practices must be of one piece with a program's goals if the goals are to be realized. In a program where goals and evaluation practices are at war, it is inevitable that the day-to-day practices will win out, leaving the rhetoric as dead promises on the battlefield.

To bring means and ends into congruence, the procedures selected for evaluating students should meet at least five criteria:

1. Evaluation procedures must be compatible with the program's overall goals and objectives. If the program seeks to promote higher-order thinking skills, evaluation may not take the form of asking for single "correct" answers on a pencil-and-paper quiz.
2. They must serve the function of the program's learning goals; that is, they should work to evaluate pupil progress along the learning dimensions that the program is trying to promote.
3. They must provide feedback to students that is more than the provision of correct answers. Feedback should be diagnostic, pointing out strengths and weaknesses, and offering suggestions for improvement.
4. They must emphasize the enablement of further pupil learning and deemphasize practices that are hurtful to pupils' concepts of self.
5. They must deemphasize practices that contribute to pupils' losing interest in the subject.

We have rejected the use of standardized and other pencil-and-paper tests as measures of pupil learning in sciencing because these tests fail on each of these criteria. They are not compatible with the goals of sciencing, as they seek to measure information acquisition within a very narrow range of alternatives. They do not serve the function of the program's goals, for they do not allow for measuring pupil growth in thinking capabilities; in problem-solving behaviors; in ability to work effectively in groups; in self-disciplined, thoughtful, responsible behavior; or in ability to design experiments, to test hypotheses, to gather data, to formulate scientific theory, to learn to err and keep trying. They do not provide information that can be used diagnostically, and consequently data from tests cannot be used to develop specific corrective or remediative teaching. Such tests may also undermine pupils' confidence in self and result in loss of enthusiasm for the subject. It is also possible that a pupil may have shown considerable growth on the learning dimensions of the program and still, for a variety of reasons quite unrelated to sciencing, receive a low score on the test. For all these reasons and more, we recommend a different set of evaluative procedures.

A discussion of evaluation cannot take place in the absence of prior consideration of a program's learning goals. (If we don't know where we want to go, we certainly won't know if we have gotten there.) Although the following list of goals has been grouped in separate categories, each learning goal overlaps with all the others, and all are bonded into a common core of what we consider to be valuable academic, social, and intellectual developmental outcomes in teaching and learning science.

Goals for a Sciencing Program

Social

1. Increased growth in independent, responsible classroom behavior
2. Increased growth in the ability to make reasoned, thoughtful choices and acceptance of the consequences of one's decisions
3. Increased growth in being a socially responsible and cooperative participant of a group
4. Increased growth in assuming responsibility for the classroom learning environment
5. Increased growth as a purposeful, productive learner and group member

Personal and Ego

1. Increased awareness of self as an individual with strengths and limitations
2. Increased sense of self as an individual with power to manipulate one's environment
3. Increased awareness of one's own capabilities to function as a problem solver
4. Increased growth of personal pride in self as a competent and skilled participant of a group
5. Increased sense of personal autonomy and ego strength
6. Increased growth as a self-initiator
7. Increased sense of self-worth
8. Increased sense of self as a "creator" and a "cognitive risk taker"

Cognitive and Intellectual

1. Increased skills in making thoughtful, accurate observations
2. Increased skills in forming reasoned and appropriate hypotheses
3. Increased skills in identifying assumptions and differentiating assumptions from fact
4. Increased skills in making comparisons and in identifying similarities and differences
5. Increased skills in classifying objects and in creating categories in which various items may be ordered
6. Increased skills in gathering data and making meaningful interpretations of the data
7. Increased skills in making decisions based on reasoned deliberation and thoughtful consideration of alternatives
8. Increased skills in creating, imagining, and inventing

9. Increased ability to be more tolerant of uncertainty
10. Increased skills in designing projects and experiments to test hypotheses
11. Increased ability to formulate and raise questions about phenomena
12. Increased understanding of the "big" scientific concepts
13. Increased knowledge base with respect to scientific information

Appreciations and Attitudes

1. Increased appreciation for science as a means for acquiring information and understanding the world and the universe
2. Increased love for science and scientific explorations
3. Increased joy in exploration, in searching, in experimentation for discovery
4. Increased ability to recognize science as a process of discovering rather than a body of information with accepted "truths"

Evaluating Students' Work in Sciencing

With the goals identified, it becomes apparent that such outcomes cannot be measured simply—and certainly not with any single pencil-and-paper test, no matter how sophisticated. Nor can such a comprehensive view of pupil growth be reflected in a single numerical score. Even the most ardent test advocates recognize the fallacy of such practice.

The evaluation practices we propose have been developed to help teachers make informed and accurate assessments of pupil growth toward the learning outcomes just identified. They should also provide diagnostic information, point to ways of remediating difficulties, and allow for pupils' growth as self-evaluators. Finally, they should provide a sound base of information from which valuable reports to parents about pupil growth can be made.

Classroom Observations   No pencil-and-paper classroom test is likely to be more effective in diagnosing pupil performance than the day-to-day observations of a trained, competent teacher. Close scrutiny of pupil behavior, in a variety of tasks, over an extended period of time—such as observing student interactions in a group, observing student problem-solving abilities on given tasks, and noting where and how difficulties arise for that student—will uncover valuable data about pupil ability and pupil learning.[7] Teachers' professional observations need to be recognized and appreciated as the source of the richest data for diagnostic work. In spite of the potential for built-in personal bias, the wealth of data from this source is likely to be infinitely more reliable to the classroom teacher in promoting pupil learning than a numerical score on any single examination.[8]

Systematic focused observations   In using so broad a screen as classroom observations, it is helpful to have some kind of "screening device"—a tool that can focus classroom observations on specific behaviors related to the learning goals of sciencing. Such a tool allows the teacher to gather specific data about pupil performance, pointing to areas of difficulty, allowing for diagnostic evaluation, and leading to suggestions for teaching.

A checklist is one such tool, and we offer one here for the teacher's use. We would hope and expect that teachers implementing sciencing programs would modify and reshape this list to reflect the learning goals in their individual classrooms.

Profile of Student Performance on Sciencing Tasks

(Diagnostic Checklist)

Pupil's Name: _____

Dates of Observations: _____ _____ _____
                            1st   2nd   3rd

Key

1 = consistently   2 = frequently   3 = occasionally   4 = rarely

	Observations		
	1st	2nd	3rd

Social Group Behavior

1. The student's behavior is independent; that is, student does not depend on me for help with every step of every problem. _____ _____ _____
2. The student is able to make reasonable, thoughtful choices and accept the consequences of these decisions. _____ _____ _____
3. The student is a responsible and cooperative participant of a group. _____ _____ _____
4. The student is helpful in caring for the classroom learning environment. _____ _____ _____
5. The student works purposefully and productively in the group. _____ _____ _____

Personal and Ego Behavior

1. The student shows that he or she is aware of his or her strengths and limitations in learning tasks. _____ _____ _____
2. The student shows that he or she can deal effectively with new situations. _____ _____ _____
3. The student shows that he or she has an awareness of self as a capable problem solver. _____ _____ _____
4. The student shows a sense of personal pride in both self and work. _____ _____ _____
5. The student shows self-confidence as a "creator" and "innovator." _____ _____ _____
6. The student shows self-confidence as a problem solver. _____ _____ _____
7. The student shows growth in self-esteem. _____ _____ _____
8. The student shows self-initiating behavior. _____ _____ _____

Cognitive and Intellectual Behavior

1. The student is able to make thoughtful, accurate observations. _____ _____ _____
2. The student is able to suggest reasonable and appropriate hypotheses. _____ _____ _____

3. The student is able to identify assumptions and differentiate these from facts.   _____ _____ _____

4. The student is able to identify similarities and differences of significance when making comparisons.   _____ _____ _____

5. The student is able to classify objects and create classification categories.   _____ _____ _____

6. The student is able to gather data and make meaningful interpretations of data.   _____ _____ _____

7. The student is able to make sound decisions.   _____ _____ _____

8. The student is able to be creative, imaginative, and inventive in working on sciencing tasks.   _____ _____ _____

9. The student is able to design projects and experiments to test hypotheses.   _____ _____ _____

10. The student is able to suspend judgment and be more tolerant of uncertainty.   _____ _____ _____

11. The student is able to formulate and raise intelligent questions about scientific phenomena.   _____ _____ _____

12. The student shows understanding of the major scientific concepts.   _____ _____ _____

13. The student shows an increased knowledge base with respect to scientific information.   _____ _____ _____

Attitudes and Appreciations Behavior

1. The student shows delight in exploration, experimentation, and discovery.   _____ _____ _____

2. The student shows a love for science and scientific explorations.   _____ _____ _____

3. The student shows an appreciation of science as a means of acquiring information and understanding of the world in which we live.   _____ _____ _____

4. The student shows increased interest in finding out and a decreased need to "know the answer."   _____ _____ _____

Self-evaluation   The importance of involving pupils in the evaluative process has long been advocated by many teachers. These teachers believe that such involvement is critical in the promotion of pupil learning. Of equal importance, these procedures allow for the shift of the locus of evaluation onto the learner. Such a shift requires that learners assume more and more responsibility for their choices and their actions and the consequences of their actions. Learners thus decrease their dependence on outside authority figures for judging their actions, for deciding whether what they do is "good" or "bad." Carl Rogers has told us that the

> most fundamental condition of creativity is that the locus of evaluative judgment is internal. The value of his product is, for the creative person, established not by the praise or criticism of others, but by himself. This does not mean that such a person is oblivious

to, or unwilling to be aware of the judgments of others. It is simply that the basis of evaluation lies within himself, in his own organismic reaction to and appraisal of his product.[9]

What distinguishes the most creative and innovative scientists of our time is their utter confidence in themselves and in their ability to move ahead to undertake experimentation with the most far-reaching, mind-boggling problems that confront them. Their inner strength imbues them with courage, drive, inspiration to create and invent, and freedom to live with risk and uncertainty. Such attributes cannot emerge in an individual who has been intimidated by the judgmental forces of others, one who must always turn to others to know: "Is this good?" "Is this right?" "Do you like this?" Persons whose locus of evaluation is far outside themselves have become crippled in their own independent functioning. Perhaps worse, they are likely to fall prey to the manipulations and coercions of others to whom they have transferred the power of judgment over their lives.

Can elementary school children play a role in self-evaluation? The data from both primary and intermediate teachers suggest that not only can they do so but that they learn to do so thoughtfully, intelligently, sensitively, and with much wisdom and insight into self.[10]

Self-evaluative procedures may occur in at least two forms. One is through oral conferencing. The teacher confers with the pupil and raises questions about his or her behavior and performance on sciencing tasks. During the raising of such questions, the teacher's tone remains neutral and nonjudgmental; the pupil is encouraged to arrive at an assessment of performance without subtle leading by the teacher. Therefore, when the teacher raises these questions, there must be no "hidden agenda"—that is, the teacher must not be making implicit judgments about what the pupil is supposed to say. The teacher does not anticipate any particular answer.

Here is a list of questions that promote a pupil's self-evaluative responses. Naturally, not all of these questions would be raised in a single conference. The teacher would select the ones that elicit the kind of information that is important in that particular session.

What science centers did you participate in today?

Tell me about the way you worked.

Tell me about some discoveries you made.

Tell me about some of the things that did not go too well for you.

Tell me about some of the things that gave you trouble.

What comments would you like to make about your behavior?

What were some of the things that you could do for yourself?

What were some of the things you needed help with?

How do you feel about your work in the cleanup of the centers?

How do you feel you got along with the other members of your group?

Tell me about any new inventions that you created.

Where do you think you need help from me?

What did you discover about the materials you worked with, and how might you account for what happened?

Tell me how you classified those objects.

What were some of the decisions you made, and how did they work for you?

Tell me about some of the experiments you conducted and what you found out.

What questions do you have about what happened?

Tell me how you think the work in science is going for you.

How do you feel about the work in science?

A second form of self-evaluation is through pupils' written reports. Students are asked to make careful and thoughtful appraisals of what they have done and the quality of their science work. Examples of some self-report forms are presented here. Teachers are encouraged to use these as a basis from which to develop an original form that is more appropriate for their own individual use. Also, as children's work in science will tend to become more sophisticated and more extensive, it is probably a good idea to modify the report forms at intervals to reflect this growth.

Self-evaluation Report, Type 1

Name _____ **Date** _____

1. In my work with my group, I am (check one) .
   [ ] usually very responsible
   [ ] mostly responsible and cooperative
   [ ] sometimes responsible and cooperative
2. In my work with my group, I (check one) .
   [ ] usually get right down to work on the science tasks
   [ ] need a little time to get down to work
   [ ] have a hard time getting down to work
3. In my work in the science centers, I (check one) .
   [ ] usually help with the cleanup and do my jobs
   [ ] sometimes help with the cleanup and do my jobs
   [ ] have a hard time getting down to helping with the cleanup jobs

4. This is what I want to say about my behavior in the group: _____

_____

_____

5. In my work on science tasks, I think I am (check one) .
   [   ] a good problem solver
   [   ] learning to be a good problem solver
   [   ] having a hard time as a problem solver

6. In my work on science tasks, I (check one) .
   [   ] have a lot of confidence in myself
   [   ] have a little confidence in myself
   [   ] am not sure about my confidence in myself

7. In my work on science tasks, I am able to (check one) .
   [   ] work on my own, with very little help from others
   [   ] work on my own, with some help from others
   [   ] work on my own, with a lot of help from others

8. This is what I want to add about the way I work on science tasks: _____

_____

_____

9. In working on thinking tasks, I am able to (check all that apply) .
   [   ] make accurate observations
   [   ] identify assumptions
   [   ] make comparisons
   [   ] classify objects
   [   ] gather data
   [   ] make decisions
   [   ] invent new things
   [   ] design projects
   [   ] make up experiments
   [   ] use my imagination
   [   ] ask good questions

10. This is what I want to add about my work on thinking tasks: _____

_____

_____

11. In my science work, I am learning that _____

_____

_____

12. When the teacher says it's time for science, I feel _____

_____

_____

13. This is what I want to add about my work in the science program: _____

_____

_____

Self-evaluation Report, Type 2: Weekly Summary

Name _____ **Date** _____

1. After thinking about my work in the science program this week, I think I need to (check one) .
   [ ] concentrate on working more responsibly in my group
   [ ] get more confidence in myself
   [ ] try to work more on my own
   [ ] concentrate more on the thinking activities with which I have difficulty:
   (check all that apply)
      [ ] observing
      [ ] identifying assumptions
      [ ] making comparisons
      [ ] classifying
      [ ] collecting data
      [ ] making decisions
      [ ] inventing
      [ ] designing projects
      [ ] making up experiments
      [ ] using my imagination
      [ ] asking good questions
2. This is what else I think I can do to improve my work in the science activities:

_____

_____

_____

3. These are the good things I'd like to say about my work in science this week:

_____

_____

_____

4. This is how I see that my work has improved since the beginning of the school
   year: _____

_____

_____

Self-evaluation Report, Type 3: Weekly Summary

Name _____ **Date** _____

1. What is your opinion of your work in the science centers this week? _____

_____

_____

2. What is your opinion of your behavior in the science centers this week? _____

_____

_____

3. What are your plans for next week in science? _____

_____

_____

4. In what ways would you describe your progress in the science activities since
   your last self-report? _____

_____

_____

Portfolios   Portfolios are an important means of gathering data about a single student's performance over time, in a particular subject area like science, and/or in overall growth and learning. A large folder, envelope, or other container is needed for each student, and classroom documents from the very beginning of the school year are placed in the folder. These documents may include children's written work, drawings, other pencil-and-paper tasks; they may include notes about science center participation (e.g., which centers were worked in, which investigations were carried out, what observations were made). Students may be the sole contributors to their own portfolios, or the portfolios may be a collaborative record, with teachers adding material they see as relevant. Portfolios provide a longitudinal record of students' growth in knowledge, attitude, and skills, revealing both quantity and quality. They offer a documented picture of how the student has been progressing.

In many classes where portfolios are used, students have ownership over them and are given choices about what they want to include. This ownership puts the student into the role of evaluator; he or she assesses and decides, "This is what I have chosen to represent my best work." Teachers may also keep their own separate records (portfolios) for each student containing those documents that the teacher deems significant. One or both methods of keeping documentation adds immeasurably to the wealth of material that profiles a student's work over the school year.

At the end of a designated interval (once a month perhaps, or perhaps at the end of a marking period), the child's portfolio is presented in a conference with the teacher (and perhaps the parent). The documents in the portfolio are examined and the quality of the student's work is discussed. Teachers who work collaboratively with children in this process will confer together about standards of performance and make explicit plans for next steps in learning.[11]

Reporting to Parents

For some teachers, ghosts of parents past loom large in their classrooms as potential critics of every action. While this may be every teacher's secret nightmare, the reality is that most parents want at least two things for their children: They want them to learn, and they want them to be happy in school. And this is true of most concerned parents, whether they live in the affluent suburbs or in the inner-city core.

Reporting to parents about pupils' learning is one of the more important of the teacher's professional functions, and we recommend that reporting about a child's work in sciencing emphasize the child's growth toward the program's learning goals. What's more, we recommend that parents be informed about these learning goals clearly and explicitly and that each child's progress toward these goals be stated as straightforwardly as possible. Parents who are given jargon-free, genuine, professionally sound teacher judgments tend to be more satisfied that they have a greater and deeper understanding and appreciation of their children and their children's classroom functioning in science.

The following recapitulation of learning goals may serve as a guide on which reports to parents may be based.

Social Dimensions of Learning in Science

1. The child's growth in functioning independently, responsibly, and cooperatively in groups
2. The child's growth in ability to make reasonable and wise choices
3. The child's growth in accepting consequences of his or her choices

Personal and Ego Dimensions of Learning in Science

1. The child's growth in his or her sense of self-worth
2. The child's growth in self-confidence
3. The child's growth in his or her ability to create and invent
4. The child's growth in self-initiative behavior
5. The child's growth in pride in self and his or her own achievement
6. The child's realistic assessment of his or her strengths and limitations
7. The child's growth in his or her feelings of power to manipulate the environment effectively

Cognitive and Intellectual Dimensions of Learning in Science

1. The child's growth in the ability to make thoughtful, accurate observations
2. The child's growth in the ability to make reasonable hypotheses

3. The child's growth in the ability to differentiate assumptions from fact
4. The child's growth in the ability to make comparisons and identify similarities and differences
5. The child's ability to classify objects and create a system of categories that works
6. The child's ability to gather data and draw conclusions based on those data
7. The child's ability to create and invent new schemes and to design projects and experiments
8. The child's growth in the ability to understand major scientific concepts
9. The child's growth in the ability to raise questions
10. The increase in the child's knowledge base of scientific information

Attitudes and Appreciations Dimensions of Learning in Science

1. The child's growth in appreciation for science and scientific investigations

Evaluation: Some Last Words

In concluding this discussion of evaluation practices, it might be helpful for us to recapitulate the beliefs at the heart of the classroom practices that have been suggested in the preceding sections.

1. Evaluation is a highly personal, very subjective process in which teachers assess student performance in terms of their own built-in biases. Biases are reduced when the teacher's judgments rely more on astute, informed observations rather than on assumptions and attributions of attitude and motive.
2. The primary purpose of evaluation is to provide feedback to students that enables them to take the next steps in growing and learning.
3. A secondary purpose of evaluation is to provide clear and well-informed feedback to parents about pupil growth, behavior, and classroom performance.
4. Feedback to students that is not usable in promoting learning may be detrimental to their growth and progress.
5. Teachers' observations of student performance in a variety of classroom contexts, over a long period of time, are likely to be more helpful in assessing student learning than formal, standardized tests. Portfolios provide important records that document an individual student's growth and learning over time.
6. Standardized and teacher-made tests often supply little data about student performance that is helpful in diagnosing weaknesses and areas where remediation is needed.
7. Some types of evaluation may be harmful to pupils' concepts of self. Those that diminish pupils' ability to grow and learn should be banished from the classroom.
8. Excessive use of teachers' judgmental, evaluative responses work to promote pupil dependency on the teacher. Such procedures militate against the development of pupil independence and growth toward personal autonomy.

9. Maturity brings with it the ability to maintain the locus of evaluation inside oneself. Teachers may work toward this goal by increasingly emphasizing self-evaluation procedures.

10. Evaluation practices that emphasize single "correct" answers lead to a false picture of science as a concern for finding "truths." True science, what we call "sciencing," is more concerned with processes of discovery, experimentation, testing hypotheses, risk taking, imagining, and searching—learning to err and to bounce back to try again.

11. Evaluation in sciencing must lead to information about pupil progress toward the stated learning goals. Practices that do not provide such information may be costly in time, money, and energy and may lack real value.

NOTES

1. Virgil Howes, *Informal Teaching in the Open Classroom* (New York: Macmillan, 1972), pp. 15–60; David W. Johnson, Roger T. Johnson, Edythe Johnson Holubec, & Patricia Roy, *Circles of Learning* (Washington, DC: Association for Supervision and Curriculum Development, 1984); Selma Wassermann, *Serious Players in the Primary Classroom* (New York: Teachers College Press, 1990).

2. Selma Wassermann, *Serious Players in the Primary Classroom.*

3. For help in setting up cooperative learning groups, see Johnson et al., *Circles of Learning.*

4. Robert Rosenthal and Lenore Jacobson, *Pygmalion in the Classroom* (New York: Holt, Rinehart & Winston, 1968), pp. 47–60.

5. Donald Schön, *The Reflective Practitioner* (New York: Basic Books, 1983), pp. 49–69.

6. Lazer Goldberg, *Children and Science* (New York: Scribners, 1970), pp. 120–130; Mary Budd Rowe, *Teaching Science as Continuous Inquiry* (New York: McGraw-Hill, 1973), pp. 510–549; Vito Perrone, "On Standardized Testing," *Childhood Education*, Spring, 1991, pp. 131–142; British Columbia Ministry of Education, *Primary Program Foundation Document* (Victoria, British Columbia: Ministry of Education, 1992), pp. 93–119; Kenneth Goodman, Yetta Goodman, & Wendy Hood, *The Whole Language Evaluation Book* (Portsmouth, NH: Heinemann, 1989); Grant Wiggins, "Assessment: Authenticity, Context, and Validity," *Phi Delta Kappan*, 75(3), pp. 200–214; Alfred DeVito, *Creative Wellsprings for Science Teaching* (West Lafayett, IN: Creative Ventures, 1984).

7. Dorothy Cohen and Virginia Stein with Nancy Balaban, *Observing and Recording the Behavior of Young Children* Third Edition (New York: Teachers College Press, 1983); *Observing & Assessing Young Children* (Toronto: Board of Education, 1983).

8. Schön, *Reflective Practitioner*, pp. 49–50.

9. Carl Rogers, *On Becoming a Person* (Boston: Houghton Mifflin, 1961), p. 354.

10. Cheryl Macdonald, "A Better Way of Reporting," *B. C. Teacher*, 61 (March-April, 1982), pp. 142–144; Carl Rogers, *Freedom to Learn for the Eighties* (Columbus, OH: Merrill, 1983), pp. 45–56.

11. For more information about the use of portfolios, see Paul Broadfoot (Ed.), *Profiles and Records of Achievement: A Review of Issues and Practice* (New York: Holt, Rinehart & Winston, 1986); Anne Davies, Coren Cameron, Colleen Politano, & Kathleen Gregory, *Together Is Better* (Winnepeg: Peguis, 1992); Donald Graves & B. Sunstein (Eds.), *Portfolio Portraits* (Portsmouth, NH: Heinemann, 1992); Andy Hargreaves, "The Maturation of Educational Measurement," *E + M Newsletter*, No. 45 (Toronto: OISE Educational Evaluation Center, 1988–89); Grant Wiggins, "Assessment: Authenticity, Context and Validity," *Phi Delta Kappan*, 95(3), pp. 200–214.

Thinking and Decision Making in Science

There are many ways to teach science. The way one chooses to teach is very much tied up with what one considers important in teaching the subject, as well as with the instructional strategies one chooses to ensure that those important learnings are effectively realized. Both of these considerations are influenced to a large extent by cognitive-emotional factors in teachers themselves—specifically, their beliefs, their perceptions of the acts we call teaching and learning, and their personalities. In teaching science, as in teaching any other subject, it is helpful for teachers to understand how their beliefs and perceptions influence their choices and how "open" and "controlling" personality characteristics tilt them toward certain teaching styles. It is also helpful for teachers to acknowledge what they consider to be the important learning goals they are after and to devise teaching strategies that are most likely to bring them to those goals.

Didactic teaching (sometimes called direct instruction) is probably the most popular and widespread means of instruction in science. Teachers who choose this approach may do so because of their concern with the importance of learning *information*. In direct instruction, the emphasis is on students' learning the *facts* of science. This is usually done via whole-class instruction, seatwork, dittos, pupil recitation—all activities geared to the same instructional end, the learners' acquisition of "scientific truths." Teachers who choose such an approach to teaching science are more comfortable with the kinds of classroom control over students' behavior and learning that direct instruction affords. Direct instruction puts the teacher at center stage; it is the teacher who plays the more active role. The students are more passive; they listen and respond to the teacher's cues and are otherwise expected to be quiet.

Although direct instruction has been hailed as effective in raising test scores,[1] an examination of the supporting research reveals that such claims go far beyond what research findings even promise or suggest.[2] Moreover, critics point to its serious shortcomings, particularly its emphasis on lower-order tasks and lack of concern for the higher processes.[3] While such limitations are serious for teaching in all subjects, they may be especially critical in the teaching of science.

Another approach to teaching science may be called "presentation" teaching. Such an approach combines information dispensing with "showing how." The teacher may do much talking, but demonstrations of how things work are also included. Teachers who choose this approach implicitly or explicitly see the acquisition of information and comprehension of certain basic scientific principles as primary learning goals. The effectiveness of this approach depends largely on the teacher's ability to present with style. Pupils' attention to the presentation is heightened if the teacher is highly entertaining, and such a talent is likely to ensure students' enjoyment of the subject, as well as their attention to the presentation.

In presentation teaching, the teacher is once again at center stage and in control of all the action. Students are listeners and observers—but there may be a higher degree of student involvement with respect to raising questions about the presentation. Presentation teaching is generally chosen by teachers who are both knowledgeable and comfortable in the subject area; they have something important to show and tell, and they enjoy doing so. Some teachers have suggested that it is important to hold the attention of pupils by entertaining them, because teachers "must compete with television" in commanding pupils' attention. In both direct instruction and presentation teaching, learning is measured by pupils' ability to store and retrieve the information about the subject accurately.

An approach to teaching science identified as inquiry grew out of the work of J. Richard Suchman, begun in 1957 at the University of Illinois. The materials Suchman developed were designed to train children in the "art of inquiry," enabling them to initiate and direct their own investigations. Suchman was concerned that most children who enter school as natural inquirers with several years of preschool experience in manipulating objects and who form concepts based on this experience lose this ability in school. In school, a different kind of learning took place, in which children were expected to keep in step with their classes and were not expected to "fool around" with materials and ideas. Students were rewarded for giving the right answers; they were expected to listen and to read what they were told to read. They were seldom given the opportunity to make decisions or draw their own conclusions. Suchman's research showed that as children moved up through the elementary grades, they asked fewer questions, proposed fewer hypotheses, and became less independent in their thinking.[4]

In response to his findings, Suchman developed a series of short film loops, each of which presented a discrepant event in science. Children view the film and begin to formulate questions about the event. They must phrase their questions in ways that allow them to gather data; the teacher may respond to their questions with answers of either "yes" or "no." As pupils gather data in this way, they begin the process of theory generation, which helps them understand the science phenomena in the film. While conducting these inquiries, children use concepts of measurement, mass, weight, motion, and pressure.[5]

The approach to teaching science currently termed inquiry has evolved beyond its original methodology. Now almost any experience that invites pupils to "mess around" with materials is often called inquiry, whether pupils are helped to make meaning from the experience or not. Perhaps such inappropriate applications of the original intent of inquiry teaching account for its loss of favor with public school officials. Inquiry teaching, like many good methodologies, has evolved in both good ways and bad.

Teachers who choose an inquiry approach in science would share the belief that the process of inquiry is at least as important as the information gathered. This approach, carried out in strict Suchman orthodoxy, would also depend to a considerable extent on the teachers' knowledge of science and on their abilities to field students' questions with accurate responses. The use of film loops instead of hands-on materials and the teacher's center-stage direction of all questions and answers in data gathering made this approach appealing to teachers who wanted to emphasize inquiry learning but also wanted to exercise extensive control of the process.

Variations of inquiry teaching are widely advocated today in several forms ("problem-solving approaches," "discovery approaches," and others) by leading science educators.[6]

The teaching-for-thinking approach we call Play-Debrief-Replay evolves from inquiry teaching, with important departures from Suchman's original conceptualization. This approach is chosen by teachers who believe that the most effective route for gathering information in science is through emphasis on the higher-order mental processes. The important difference is that teachers are more comfortable in allowing pupils to play active roles in their own learning. Though they are always "in charge" in their classrooms, they do not need to exercise control over every learning situation. They understand that important learning may occur in a classroom in which children are actively engaged, working cooperatively in small groups, in productive problem solving. They share the view that concept development best results from pupils' hands-on experiential learning, as advocated by the current AAAS report on the need for reform in science teaching.[7]

Teachers who choose this or other inquiry-based approaches do not think of science as simply being concerned with the presentation of a body of information about science or the learning of "scientific truths." They see science teaching as involving the process skills of learning to gather information; to observe, study, and classify; to speculate, hypothesize, and generate theories; to test ideas and reject previously held assumptions in the face of new and contradictory evidence; to design investigations and experiments; and to interpret data intelligently.[8]

In this approach, process skills are emphasized over "correct answers," the *search* for answers becomes more important than the answers themselves, questioning answers is more important than accepting them at face value, and greater tolerance for ambiguity, rather than closure, is cultivated.

In this evolution of inquiry teaching, more opportunities are extended for pupils to examine decisions requiring scientific judgments, and one important goal is to help pupils make decisions about matters of science with intelligence, sensitivity, and growing wisdom. This chapter will make more explicit how the Play-Debrief-Replay approach to teaching science, introduced in Chapter 1, lends itself to the goals and instructional strategies of teaching for thinking and decision making in science.

LEVELS OF THINKING

It will likely not come as news that the various mental acts that we call thinking differ greatly. For example, when we are asked to come up with the names of three major cities in Europe, the name of the team that won the World Series in 1986, the chemical symbol for iron, or the definition of photosynthesis, we are thinking. Such activities call for the recall of information, and such information retrieval, no matter how hard we have to work at remembering, requires that we function at lower cognitive levels.

When we think about a vacation we had last year, a movie we saw and liked, or a favorite piece of music, we are also thinking. This kind of thinking, however, is not very taxing in terms of intellectual rigor. It does not require sophisticated cognitive processing, or any generative act.

Planning for a vacation in Spain, thinking about which three couples might make an interesting group of dinner guests, thinking about organizing the Saturday chores— these acts also require thinking. While such acts require some planning and problem solving, the quality of thinking that is called for is not excessively rigorous in terms of cognitive demands.

By contrast, raising enough money to buy a new car, deciding whether it is more advantageous to buy a new house or stay where you are, selecting and implementing a healthful diet that will ensure that you lose 20 pounds, designing and building a small seaworthy boat, designing a Parents' Night program to inform parents about your new sciencing curriculum and generate their interest and support—such activities involve higher-order functioning. They require planning and problem-solving tasks of greater complexity. In such activities, ideas and strategies need to be created and implemented, and the evaluation of results is implicit.

At even higher levels of cognitive functioning are activities that call for designing investigations, creating new schemes, and extensive original thinking. Such problems or exercises call for functioning at very high, sophisticated levels and involve tasks that are very complex. Such activities would include designing an experiment to test the use of vitamin C as an effective remedy for colds, designing a new evaluative system that would assess pupils' growth in cognitive skills, or finding a cure for a terminal or degenerative disease.

From these examples it can be seen that there are various levels of thinking. Some school tasks require the retrieval and recall of information. This is sometimes called "lower-order" thinking. These activities require no originality on the part of the thinkers. Some work called thinking calls for simple calculation and minimal processing of information. This too occurs at lower cognitive levels and requires minimal originality or creativity. Some work called thinking requires pupils to come up with the answer the teacher seeks. Such activities once more call for little originality or creativity and occur at lower levels of the cognitive scale. Other activities called thinking call for imagining, creating, making decisions, planning, evaluating, solving problems, or designing investigations. These require much originality and the ability to process information, to create schemes, to take cognitive risks. These thinking activities require higher-order cognitive functioning. Differences are also seen in the significance of what is being thought about.

An effective sciencing program is dependent not only on the teacher's awareness of the differences between activities that call for students to function at lower or higher cognitive levels but also on the incorporation of higher-order tasks into the science curriculum.

Higher-order tasks are inquiry-oriented, and most of them are open-ended. They do not lead students to a predetermined, correct answer or answers. Usually, many different responses are acceptable and appropriate. Lower-order tasks generally lead to "correct" responses, and the purpose of these tasks is to help pupils arrive at that answer.

For example, in a higher-order task, pupils might be asked to develop hypotheses to explain why 2 feet of snow had collected on one side of a street and 3 feet on the other. In such a task, the process of generating several appropriate, thoughtful explanations is what is emphasized, and no "correct" answer is sought. A lower-order task might require students simply to calculate how many inches of snow had accumulated on each side of the street.

Higher-order tasks are rooted in the kinds of mental operations that demand the processing and generation of information, intelligent observation, and critical discrimination. Louis Raths calls such mental functions *thinking operations,* and he identifies 13 of them:

1. Comparing: looking for similarities and differences
2. Observing: making visual, auditory, and tactile observations of data
3. Classifying: examining an assortment of items, sorting them, and categorizing them to some purpose
4. Imagining and creating: inventing new ideas, new techniques, and new apparatus; tapping the inner resources of inventiveness
5. Hypothesizing: coming up with a variety of appropriate explanations for a particular question, problem, or dilemma
6. Evaluating and criticizing: making judgments and offering opinions based on formulated criteria
7. Identifying assumptions: differentiating between what is observably true and what is taken for granted
8. Collecting and organizing data: locating information, locating sources, examining and culling relevant data, and developing procedures for the assembling of the data
9. Summarizing: condensing the essential meanings from a body of data
10. Coding: using a shorthand system to identify certain patterns of thinking that may be counterproductive to effective cognitive functioning
11. Interpreting: explaining the meanings of an experience; reading into the data and extracting supportable conclusions from them
12. Designing problems and investigations: identifying problems, hypothesizing, collecting and organizing data, testing hypotheses, and evaluating results
13. Decision making: examining the beliefs, attitudes, and feelings that lie behind the choices we make and examining the consequences of personally made choices[9]

The examples that follow show how these thinking operations are incorporated into the investigative play stage of the sciencing program. Children work with these higher-order tasks in small groups, devising their own systems of generating data. Sometimes the tasks might involve photographs, models, or illustrations instead of manipulative materials. While such materials are also productive for generating ideas and are advocated for use in examining value issues involved in scientific decision making (to which topic we will return shortly), the use of hands-on, experiential materials should take precedence, especially in the first stages of concept building.

Example 1: Comparing

Present the pupils with a balloon and an air pump. Ask them to study the items and to conduct some investigations with them. Then ask them to discuss how these two items are alike and how they are different.

Example 2: Identifying Assumptions

Ask the children to take their own pulse and to record their pulse rate for a period of 1 minute. Then have them talk together and compare their pulse rates with one another. Ask them to identify some assumptions they have made in recording their pulse rates.

Example 3: Imagining and Creating

Present the pupils with the following activity: Each year the city of Nanaimo, British Columbia, has a bathtub race. Each participant builds a bathtub boat that can be propelled across the Straits of Georgia, a distance of 30 miles. Ask the pupils to work together to design a bathtub boat that might win this race. Ask them to build a model of it, using whatever materials are available in the classroom.

Example 4: Classifying

Gather a collection of tools or other implements, such as rope, hammer, ruler, shears, pulley, pliers, drill, pump, wrench, extension cord, battery, saw, hose nozzle, light bulb, and stapler. Ask the pupils to work in groups and to classify the items. Ask them to give each group a name that would identify the characteristics shared by the items in each group. Have them suggest purposes such a classification system might have.

Example 5: Suggesting Hypotheses

Present a group of children with a nail, knife, or other object that is rusted. Ask them to examine the object and to generate hypotheses that would explain how the rusting occurred.

Example 6: Observing

Present the students with one or more pieces of plastic. Ask them to work together to study the plastic. Ask them to talk together about what they observed. Then ask them to list ten observations they made about this material.

FREEDOM TO CHOOSE

In both direct instruction and presentation teaching, most important decisions and matters of judgment reside in the teachers' domain. Implicitly and explicitly, teachers carry the burden not only of knowing but of deciding as well. Since the most important judgments are made by teachers, students have little opportunity to get serious practice in the skill of making judgments as it relates to science. They are given little practice in examining data intelligently and in using data to arrive at thoughtful, data-based decisions. While that may not seem much of a problem at first glance, consider the implications of students having such limited opportunities to examine scientific issues with values dimensions. Edward B. Fiske, writing about "scientific literacy" in the *New York Times Education Supplement,* states:

> Citizens are routinely finding themselves facing decisions that require scientific judgments—from national policies on nuclear power and "Star Wars" to personal decisions about the risks of sexually transmitted diseases. But there is uneasiness that many Americans are ill equipped by their science educations to make such decisions intelligently.[10]

Citing data on the lack of scientific literacy in the general adult population, Fiske points to the study of 2000 adults, conducted by Jon D. Miller at Northern Illinois University, in which more than 2 out of 5 agreed that "space shots have caused changes in our weather and that some numbers are especially lucky for some people." More than a third of those interviewed agreed that "science tends to break down people's ideas of right and wrong."[11]

The burden of becoming scientifically literate—of becoming informed about the value issues surrounding scientific decisions—belongs to every citizen of a democratic society. It is, in fact, the primary mission of the group of scientists and educators whose work on Project 2061 pointed to the urgent need of "scientific literacy . . . as a central goal of education."[12]

Life in an advanced technological society is driven by scientific decision making: Should world population be controlled? Should we encourage the building of supersonic aircraft? Should a new form of life, created in a laboratory by combining genetic material from two different species of bacteria, be released in the environment? Should the black bear population be systematically extinguished to protect national park visitors? Should scientists be free to conduct experiments on live animals? Should the chemical plant get rid of its toxic waste in your community? Is the incidence of "Gulf Syndrome" related to veterans' exposure to toxic gas? Are hormone-injected cattle and poultry good for us to eat? Should we allow the nuclear power plant to be built in the next town? Should we vote for candidates who support or oppose defense expenditures for weapons in space? What should be done about oil spills in the oceans?

If we decide to accept the burdens of studying these issues, of becoming informed and exercising our own judgments about them, we must provide a place in our science curriculum for opportunities for students to acquire such skills as are needed to carry that responsibility. If we choose to unburden ourselves of that responsibility, we give power and control over our lives to the "experts" who will make the decisions for us, and we will have to learn to live with the consequences.

We may, of course, leave all these decisions to the experts. Yet René Dubos tells us that although "scientists are valued as sources of expert information, there is a widespread feeling that their scientific expertise does not necessarily qualify them for decision-making in problems of social concern."[13] He goes on to say:

> In practically all, if not all, cases, the decision to use or reject a scientific technology involves complex factors such as economic growth and national prestige, a variety of experiences affecting the quality of life, and other values that cannot be defined in scientific terms. Specialized technical knowledge is essential because it helps to forecast the probable consequences of certain courses of action, but it is not sufficient to formulate practical policies because these always involve choices as to what is socially desirable or objectionable. Because of their social awareness, perceptive and critical laymen can often contribute as much as professional scientists to the formulation of public policies concerning science. In many situations, indeed, laymen even have an advantage over scientists in this regard because their overall view of human problems is not distorted by the parochialism which commonly results from technical specialization.[14]

It is true that scientists may be experts in their individual fields, but they are also human, subject to the same human failings found in the rest of us. "Psychological processes powerfully influence and constrain the quality of scientific inquiry,"[15] and the notion of human bias and prejudice is not entirely absent from all scientific endeavors.[16]

In a democratic society we have many options, and we are asked to choose from among them. We are encouraged to study, to examine the issues, to think for ourselves, and to make up our minds. We may exercise these options through the ballot box and through other powerful devices, and we are encouraged to do so. Such action on the part of society at large may be for the better or for the worse, depending on whether those who act do so out of informed consensus or out of their own prejudices and vested interests.

David Gardner, former president of the University of California, has written:

> There is something anomalous, incongruous even, in the contrast between the scientific texture of our culture and the scientific ignorance of our people. Not everyone needs the

education and training it takes to prepare one to be a theoretical physicist or a marine biologist. But if the average person has little or only the most rudimentary acquaintance with the character and place of science and technology in our lives, society and culture, then as a people we cannot comprehend the context within which we are living. Nor can we, as individuals, comprehend the consequences of our actions either for ourselves or for others.[17]

By actively confronting value issues in science, students will come to a greater understanding of their own beliefs and feelings with regard to these issues and the beliefs and feelings of others—both their peers and the adults who are making the decisions that affect their lives. They will be empowered to deal not only with what is but, more important, with the what "ought to be." In that way, they will grow more responsible, more knowledgeable, and therefore better able to play active roles in making the world a more desirable place in which to live. George Pugh has written that if we are to enjoy a future where life will be worth living, there "is need for deliberate education in human values."[18]

IMPLICATIONS FOR THE TEACHER

A hands-on, experiential teaching-for-thinking program in science calls for the active involvement of pupils. Instead of prizing and rewarding conforming, passive pupil behaviors, teaching for thinking requires pupils to function independently and responsibly on their own. Instead of learning dependency on the teacher as the source of knowledge, direction, and control, the students are required to become problem solvers and to work out learning problems autonomously. Instead of learning conformity and acquiescence, pupils learn challenging, inquisitive behaviors. Is this what we really want? Do we really want students to become more critical and more questioning, less accepting of what we say is true? Do we want more autonomous behaviors in our classrooms and less dependence on the teacher as the authority? Do we want classrooms in which children may exercise choice, in which they are free to differ with us, without being condemned for it?

We cannot have both a teaching-for-thinking program in science and conformity. We cannot have learning to choose and yet avoid controversy. We cannot make all the decisions for students and exercise all the controls over their learning and yet expect them to learn to do these things for themselves. We cannot have an experiential science curriculum emphasizing thinking without the mess that is an adjunct of any productive and creative act.

In making the choice about how to teach science, the teacher is at a critical crossroads. To choose teaching for thinking may mean relinquishing long-held, deeply entrenched beliefs about teaching. It is likely to mean taking some risks. It is more than

likely to mean creating classroom conditions that are markedly different from what is seen in other classrooms.

It may mean some rough roadways, for most new paths do not follow a straight and smooth route. Few of us learn to walk without falling. Yet the rewards for such a choice are great: classrooms in which students are purposefully and productively engaged in scientific inquiry, where knowledge is being generated, where children are learning to make choices. Teaching for thinking may be a choice worth considering, but only you can decide that for yourself. Should you make that choice, we hope that the rest of this book will serve you well.

PLAY–DEBRIEF–REPLAY: INSTRUCTIONAL STRATEGIES EMPHASIZING THINKING AND DECISION MAKING

Investigative Play: Concept Development Through Hands-on Experience

One of the most important goals of science teaching is the development of conceptual understanding. As concept development occurs, so does increased scientific awareness, and on this very solid foundation a substantial knowledge base is built.

Concepts do not grow well in the one-dimensional garden of listening. They are more readily developed through three-dimensional, concrete experiences. Take, for example, the study of water. We can come to learn something about water from hearing these facts:

Water is colorless and tasteless.

It freezes at 32° Fahrenheit.

It boils at 212° Fahrenheit.

Its chemical symbol is H_2O.

However, knowing such facts about water hardly contributes to our understanding of the larger meanings about water: how it "works," how it affects living and nonliving things, how it is like other substances, how it is different from them. (What's more, such facts presented as "scientific truths" are already misleading. For example, due to certain minerals in the ground, some tap water is far from tasteless, as some children's experience will tell. Also, the temperature at which water boils and freezes varies with other factors, such as altitude.)

Concepts about water begin to be formed in the bath when we are babies—when Mommy soaks up the washcloth and sprinkles droplets playfully on our hair, when we suck it out of a bottle and register disappointment at its not being milk. We develop concepts about water from touching, tasting, and smelling; by making tea and putting ice in lemonade; by squirting the hose and spilling the jug; by dissolving sugar in it; by seeing plants die for lack of it; by making bubbles; by quenching thirst with it. To experience water in its many contexts is to grow to greater conceptual awareness. It also follows that when our experiences have been real, it is much easier to acquire "the facts." Having seen water, touched water, and tasted water, it is easier to *know* water. Our knowledge base is greatly expanded when it is built on the solid foundation of experience, leading to concept development.

Investigative play provides the forum for such concept development. Here's an example of how this might occur. The teacher sets up the conditions in which investigative play on one aspect of studying water takes place by creating a center containing one or two large plastic basins of water and a variety of objects: sponges, chalk, Ping-Pong balls, modeling clay, aluminum foil, containers with removable lids, bits of wood, clothespins, stones, shells, Styrofoam chips, plastic dishes and cups, nails, paper cups, glass jars. An "activity card" is placed in the center to give some direction to the investigations and to encourage some original work as well; for example:

- Use the materials in this center and make some observations about things that sink and things that float.
- Try as many investigations as you can think of.
- Talk with each other about your ideas.
- Then make a record of what you observed.

There may be other ways to use the materials in this center. Try some of your own investigations and see what happens.

The children are arranged in groups. One group, working cooperatively in the sinking-and-floating center, proceeds to play with the objects in the water and carry out investigations. Some teachers have observed that it may take as many as three play sessions before children are ready to move into more focused investigations and that such freer play is likely to be an important first step. They advise that children should not be rushed through free play into focused play and that these stages be allowed to run their natural course.

A teacher who observes the children carrying out investigative play in the center will be able to see how these activities elevate conceptual understanding through hands-on experience. Children working with these materials may be seen carrying out the higher-order operations of observing and gathering data, testing hypotheses, generating theories, interpreting data, and extracting scientific principles. All these acts work to develop concepts of sinking and floating capabilities and broaden pupils' conceptual base about water. We call this process sciencing: investigative play emphasizing higher-order operations that promotes concept development through hands-on experience. (Chapter 4 presents examples of 60 investigative play activities for the elementary school classroom.)

Debriefing: Extracting Meaning from Play

As the Play stage provides for direct, hands-on experience in manipulating scientific variables, the teacher's interactions with students during the subsequent Debriefing stage work to help pupils make meaning from their play experiences. This is done through the teacher's skillful use of questioning strategies that elevate pupils' deeper consideration of data and promote concepts and principles based on experiential play. As the teacher questions students about their work, the questions used may raise levels of awareness, require pupils to analyze their ideas, call for deeper reflection about certain issues, and ask for value issues to be examined. When the teacher's interactions call for these higher-order responses, pupils' thinking is enhanced.

Of course, a teacher interacts with students in many ways. Interactions may inhibit pupil thinking. They may delimit thinking. They may be unrelated to the thinking activity in that they manage behavior.[19]

Learning to use interactions that call for higher-order mental processing in debriefing science activities is a challenging task for many teachers who have been trained to use other teaching styles. These new interactive skills are not acquired instantly. They require the development of certain attitudes as well as specific skills. They require the ability to discriminate between questions and responses that call for thoughtful reflection and ones that reduce such opportunities. They require the ability to let go of the need to lead the pupils to acquire specific content. They require the ability to keep from making evaluative judgments of what students say and do. They require a commitment to the development of the necessary skills through classroom practice. Finally, they require a nondefensive attitude on the part of the teacher in the ongoing analytic examination of teacher-student interactions. As you can see, the requirement to practice is essential.

Use the following guidelines to examine and monitor your teaching-for-thinking interactions during Debriefing sessions. Begin to notice the relationship between your questions and the effects that they have on the students' responses.

Some types of interactions inhibit pupil thinking.

This may occur in a number of ways. One is when the response has inadvertently brought closure to the student's cognitive processing. The effect of closure is that the student is no longer encouraged to think about the issue. The burden of processing has been lifted. Closure occurs in the following instances:

- When the teacher agrees with the student: "You are right, Frank. Carbohydrates are foods that are made up of some form of sugar or starch."
- When the teacher disagrees with the student: "No, Rosa. You can't get that kind of reaction from the procedure you used."
- When the teacher doesn't give the student a chance to think
- When the teacher expresses a personal opinion: "If you had heated the water first, before you tried to dissolve the sugar, you might have had an easier time of it."
- When the teacher does the thinking by telling or showing the student what to do: "Try it this way, Marvin. You'll see you'll get much better results."
- When the teacher talks too much
- When the teacher cuts the student off and does not let the student continue with the formulation of the response

Closure also occurs when the teacher's response has undermined the student's confidence in his or her idea. The effect of undermining responses on the students is that they become afraid to offer new ideas, opinions, and thoughts for fear that they might be put down. Here are some examples of responses that accomplish this:

- "Where on earth did you get the idea that ice crystals form from salt?"
- "We don't have time to discuss solar energy now, Fiona."
- "We're not interested in what you found, Charlie."
- "That's a stupid question, Bernard. I'm surprised at you."
- "Obviously you weren't listening, Audrey; otherwise you wouldn't be saying that."
- "Now, Mei-Li, let's remember that certain animals do *not* make good house pets."

In examining pupils' belief statements, closure may also occur in these circumstances:

- When the teacher agrees or disagrees with the belief
- When the teacher injects his or her own opinion
- When the teacher challenges the student harshly and puts him or her on the defensive

Some types of interactions reduce students' opportunities to think.

Certain interactions require that students retrieve information. While this is also a form of thinking, it is considered to be thinking at a lower level of cognitive functioning. This type of thinking requires no initiative and no originality. The student has merely to recall information; he or she does not have to process it. Most of these interactions require students to come up with single correct answers. The student's thinking is limited by the parameters set by the expected answer.

Such limiting interactions have certain observable effects on students' responses. For example, students who have become habituated to such interactions grow to feel very secure in the "right-answer context," and they may initially have a most difficult time tolerating the ambiguity necessary for cognitive processing. Considered reflection may make them very uneasy. They don't want to suspend judgment. They want *answers.* Isn't it the answers that really count?

In debriefing the investigative play activities, be especially alert for interactions that reduce opportunities for students to think. For example:

- Looking for a single correct answer: "What are the names of the three main systems of the human body?"
- Looking for the single correct procedure: "Look at the way Minnie is siphoning the water."
- Leading the student to the right answer or giving clues to the right answer: "Remember when we talked about skeletons, yesterday, we said that the bone structure was . . . what?"
- Using voice inflection to "clue" pupils to the right answer: "Feel the rocks. Do they all *feel* the same?"
- Leading students to a particular line of thought: "Can a fish live on land?"

In debriefing activities in which value issues are under discussion, the teacher reduces opportunities for pupils' thinking in the following ways:

- By leading students around to the teacher's point of view: "I know that you really didn't mean that, Harry."
- By using voice inflections that reveal the teacher's bias: "Do you *really* think that is good, Anita?"
- By raising tangential questions that sidetrack the discussion: "I know you have been

commenting on the need for recycling waste, Sylvester, but what about the amount of garbage in this class?"

Some types of teacher interactions call for students to think more deeply about their ideas and consider the value issues underlying certain choices. When students are required to do this, they are being asked to function at higher cognitive levels.

Some interactions call for students to reflect on their ideas. These reflective responses require that students examine the face value of an idea or belief, reconsider it through cognitive processing, and assume responsibility for it. Reflective questions and responses are the *core* of teaching-for-thinking interactions and are used extensively during Debriefing.

Emphasizing reflective responses in the debriefing sessions will yield fruitful results. It will first of all communicate to the students that you are listening to their ideas. It will indicate that students' ideas are being respected and valued. It will indicate to them that it is safe for them to express an idea without fear that what they offer is being judged negatively. Such acceptance of students' ideas creates a generative climate for promoting thinking and the examination of choices in science. Reflective interactions will, of course, do much more. They will require that students think about what they are saying and identify the beliefs they hold that shape their opinions.

Asking students to present their ideas, points of view, and opinions also falls under the category of reflective responses. This is done by attending to those ideas in the ways just described. For example:

• Teacher reflects or paraphrases the student's idea:

STUDENT: I put the animals that live on land and those that live in the ocean in different categories.
TEACHER: Animals that live on land were placed in one category and animals that live in the water were put in another category.

STUDENT: A grasshopper has wings but it doesn't fly.
TEACHER: You found that grasshoppers are not flying insects.

STUDENT: The whales. I think we have to do something to save the whales.
TEACHER: You are concerned about the whales. You believe not enough is being done to protect them.

• Teacher interprets what student is saying:

STUDENT: They're doing experiments with dolphins and they are finding that dolphins can understand language. They can understand what we are saying.

TEACHER: That idea seems to go against our old belief that animals are "dumb." Now we seem to be finding that dolphins have intelligence.

Some teaching-for-thinking interactions require that students analyze their ideas. These analytic responses call for deeper examination and greater cognitive risk and therefore produce greater tension. Responses that require analysis should be sensitively interspersed with reflective responses and should be stated in nonthreatening ways. In Debriefing, the highest percentage of responses would fall into the reflective category. A much smaller percentage of responses would fall into the analytic category. Here are some examples of responses that require pupil analysis:

- Asking for examples:

  "You said that we eat protozoa, Bobby. Can you give me an example of what you mean?"

  "You said that we should support additional public transportation. Can you give some examples of what you think would be appropriate?"

- Asking where the idea came from:

  "It seems to me that you are saying that dinosaurs are not reptiles. I'm wondering how you came to that idea?"

  "You think we should abandon the automobile altogether. Did you read something that gave you that idea?"

- Asking for a summary:

  "I have heard you describe how the respiratory system works. Now would you please summarize those ideas?"

  "You've been describing the effects of pollution from automobile exhaust. Please summarize your ideas, Melvin."

- Asking about inconsistencies:

  "You have been talking about the dangers of using pesticides, Leon. You have also said that it's the best way to control vermin. Is there an inconsistency between those two ideas?"

- Asking that an assumption be identified:

  "You think that the reason the eggs did not hatch was that there was insufficient light in the incubator. What assumptions are you making?"

  "You think we should abandon the automobile altogether. I wonder if there are some assumptions that need to be identified."

- Asking about alternatives:

"You've suggested that we might spray the plants with pesticides to get rid of the fungus but that this procedure may be harmful to humans. What might be some alternatives?"

- Asking that comparisons be made:

"How does wind power compare with solar power?"

"In what ways does wood compare with concrete as a building material?"

- Asking that data be classified:

"You've put together a large list of foods that most of us eat for breakfast. How might such foods be classified?"

"What does such a classification tell us about our eating habits at breakfast?"

- Asking for supporting data:

"You've talked about the dangers to the environment caused by using fossil fuels. What data support that idea?"

A third category of teaching-for-thinking interactions involves challenging questions. These interactions are the most aggressive and potentially the most demanding. They require that students extend their thinking much further—into new and unexplored territory. They require that students go "out on a limb" in affirming their beliefs and values. Here students are at the greatest cognitive risk and consequently under still greater tension. In Debriefing, challenging questions make up the smallest percentage of total responses. They are always used thoughtfully and sparingly—and only when the teacher thinks that the student has reflected on the idea, has examined it in depth, and is now cognitively ready to make a leap. The overuse of challenging questions may be counterproductive to enabling the student to examine and work out ideas fully, since they have the effect of moving the discussion out of the realm of the original statements into the examination of new issues and ideas.

Questions that challenge students' thinking and move the discussion into the examination of new issues include these:

- Asking the student to generate hypotheses:

"What hypotheses can you suggest to explain why the spider can walk across the ceiling without falling?"

"What hypotheses can you suggest to explain why people smoke in the face of data about the hazards of smoking?"

- Asking the student to interpret data:

"On the basis of your observations of the squid's shape, what can you tell about the way it might move through the water?"

"The graph shows that the people in the poorest countries seem to have the highest birth rates. What are the implications of these data?"

- Asking the student to make judgments and to provide criteria for those judgments:

"You said that the current program for environmental protection is weak, Margo. Can you describe what you see as the major weaknesses?"

"What is your opinion of the government's toxic waste program? What do you see as its major weaknesses and strengths?"

- Asking the student to apply principles to new situations:

"If heavy objects sink, how do you explain the fact that large boats do not sink?"

"If the Chinese are successful in restricting parents to one child per family and thus reduce the national birth rate, how do you suppose such procedures might apply in India?"

- Asking the student to formulate a way to test a theory, prediction, or hypothesis:

"You said that taking vitamin C in large doses is a good way to cure a cold, Sancho. How would you test that idea?"

- Asking the student to make predictions:

"What do you suppose will be the effect of computer games on the way children play?"

"Will this be good? What are your opinions?"

- Raising a new idea or asking a question that opens up a new line of inquiry:

"You were talking about how the farmland in the delta area has given way to suburban housing, Franco. In what way might that relate to the future food market?"

"What are the implications of all this development for the community?"

- Asking students to examine their position with regard to the value issues that are imbedded in their statements:

"How might this affect our lives?"

"How much thought have you given it?"

"Is this something you care a lot about?"

"Why would this be important to you?"

"How do you translate that belief into action?"

Some responses are not directly related to the teaching-for-thinking inquiry. These include responses dealing with classroom management, behavior management, teacher's speech patterns, and the like; for example: "Willy, will you speak a little louder?" "Please erase the boards now." "Gary, you've had your hand up. What did you want to say?"[20]

Cognitive Play: Opportunities for Students to Learn to Choose

Knowing how to choose wisely is probably what distinguishes mature adults from the immature. We associate immaturity with indecisiveness, with the inability to make up one's mind, with the inability to take action. We also associate immaturity with the need to turn to others for help in decision making. "What should I do?" and "Please tell me what to do!" are signs of certain deficiencies in adulthood. When these are persistent behaviors in adults, we see these people as diminished in their capacity to function maturely, to take charge of their lives.

As some adults are dysfunctional in their ability to choose, others seem to make choices based on whim or caprice. "Foolish choices" is how we describe them, and even though foolish choices may end up presenting certain difficulties for the chooser, repeated patterns of foolish choices do not seem to prevent the same patterns from recurring. Learning that one's choice has been foolish and has ended in disaster does not necessarily equip us to choose wisely in the next round.

Learning to choose wisely is almost certainly a learned skill, born of many, many experiences with choosing. Although few data have been collected from research in this area, what data we do have suggest that decision making is informed by the skills of higher-order thinking, which include the ability to analyze, observe, compare, gather and interpret data, evaluate critically, and suspend judgment until most of the data are in.[21] Wise decisions are also very much dependent on the ability to free oneself from one's prejudices and from a tendency to behave impulsively, "without thinking." What helps us through the maze of uncertainty about *how* to decide is our ability to consider the various aspects of the situation thoughtfully and analytically and to have some view of the consequences that certain courses of action will bring.

Choosing wisely is not easy. In a world in which we are constantly bombarded with options, we make hundreds, perhaps thousands, of choices each day. Some of these decisions are inconsequential (Shall I wear the red dress, or the blue? Shall I have toast or cereal?); some are of greater import (Shall I read the students' papers after school, or shall I take them home to read this evening? Shall I study for the exam this weekend or go skiing?). Some decisions we make have even greater consequence for us or for others (Shall I support the referendum to curtail housing development in our town? Shall I join the demonstration against the opening of the nuclear power plant? Which candidate deserves my vote?).

Having to make lots of choices can be quite fatiguing, and when the decisions have greater consequence, the act of choosing may be fraught with uncertainty. Teachers, for example, are said to make more than 1000 decisions each teaching day; that likely accounts for the fatigue teachers feel at the end of the week and for the need for some extended vacation time interspersed throughout the school year. Decision making is hard work, and we need an intermission from it, lest we burn out.

Though choosing plays a very major part in our lives, learning to choose wisely does not seem to appear on any list of skills that schools consider worthwhile as part of their stated educational objectives. Perhaps it has been assumed that learning to choose is a by-product of other learning. This is a dubious assumption. Perhaps it is assumed that pupils will have many opportunities to choose in most classrooms anyway, so there is no need for additional attention. That, too, is an assumption that does not stand up in the presence of facts.[22] The data from the Jackson and Goodlad studies show that in most classrooms it is the teacher who makes the important decisions and the students who are expected to follow obediently. Those who would question the teacher's decisions or who would argue for other alternatives are considered rebellious or naughty.[23] In some cases, involving children in decision making may mean trying to manipulate them into accepting a decision already made:

TEACHER: You may choose an activity that you'd like to do this afternoon.
PETER: Let's go out to the playground.
TEACHER: No, Peter. We can't do that.
BILL: Let's play Heads Up in the classroom.
TEACHER: That would be too noisy, Bill.
FRED: Let's have reading.
TEACHER: That's a good idea.

We are suggesting that teachers consider giving pupils more opportunity in classrooms to learn to make thoughtful choices and that this should occur with regularity in the science curriculum. In the Play stage, pupils will, of course, be making choices about performing certain investigations, about the nature of the inquiries, and about the way they work with each other. Such activities will certainly provide much practice in learning to choose, as it relates to problem solving in science and in interpersonal relationships. Play may also provide opportunities, particularly for middle and upper elementary pupils, to work with materials that call for discussion on science issues with value dimensions. This kind of play moves from the hands-on manipulation of material into the realm of cognitive "minds-on" play, where groups discuss and play with ideas. Not only does this kind of play allow pupils to examine value-related issues, but it also opens up opportunities for thoughtful discussion, for the gathering of relevant data, for the development of informed opinion, and for the identification of beliefs with regard to the issues. Through such a process, children may grow as more intelligent decision makers.[24]

In "minds-on" play activities, pupils are presented with some primary data such as a photograph, an illustration, an article, a story, a news event, a case study. Play groups are formed; however, the play takes the form of an examination of the data and discussions in the group based on a series of value-related study questions. Chapter 4 contains many examples of how teachers may engage pupils in decision-making experiences related to certain science topics; here are some additional examples of how these ideas are translated into classroom activities.

Examples of Decision-making Activities for "Minds-On" Play

Example 1

Present the pupils with a photograph of animals in an experimental laboratory for medical research.

Study questions:

Should scientists be permitted to do scientific experiments with live animals? What are your views on this?

What animals should be used? What animals should be exempt?

What are some advantages of such experimentation? What are some disadvantages?

What guidelines would you set for scientists who do these experiments?

Example 2

Present the pupils with a photograph or illustration of pesticides used in agriculture.
Study questions:

Should pesticides be banned? What do you think?

What are some advantages of pesticides for farmers? What are some advantages for you and your family?

What are some disadvantages for the farmer? For you and your family?

What might some consequences be for farmers and for consumers if pesticides were banned? Would it be worth it?

Example 3

Present the pupils with a photograph of a beach and water birds after an oil spill.
Study questions:

What happens when an oil tanker breaks up in the sea? What are your ideas?

What are some consequences for the beach, the residents, the water birds, the fish, the ocean?

We need to move the oil from where it's taken from the ground to where it is refined. Don't we need the tankers to do this?

What alternative courses of action might be considered?

What would be some consequences of the actions you are considering?

Example 4

Present the pupils with a photograph of the local garbage dump.
Study questions:

Where does the garbage go when it is collected? Is this a good place for it? What are your ideas?

What do people throw away? How much is thrown away? Is this good?

What happens to garbage? What are your ideas?

Example 5

Present the pupils with an illustration of laundry detergent and a washing machine, and describe the following situation: Brand X laundry detergent has a lot of pollutants, but Mrs. Jones uses it because it gets her clothes looking cleaner. Brand Y laundry detergent has no pollutants, but Mrs. Jones doesn't use it because it doesn't get her clothes looking clean.
Study questions:

What should Mrs. Jones do? What are your ideas?

Should there be laws that prevent people from using the laundry detergent of their choice? What are your ideas on this?

Should people have freedom of choice when it comes to using things that might be harmful to the environment? What are your ideas?

Debriefing: Interactions to Analyze and Inform Decision Making

The value dimensions of investigative play activities are examined during Debriefing as well. Once again, the way teachers respond to students' statements may encourage or discourage this examination. All the types of responses identified as teaching-for-thinking interactions are relevant to the examination of value issues. The shift in interactional emphasis is on flushing out students' belief statements and ideas and using the interactive process to hold up these beliefs to critical analysis. This is done in nonthreatening ways, so that the student feels invited to examine rather than under interrogation.

The backbone of the teacher-student interactions in examining students' beliefs is the reflective response. Such responses attend directly to the students' belief statements, so that their ideas are held up for their reflection and subsequent consideration; for example:

TEACHER: What are your views on the use of pesticides?

HUGO: Well, they make everybody sick. We should just get rid of them.

TEACHER: You're saying that they're no good, and we'd be better off if we simply did not use them.

As the teacher follows through with this interactive process, students are invited to examine each belief from a variety of perspectives. Where did the belief come from? What data support it? What assumptions are being made? What might some consequences of such an action be for specific groups of people (farmers, consumers, business owners, commuters, etc.)? Such interactions, sensitively carried out, help to inform the child's belief and pave the way for continued examination. In this process, the teacher maintains a neutral position, so that the student is free to think his or her own thoughts and to make up his or her own mind. That does not mean that teachers *never* offer their own views; they just do not do so at this time.

Using teaching-for-thinking responses to help students examine their beliefs about issues in science will enable them to reflect on what they really believe, what data support those beliefs, what is important in their lives, what they care about, and what they stand for. Despite widespread discussion of "values clarification," values do not magically emerge from such questioning strategies. What does happen is that students begin to reflect on their points of view, building habits of thinking about the issues. When beliefs are informed by reliable data, when we have subjected them to critical analysis, we are more likely to behave in more responsible and consistent ways. Informed beliefs help us to make intelligent decisions.

Here are some reminders that may be helpful as you carry out this interactive process in which beliefs are examined:

- When you help students to reflect on beliefs, you do not impose your own beliefs on them. You give students opportunities to express their own points of view, and you accept those opinions.
- When you help students to reflect on beliefs, you do not manipulate them or

lead them to accept certain beliefs. You allow students to make up their own minds.

- When you help students to reflect on beliefs, you are communicating a very great regard for them and for their ideas. Implicit in what you are saying is, "I hold you in such high regard that I am able to allow you to make this decision on your own."
- When you help students to reflect on beliefs, you allow them to determine for themselves what it is they really stand for. As you do this, you might help the student to reaffirm a position that is discrepant with your own beliefs.
- When you help students to reflect on beliefs, you are holding up a verbal mirror so that they may see and hear their beliefs more clearly.
- The student may express a point of view or belief that is truly repugnant to you. If you cannot maintain a neutral and accepting position, you may be tempted to step outside of the reflective process and express your own opinion about the matter. Although it is important for teachers to show themselves as persons who have strong values of their own and to disclose their own attitudes, ideas, and beliefs to students, this practice is not considered effective in helping pupils to reflect.[25]
- The effect of the reflective response may initially be to create cognitive dissonance in the student's mind. In attempting to resolve this dissonance, the student comes to a clearer understanding of the belief through a process of mental sorting.
- When teachers begin to use reflective responses with students, the initial effect may be to raise the level of the students' anxiety. Students who have been conditioned to come up with the "right" answers may initially become uncomfortable in the presence of reflective questions, where no specific answer is expected. It may take several weeks before students feel safe about expressing different points of view and understand that many opinions are acceptable.
- Reflective responses are never used to threaten, coerce, badger, or hurt a child in any way.
- Reflective responses are only one of several types of interactions that teachers use in their classrooms. It would be wrong to assume that once teachers had learned to use reflective responses skillfully, they would use these responses to the exclusion of all others. There are times when teachers are called on to be directive. There are times when teachers are required to make judgments. There are times when teachers may wish to express a strong point of view of their own. All these responses remain in the teacher's repertoire. Reflective responses are one additional resource.

LEARNING TEACHING-FOR-THINKING INTERACTIONS: TOOLS FOR THE TEACHER

We have said that learning to debrief the sciencing activities using teaching-for-thinking interactions does not occur from a single reading or from a short burst of classroom activity. To move to mastery levels of using reflective, analytic, and challenging interactions, to use these skillfully and effectively in generating the conditions that lead to the improvement of thinking and choosing skills, requires thoughtful attention and considerate study. It requires commitment to practice and objective analyses of your interactions and your ability to build growth gains into new performance levels. For your work in this area we offer you the following tools:

1. A coding sheet to help you examine your teaching-for-thinking responses. As you listen to yourself interact with pupils during the Debriefing exercise, use the coding sheet to keep a record of the types of responses you hear yourself making. When you have completed the coding, tally the responses to obtain a profile of your overall teaching-for-thinking interactions. The more you do this, the more self-aware you will grow in your interactive style, and the more you will grow in your use of higher-order responses.

2. An analysis sheet to help you to focus on the strengths and weaknesses of the Debriefing interactions. It will help you pinpoint areas of needed growth and identify where you must concentrate your energies in subsequent practice sessions. It also requires that your responses be laid out on a grid, so that the response pattern may be examined.

3. Guidelines for attending, to identify strategies that will enable you to pay more careful and thoughtful attention to students' statements. Learning to attend is a critical aspect of an effective reflective response.

4. Some suggestions for undertaking a self-training program.

We also provide samples showing how all these tools are used.

Coding Sheet

A. Responses That Inhibit Student Thinking

Responses that bring closure:
Agrees/disagrees _____
Doesn't give student a chance to think _____
Tells student what teacher thinks _____
Talks too much _____
Teacher does the explaining _____
Cuts student off _____
Heckles/is sarcastic/puts student down _____
Gives other closure response _____

B. Responses That Limit Student Thinking

Looks for single, correct answer/method _____
Leads student to "right" answer _____
Tells student what to do _____
Gives data _____
Gives other limiting response _____

C. Teaching-for-Thinking Responses

a. Responses that promote reflection:
Repeats statement _____
Paraphrases statement _____
Asks for student's idea _____
Asks for more information _____
Accepts student's idea nonjudgmentally _____
Other responses requiring reflection _____

b. Responses that promote analysis:

Asks for an example _____
Asks about assumptions _____
Asks for a summary _____
Asks where the idea came from _____
Asks why the suggestion is good _____
Asks about alternatives _____
Asks that comparisons be made _____
Asks for data to be classified _____
Asks what data support the idea _____
Other responses requiring analysis _____

c. Responses that challenge:

Asks for hypotheses _____
Asks that data be interpreted _____
Asks for criteria to be identified _____
Asks that principles be applied to new situations _____
Asks for predictions _____
Asks how a theory may be tested _____
Other challenging responses _____

D. Unrelated Responses
Classroom/behavior management _____
Speech/mannerisms _____
Other unrelated response _____

Use the code letters for these responses (A, B, Ca, Cb, Cc, D) in analyzing Debriefing sessions.

Analysis of a Debriefing Session

1. Describe the Debriefing session in general terms.

2. How would you characterize the responses of the students?

3. To what extent were you able to attend to students' statements and reflect their ideas accurately?

4. What were some of the best features of this Debriefing session?

5. What did you perceive to be some weaknesses of your interactions?

6. What new insights did you acquire about teaching-for-thinking interactions from this Debriefing session?

7. What specific aspect of your teaching-for-thinking interactions needs more practice in the next session?

8. Debriefing response pattern: Plot each response to a student's statement on the grid. This will enable you to examine your response pattern.

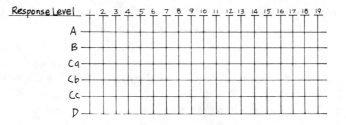

Then ask yourself:

Am I using reflective responses as my primary interactive mode?

Am I challenging too often?

Am I using too many "limiting thinking" responses?

Does my response pattern show a strong core of teaching-for-thinking interactions?

Guidelines for Attending

For teaching for thinking interactions to be effective, it is important that the teacher be able to attend thoughtfully to the students' ideas. This includes the ability to listen to the idea, to make meaning of what is being said, and to free oneself from the desire to comment on or to judge it. Your ability to attend thoughtfully and intelligently will increase as the following conditions are met.

1. You are able to make and hold eye contact with the student speaking.
2. You are able to listen to and communicate respect for the student's idea.
3. You are able to free yourself from the need to evaluate the student's idea, either in tone or in word.
4. You are able to avoid commenting on the student's idea reactively or presenting your own idea.
5. You are able to make meaning of what the student is saying.
6. You have an awareness of any affect (verbal or nonverbal) being communicated by the student.
7. You are especially aware of indicators of stress being shown by the student.
8. You can formulate a response that thoughtfully reflects the meaning of the student's statement.
9. You are able to make the student feel safe, nondefensive, and nonthreatened in expressing ideas.

Suggestions for Professional Development

1. Call a group of students together for a Debriefing session, after they have had a good opportunity to participate in the Play stage with sciencing materials.
2. Set up a tape recorder so that you may make a recording of your Debriefing interactions. Begin to talk with the students about their work in the science center, and concentrate on attending to their statements. Emphasize the use of reflective responses. Record the session. Let the Debriefing session run for 8 to 10 minutes.
3. Play the tape back after school. Use the coding sheet to tally the kinds of responses you hear yourself making.
4. Use the analysis sheet to assess the Debriefing session.
5. Commit yourself to at least three Debriefing sessions per week, recording at least one of them.
6. Keep your coding sheets and analysis sheets in a folder so that you may have an ongoing record of your professional development in teaching-for-thinking interactions.

Samples

Sample Debriefing Transcript Emphasizing Thinking[26]

SCIENCING, GRADE 6
"LOCUSTS"

	Response Analysis
TEACHER: You were making some observations of locusts this morning. Would you tell about some of the observations you made?	(1) Asks for students' ideas
LEANNE: Well, it was weird. Their eyes are way over on the side.	
TEACHER: You observed that the eyes were in an odd place—way over at the sides.	(2) Promotes reflection by paraphrasing
LEANNE: Yeah.	
TEACHER: Do you have any ideas that might explain why the eyes are at the side?	(3) Asks for hypotheses to be generated
LEANNE: So that they can see in front and in back of them. If anything is approaching them fast or something.	
TEACHER: What might be some advantages of that, Leanne?	(4) Asks for analysis
LEANNE: It would be for protection, I think.	
TEACHER: So having the eyes there and being able to see in both directions would be a protective device for this animal.	(5) Promotes reflection by paraphrasing
LEANNE: Uh-huh.	
TEACHER: I see.	(6) Accepts nonjudgmentally
Are there other observations that you made?	(7) Asks for students' ideas
GRAEME: I saw those two things sticking up out of his head.	
TEACHER: Do you have any ideas about them?	(8) Asks for student's ideas
GRAEME: Antlers, I think.	
LILA: Feelers. Antennas.	
TEACHER: Graeme, you call them antlers and Lila calls them feelers or antennae.	(9) Calls for reflection by repeating the statements
GRAEME: Antennas.	
TEACHER: You think they are antennae.	(10) Promotes reflection by repeating statement
GRAEME: Yeah.	

TEACHER: Any ideas about what they might be for?

(11) Asks for hypotheses

LILA: They're to feel. To feel around.

TEACHER: Have you seen them used in that way?

(12) Limits thinking; looks for answer

GRAEME: I was watching them feel around with those things. Like when you are in the dark, feeling around with your hands in front of you.

TEACHER: The antennae are used to signal to the locust about what lies in its path.

(13) Promotes reflection by paraphrasing

GRAEME: Yeah. Like if there's something good to eat or something.

TEACHER: Sends it the message.

(14) Paraphrases

GRAEME: Yeah.

TEACHER: There's something I was wondering about. Why might a locust need antennae to feel with, if it has eyes that see in both directions?

(15) Challenges: asks that data be interpreted

CLAUDIA: Well, the eyes are on the side, so they can only see this way. They can only see that way. The antennae are to feel and they can just feel in front of them, because, um, I've never seen their eyes move around to the front of them.

TEACHER: The eyes seem to have a limited range, is that what you're saying?

(16) Promotes reflection by paraphrasing

CLAUDIA: When Gavin puts his finger by his locust, he puts his antennae down. He doesn't turn around to see what's there.

TEACHER: So that observation is what you are using to support your theory.

(17) Promotes reflection by attending to the main idea of her statement

CLAUDIA: Yeah.

TEACHER: I see.

(18) Accepts nonjudgmentally

Any other thoughts to share?

(19) Asks for students' ideas

(Session continues in this fashion for another 10 minutes.)

Sample Coding Sheet for Transcript of "Locusts"

A. Responses That Inhibit Student Thinking

Responses that bring closure:
Agrees/disagrees _____
Doesn't give student a chance to think _____
Tells student what teacher thinks _____
Talks too much _____
Teacher does the explaining _____
Cuts student off _____
Heckles/is sarcastic/puts student down _____
Gives other closure response _____

B. Responses That Limit Student Thinking

Looks for single, correct answer/method _____ *(12)* _____
Leads student to "right" answer _____
Tells student what to do _____
Gives data _____
Gives other limiting response _____

C. Teaching-for-Thinking Responses

a. Responses that promote reflection:
Repeats statement _____ *(9)*, *(10)* _____
Paraphrases statement _____ *(2)*, *(5)*, *(13)*, *(14)*, *(16)*, *(17)* _____
Asks for student's idea _____ *(1)*, *(7)*, *(8)*, *(19)* _____
Asks for more information _____
Accepts student's idea nonjudgmentally _____ *(6)*, *(18)* _____
Other responses requiring reflection _____

b. Responses that promote analysis:

Asks for an example _____
Asks about assumptions _____
Asks for a summary _____
Asks where the idea came from _____
Asks why the suggestion is good _____ *(4)* _____
Asks about alternatives _____
Asks that comparisons be made _____
Asks for data to be classified _____
Asks what data support the idea _____
Other responses requiring analysis _____

c. Responses that challenge:

Asks for hypotheses _____ *(3)*, *(11)* _____
Asks that data be interpreted _____ *(15)* _____
Asks for criteria to be identified _____
Asks that principles be applied to new situations _____
Asks for predictions _____
Asks how a theory may be tested _____
Other challenging responses _____

D. Unrelated Responses

Classroom/behavior management _____
Speech/mannerisms _____
Other unrelated response _____

Use the code letters for these responses (A, B, Ca, Cb, Cc, D) in analyzing Debriefing sessions.

Sample Analysis of a Debriefing Session

1. Describe the debriefing session in general terms.

   The pupils had been observing the behavior of 8 locusts in
   a large glass container with an open top. When they came to
   the Debriefing session, they seemed eager to share their
   ideas. All 8 pupils volunteered ideas throughout the
   12-minute session, and no behavior management was
   required.

2. How would you characterize the responses of the students?

   The responses of the students were, generally,
   thoughtful. They were responsive to my questions, and
   they were able to show that they could make meaning from
   what they observed. Even though I used several
   challenging questions (I did not intend to use so many),
   the pupils responded to these thoughtfully. They were not
   stymied by them.

3. To what extent were you able to attend to students' statements and reflect their ideas
   accurately?

   I'm learning to do this more and more. I think I attended
   well. I tried to stay with reflective responses
   throughout but was not entirely successful. At one point I
   heard myself saying, "Have you seen it used in this way?"
   Not good. I think I used too many challenging responses,
   although each time I used one, it did get a response.

4. What were some of the best features of this Debriefing session?

   I liked the fact that everyone in the group had something
   to say. I liked the fact that I didn't have to urge them to
   talk. They seemed to feel safe in expressing their
   thoughts.

5. What did you perceive to be some weaknesses of your interactions?

   I am still not quite comfortable in this mode and have to
   grope to come up with an appropriate response. Also, I
   jump into challenging questions too quickly.

6. What new insights did you acquire about teaching-for-thinking interactions from
   this Debriefing session?

Reflective questions are effective for generating
pupils' ideas. I don't have to keep challenging them all
the time for them to do some productive thinking.

7. What specific aspect of your teaching-for-thinking interactions needs more practice
in the next session?

Attend, apprehend, and reflect. Attend, apprehend, and
reflect. Attend, apprehend, and reflect!

8. Debriefing response pattern: Plot each response to a student's statement on the grid.
This will enable you to examine your response pattern.

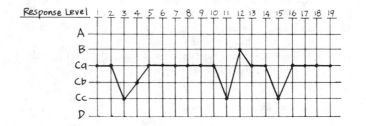

Sample Debriefing Transcript Emphasizing Decision Making

SCIENCING, GRADE 3
"GARBAGE"

**Response
Analysis**

TEACHER: You were out on the playground this afternoon just after
lunchtime making observations of the condition of the
playground. Some of you took some notes, and others
made some illustrations. When you came back into the
classroom, some of you said that the litter and trash on
the playground was "disgusting" and suggested that the
principal should take some action. What ideas do you
have about that?

HEATHER: I think what might be a good idea is if the principal
might have an extra recess or something and called everybody out and everybody would have to pick up some
kind of litter.

TEACHER: You think the principal should require all the students   (1) Reflects student's
to come out and participate in picking up the litter.   belief statement

HEATHER: Uh-huh.

RAY: I think they should just not let them have the privilege of having more recess, or make them go home for lunch if they just drop their litter around everywhere.

TEACHER: You think the principal might take action that would deny some privileges.

(2) Reflects student's belief statement

RAY: Uh-huh.

TEACHER: You think that would be a good thing to do.

(3) Asks student if this idea is good

RAY: Uh-huh.

CLAUDIA: Or you could do what they did at our other school. There's four classes and each class is responsible for a different part of the school grounds. Whoever picks up the most litter gets points for their class.

TEACHER: So there might be a competition and the students would win points for their class.

(4) Reflects student's belief statement

CLAUDIA: Yeah, because they might do that because they want to get a lot more points for their class.

TEACHER: It's a good idea for pupils to clean up the litter in order to win points.

(5) Asks student if this is a good idea

CLAUDIA: Uh-huh.

TEACHER: You like that way of doing it?

(6) Asks student to affirm that position

CLAUDIA: Uh-huh.

DAVID: Not have an extra recess to do it—pick up all the litter. They should go out for lunch and have fun and play around but instead of doing that have—pick up their litter at lunch.

TEACHER: I'm not sure I quite understand your idea, David. Can you help me? Are you saying they should not have their lunch period but would instead have a period to pick up the litter?

(7) Asks student for more information

DAVID: No. Well, there's 45 minutes for lunch and they should just have part of that time to pick up the litter. Everybody would have to pick up a certain amount. I don't think they should get an extra recess for that.

TEACHER: So what you're saying is that there should be some penalties involved for people who leave their litter around.

(8) Interprets what student is saying

DAVID: Yes.

TEACHER: I see. Thank you, David.

(9) Accepts idea nonjudgmentally

Here's another question. Why do you suppose students leave their trash on the playground?

(10) Asks for hypotheses to be generated

COLIN: 'Cause they're too lazy to put it in the trash can or they just can't find one, so they throw it on the school grounds.

TEACHER: You think it's a question of laziness.

(11) Reflects student's belief statement

COLIN: Uh-huh.

CLAUDIA: Or, like, say they're playing with their friends or playing on the swing, but if they get off the swing, somebody else will get on the swing, so they just throw it any old place so they can keep the swing.

TEACHER: You seem to be supporting what Colin is saying, Claudia, that it's a matter of laziness or being too busy. They just don't want to stop their playing to take their litter to the trash can.

(12) Interprets student's belief statement

CLAUDIA: Uh-huh.

HEATHER: I think sometimes it's a matter of what they think is more important. Like, it's more important for me to play with my friends than go and put the litter in the garbage.

TEACHER: It's a question of priorities, Heather—what you see as more important, and it's more important for you to play with your friends. You would do that first rather than take your litter to the trash can.

(13) Reflects student's statement

HEATHER: No, that's not what I'd do, but that's what some kids do.

TEACHER: Some kids do that. But your priorities would be that you would take the litter to the trash can first, then play with your friends next.

(14) Reflects student's statement

HEATHER: Most of the time.

TEACHER: Where did those priorities come from, Heather? Can you tell us about it?

(15) Asks where student got those beliefs from

HEATHER: Because when we went to Disneyland, somebody drops something on the ground and somebody picks it up and I was thinking, why should somebody do that for you when you could do it yourself?

TEACHER: In other words, when you were in Disneyland and you saw somebody picking up after the crowds of people, it made you stop and think, "Why do people behave that way?"

(16) Reflects student's statement

HEATHER: Yes. It was just what I felt when I went to Disneyland.

TEACHER: And that helped you come to some opinions that you now have about littering.

(17) Asks student to affirm the statement

HEATHER: Uh-huh. And some of the commercials. Like that commercial when the Indian sees somebody throw their garbage out of the car window.

TEACHER: I don't know about that one, Heather. Would you tell me about that one?

(18) Asks for more information

HEATHER: Well, there's this Indian and he's walking by the road and then this lady drives by in her car and she throws a bunch of garbage down and it lands right by his feet.

TEACHER: I see.

(19) Accepts
nonjudgmentally

HEATHER: And what I thought was, what he was thinking about. When they lived there, there was no litter and they kept it pretty clean. And I was just thinking about what had happened.

TEACHER: Are you saying that when the white people took over this land from the Indians, they made some changes that the Indians would not necessarily have approved of?

(20) Interprets
student's belief
statement

HEATHER: Uh-huh.

TEACHER: I see. Thanks for sharing your ideas, Heather. Does anyone want to say anything more?

(21) Accepts
nonjudgmentally and
invites additional
discussion

CHOOSING A WAY TO TEACH SCIENCE: A RECAPITULATION

We began this chapter by stating that there are many ways to teach science and that the way one chooses to teach is very much a reflection of what one considers important in teaching the subject. Choice of approach and of methods is also, to a considerable extent, a reflection of each teacher's beliefs about how pupils learn and of the way the teacher conceptualizes the teaching-learning process.

In this chapter we also presented several more familiar approaches to teaching science and addressed what we believe to be some of the advantages and limitations of each. The approach we recommend, for all the reasons we have given throughout this text, is the one that incorporates pupils' active involvement in science learning with instructional strategies that emphasize the higher-order mental functions. Teachers do not learn such teaching methods simply by reading about them; these methods need to be put into practice in the classroom and continually refined by long-term application. We realize that it is asking a lot of teachers to commit themselves to such practice—yet each of us, no matter how crowded our daily schedules are, does manage to make time to do those things that we consider most important. Only you can decide if teaching for thinking in science is important. Consider these scenarios before you make up your mind.

Scene 1

This is the Archive School. Observe Mr. Finster teaching science to his grade 6 class. The lesson is "Squids."

TEACHER: Now, boys and girls, I want you to listen to this and take some notes. We are going to have a test on this tomorrow. *(Reads from his text)*
"The squid is a ten-armed marine animal belonging to the order Ceph-

alopoda, in the phylum Mollusca." Now, you remember what that means. We had that yesterday. "Squids are active and carnivorous animals found in every sea, where they prey on fishes and crustaceans. Some of them live on the surface, while others stay at great depths. They swim quickly by means of fins, but when greater speed is necessary, they propel themselves backward by forcing jets of water from the mantle cavity through their 'siphons.' When defending themselves, they can disappear behind a cloud of sepia or 'ink,' which they expel from special sacs within their bodies. The bodies of squids are usually long, conical, and provided with ten tentacles around the mouth. The shell is inconspicuous and located inside the body. *Architetuthis princeps,* sometimes reaching 50 feet between the ends of the tentacles, is the largest known invertebrate." I'll write that name on the board, so you can get the spelling right. "*Loligo pealii,* about 1 foot long, is the common squid of the Atlantic coast. *Loligo opalescens,* the common squid of the Pacific, is the species popular in the Chinese markets." I'll write all these names down, so you can copy them. Any questions?

Scene 2

This is the Dusty Roads School. Observe Mrs. Pointer teaching science to her grade 5 class. The lesson is "Squids."

TEACHER: *(passing out the worksheets)* Now, boys and girls, I want you to read the paragraphs and answer the questions at the bottom of the page. If anyone has any trouble reading any of the words, because some of them may be a little hard for you, raise your hands and I'll come over and help you with them. You have ten minutes to finish this exercise.

Worksheet Exercise

Class: Cephalopoda
The cephalopods, commonly known as the squids and octopuses, are the most highly developed of all mollusks. They have a large head with eyes and a mouth with horny jaws and a radula. Eight or ten arms or many tentacles surround the mouth. All cephalopods are free swimming. They range in size from a few inches up to 28 feet. The sexes are separate, and fertilization is internal. The eggs are covered by gelatinous capsules and hatch into miniature adults. All cephalopods are marine animals.

The squids have a reduced internal shell. In octopuses, the only vestiges of the shell may be a few calcareous plates. The nautiluses (for living species of a single genus forming a separate order of cephalopods) resemble snails in having a coiled, external shell, but the space inside the shell is divided into compartments by walls. The cephalopods were much more varied and numerous in ancient times, when approximately 10,000 species occurred; today, only 400 species exist.

1. Mollusks are in the class called _____

2. All mollusks live in _____.

3. The class of animals is called cephalopods because _____.

4. Three types of cephalopods are _____ , _____ , and _____.

5. The shells of squids may be found _____.

Scene 3

This is the Pathway School. Observe Mrs. Intrepidus teaching science to her grade 4 class. The lesson, once more, is "Squids."

The teacher purchased 2 pounds of squids for $3.50 in the local supermarket. She brought them into the classroom and gave them out, one squid for each pair of children. With newspapers protecting their desks and a good supply of paper towels, the pupils were instructed to make some observations of the squids. Many of them, on their own initiative, obtained some knives and scissors and began to do dissecting, laying out the parts of the animal. One pair of children was examining parts more closely with a hand-held magnifying glass. The observing activity lasted for about 20 minutes. The teacher called the students up, after a general cleanup, for the Debriefing.

TEACHER: Now, boys and girls, tell me about some of the observations you made about this marine animal.

NOTES

1. Barak Rosenshine, "Context, Time, and Direct Instruction," in *Research on Teaching*, ed. Penelope L. Peterson and Herbert J. Walberg (Berkeley, CA: McCutchan, 1979); Bryan Cole, "Integrating Site-Based Management and Effective Schools Research for Policy Development," *Journal of School Leadership*, 3(3) (1993), pp. 228–245.
2. Larry Cuban, "Transforming the Frog into a Prince: Effective Schools Research, Policies and Practice at the District Level," *Harvard Educational Review*, 54 (1984), pp. 129–151.
3. Larry Cuban, "Persistent Instruction: Another Look at Constancy in the Classroom," *Phi Delta Kappan*, September 1986, pp. 7–11.
4. Ronald D. Anderson et al., *Developing Children's Thinking Through Science* (Englewood Cliffs, NJ: Prentice Hall, 1970), p. 175.
5. J. Richard Suchman, *Developing Inquiry* (Chicago: Science Research Associates, 1966).
6. Mary Budd Rowe, *Teaching Science as Continuous Inquiry* (New York: McGraw-Hill, 1973); Lazer Goldberg, *Children and Science* (New York: Scribner, 1970); Anderson et al., *Developing Children's Thinking*; Arthur Carin and Robert B. Sund, *Teaching Science Through Discovery*, rev. ed. (Columbus, OH: Merrill, 1984); Robert Beichner & Daniel Dobey, *Essentials of Classroom Teaching: Elementary Science* (New York: HarperCollins, 1994); Willard Jacobsen and Abby Bergman, *Science for Children* (New York: HarperCollins, 1991); Ralph

Martin, Colleen Sexton, Kay Wagner, and Jack Gerlovich, *Teaching Science for All Children* (New York: HarperCollins, 1994); American Association for the Advancement of Science, *Benchmarks for Scientific Literacy* (New York: Oxford, 1993); Robert M. Hazen and James Trefil, *Science Matters: Achieving Scientific Literacy* (New York: Doubleday, 1990); Eleanor Duckworth, *Science Education: A Minds-On Approach for the Elementary Years* (Hillsdale, NJ: Lawrence Erlbaum, 1990).

7. American Association for the Advancement of Science, *Science for All Americans Summary* (New York: Oxford, 1989).

8. AAAS, *Science for All Americans* (New York: Oxford, 1990).

9. Louis E. Raths, Selma Wassermann, Arthur Jonas, and Arnold Rothstein, *Teaching for Thinking: Theory, Strategies and Activities for the Classroom* (New York: Teachers College Press, 1986), pp. 5–24.

10. Edward B. Fiske, "Searching for the Key to Science Literacy," *New York Times Education Supplement*, January 4, 1978, p. 20.

11. *Ibid.*, p. 21.

12. AAAS, *Science for All Americans Summary* 1989, p. 3.

13. René Dubos, "Scientific Knowledge and Social Wisdom," in Lazer Goldberg, *Learning to Choose* (New York: Scribner, 1976), p. xiv.

14. *Ibid.*, pp. xvi–xvii.

15. Michael Mahoney, "Self-deception in Science," quoted in "Research on Researchers and a Science of Science," *Phi Delta Kappan*, November 1986, p. 245.

16. Stephen Jay Gould, *The Mismeasure of Man* (New York: Norton, 1981).

17. David Gardner, "Education Watch," *New York Times*, April 6, 1986, Section 4, p. 24.

18. George E. Pugh, *The Biological Origin of Human Values* (New York: Basic Books, 1977), pp. 442–443.

19. Selma Wassermann, *Asking the Right Question: The Essence of Teaching* (Bloomington, IN: Phi Delta Kappa, 1992).

20. For an extended discussion of teaching-for-thinking interactions, see Raths et al., *Teaching for Thinking*, pp. 163–194.

21. Jack Fraenkel, *Helping Students Think and Value*, 2nd ed. (Englewood Cliffs, NJ: Prentice-Hall, 1980); Province of Alberta, Department of Education, *Experiences in Decision Making* (1971); Goldberg, *Learning to Choose*.

22. Philip Jackson, *Life in Classrooms* (New York: Teachers College Press, 1990; originally published 1968); John Goodlad, *A Place Called School* (New York: McGraw-Hill, 1983).

23. Victor Goertzel and Mildred G. Goertzel, *Cradles of Eminence* (Boston: Little, Brown, 1962), pp. 277–278.

24. Louis E. Raths, Sidney B. Simon, and Merrill Harmin, *Values and Teaching*, 2nd ed. (Columbus, OH: Merrill, 1980), pp. 26–35.

25. *Ibid*, p. 22.

26. The authors acknowledge the contribution of Brian Hodgins in the making and transcribing of the "Locusts" Debriefing session.

60
Sciencing
Activities

Science is everywhere around us, from the early morning fog that immobilizes the airport to the burned toast, from the flooded carburetor to the first robin of spring, from your personal home computer to the 5 pounds you gained on your summer vacation. Whether it's pearls or butterflies or popcorn, it's science. Whether it's the weather, toxic waste, or the moon, it's science. Whether it's gravity or oil spills, it is still science.

What can children do that will increase their understandings of science? Everything! The options are unlimited. Selecting sciencing activities from such a vast pool of resources as the planet Earth necessitates the identification of a few criteria.

In this chapter we have included 60 potentially rich sciencing opportunities for elementary-grade students. These activities reflect the criteria we believe to be fundamental to good science teaching that we spelled out in Chapter 1. All activities emphasize cooperative work in investigative play. All activities are experientially based and require active hands-on involvement with the materials. All activities are based on certain "big ideas" integral to science curricula for the elementary grades.[1]

None of the activities leads children to find "right" answers, nor does any activity stress the acquisition of specific information. Instead, activities require pupils to exercise their higher-order thinking skills—to compare and observe, to classify and interpret data, to suggest hypotheses and examine assumptions, to imagine, invent, and create. The activities are not arranged sequentially. They are not intended to be followed *ad seriatim* from 1 to 60. We are suggesting that conceptual learning is promoted even as the teacher selects activities in a nonlinear, nonsequential pattern. This may appear to be at variance with teachers' perceptions of how a curriculum must be structured. It may be at variance with the arrangement of many curriculum textbooks. However, our experiences with teachers and children in Project Science-Thinking, a 2½-year field research study, have shown that children do not need to proceed from topic to topic in a textbook progression to develop conceptual understanding. Important concept learning may occur via a nonsequential process, as happens through the firsthand experiences of preschoolers. What appears to be the critical variable in promoting conceptual growth is not the "correct" sequencing but how connections are made and meanings are thus built.

Play-Debrief-Replay provides an instructional paradigm for the sciencing activities. This structure allows for extensive experiential investigative play with a variety of science materials. Work in groups promotes interactive discussion on the phenomena under investigation. Students observe each other's trials, comment, provide feedback, offer suggestions, and generally "wash through" their ideas in this primary investigative arena. The activity cards focus inquiries on the higher-order mental processes. Through Debriefing the teacher enables students to make connections and search for meanings from their play experiences. Through this process pupils expand their base of knowledge in science as well as their awareness of how science affects our lives. Replay invites pupils to reexamine their findings, to solidify concepts, and to develop new conceptual frameworks. To an untrained observer, the surface impression of Play-Debrief-Replay in progress may appear disorganized and messy, but to the trained professional, the organizational structure of the learning experiences is clear.

INTRODUCTION TO THE ACTIVITIES

How the Activities Are Grouped

Even the most cursory perusal of the activities section will reveal that activities have not been grade-ranked. That is, we have not indicated that such and such an activity is suitable for grade 4 pupils, while another is more suitable for grade 3 pupils. Although such an omission may be at variance with customary practice, we feel there is a good case for such variance.

First, we believe that the assigning of scientific content to a particular grade level (for example, if it's air pressure, it must be grade 3) is an invented idea with little empirical evidence to support its use. Carried into rigid grade-level application, such practice may be more counterproductive to pupil learning than it is enabling. As far as we know, the study of air pressure at the grade 3 level has nowhere been writ in stone as sacrosanct, and in no way will pupils' scientific learning be impaired if air pressure is studied at grade 3 or 4 or 5 or 6 . . . or even at the high school or university level.

Assumptions have been made that if air pressure is not successfully taught and learned in grade 3, the successful teaching and learning of properties of matter, scheduled for grade 4, will seriously suffer—something akin to the domino theory. Such "educational principles" do not stand up under critical or empirical scrutiny; they are traditions that continue to endure long after their educational value has been in disrepute. In fact, the AAAS report, *Benchmarks*, presents science as "a compendium of specific science literacy goals that can be organized however one chooses."[2] Rather than a series of topics that follow in rigid sequence, *Benchmarks* advocates the increasingly sophisticated examination of certain "big ideas" related to the same topics, as students advance through the grades.

Second, we believe that almost any scientific investigation may be undertaken effectively, productively, and intensively at virtually any grade level. Although different age groups are likely to approach a sciencing activity differently, depending on level of sophistication; background of experience with science; experiences as thoughtful, trained observers; and other variables, each age group nevertheless has a great deal still to learn about the particular scientific phenomena integral to each sciencing investigation. In other words, air pressure can and should be studied throughout science, since, obviously, the more we study, the more we are likely to know. If we can learn to examine critically the traditions that bind us and open our minds to a more thoughtful approach to the relationship between content and grade level, perhaps we may also disabuse our students of the repugnant attitudes formed by such practices, which inevitably lead to the closing off of further inquiry. ("Oh, air pressure. We had that in grade 3. In grade 4 we study properties of matter.")

The truth is that the littlest children can be profitably engaged in a scientific inquiry on air pressure; so may more sophisticated sixth graders. The differences are found in the sophistication of the explorations, and it is enormously satisfying to see how different age groups can and do undertake different, productive investigations with the same materials.

Having made what we hope is a credible case for the consideration of sciencing activities above and beyond grade-level concerns, we now offer one small caveat. There are likely to be some sciencing activities that for a variety of reasons (teacher's preference, prescribed content for the grade, grade-level assessments, pupils' prior experiences, ability levels, etc.) are more or less suitable for some groups of children. It is possible that the sophistication of some materials or inquiries do not lend themselves easily to some primary graders. Once again, we suggest that the teacher make the choice, that the choice be based on clearly identified criteria, and that these criteria relate to promoting pupils' learning in science.

Instead of grade-ranked activities we have chosen to categorize them according to teachers' expressed concerns:

Category A, "Wet, Wetter, Wettest," contains activities involving investigative play with water. This is likely to mean spillage—on tables and perhaps on the floor as well. We'd like you to know this just in case such activity creates a problem for you.

Category B, "No Fuss, No Muss, No Sticky Mess," contains activities that are generally dry and safe and will not leave a mess on the table, on the floor, or around the room. If you begin with concerns about such by-products of sciencing as the mess, you are likely to want to choose, initially, sciencing activities from category B.

Category C, "Who's Afraid of Spiders?" contains activities that some teachers consider more high-risk. They may involve greater mess, the use of more dangerous materials (such as heat sources), more difficult access of materials, or personal distaste on the part of teacher or pupils.

The physical sciences are heavily represented in category A. Biological and physical sciences are emphasized in categories B and C. An index of the activities in each group is found on the introductory pages for each category.

Presentation of the Activities

Each activity has been presented in a single format, to allow for its clear application to the classroom. The format provides detailed information about how the activity is translated from the page of this book into classroom practice. Each activity, therefore, contains the following information:

1. Activity Card   Directions to focus the students' investigative play are presented in the form of an activity card. It is suggested that you print these directions on cards, to be placed in the investigative play center. If necessary, the language may be modified so that the directions are more easily understood.

Most activity cards also include directions that allow pupils to go beyond the suggestions to create their own investigations. These more open-ended suggestions call for greater self-initiating behaviors and may not prove fruitful for some pupils at first. However, as pupils gain skill in these exercises, they will eventually be able to conceive and conceptualize more sophisticated investigations and extend their work into more original inquiries. These more original investigations should, of course, be greatly encouraged.

2. Materials   A comprehensive list of the materials needed to conduct investigations is provided.

3. Thinking Skills   The thinking operations discussed in Chapter 3 that are emphasized in each inquiry are identified.

4. Big Ideas   Those important science concepts that are being examined in the investigations and debriefing activities.

5. Notes to the Teacher   Information to facilitate the implementation of each activity is provided.

6. Debriefing   Examples of questions that call for pupils to reflect more thoughtfully about their inquiries are included. These should be used selectively—that is, in a way that attends thoughtfully to the students' statements. It is not intended that all the questions listed for each activity be used in one single Debriefing session. They are not a "course of questions to be covered" but rather give examples of higher-order questions that may be used. Specific suggestions for effective questioning during Debriefing sessions are found in Chapter 3.

7. Extending   When students have had sufficient time to carry out initial investigative play, the teacher may wish to extend the inquiries to provide for more substantive investigations. Specific ideas are offered as to how this might be done. Also, the use of questions calling for pupils' examination of value issues related to work in science are included. (Again, see Chapter 3 for a more complete discussion of how this is done.)

8. Creating As children's interest in each activity draws to its natural close, some culminating experiences may be appropriate. Activities that integrate science with other areas of the curriculum and emphasize more creative work and problem solving are included.

Choosing Activities

Faced with 60 sciencing activities, the caveats in the introductory section of this chapter, the absence of grade-level guidelines, the need to acquire materials, the newness of such an approach, and the possible feelings of anxiety that all of this has begun to generate, how should you choose your sciencing activities? We offer some ideas that may be helpful. But underlying all of them is our belief that each teacher is the best possible judge of what constitutes an appropriate activity for his or her own students. To that end, we do not suggest or advise that Activity 12 is better or worse than Activity 46; that you must include at least six activities from category C; that a good science program (like a good Chinese dinner) needs 5 from category A, 10 from category B, and 8 from category C! We say instead, here are some ideas that we offer for your consideration. Use these, identify your own criteria, and then make selections that seem reasonable for you.

In making the choices, ask yourself these questions:

- Will I be able to obtain the materials easily enough? How much work or stress will be involved in gathering the materials?
- Do the big ideas being examined relate to the science concepts specified by my school district for teaching science?
- Does the content of the activity relate to the science content prescribed for my grade? If not, will I be able to justify its choice in an educationally sound argument to any potential naysayer?
- Will my pupils be able to function successfully on this task without excessive teacher direction? Does the activity call for very high levels of independent functioning on the part of my pupils? Will my pupils be able (with some help from me) to meet the challenge of this activity? Does this activity ask much more than my students are able to give at this stage of their work? (Am I sure that I am not underestimating their ability?)
- Does the thought of trying this activity intimidate me? Is this a high-risk activity for me? What is there about it that causes me concern?
- Does this activity involve the use of live animals? Am I clear about the ethical considerations that surround the study of live animals in the classroom?

It is probably a good idea to choose, at first, activities that feel comfortable and safe, ones whose materials don't require massive amounts of energy to acquire, ones that are not likely to invite disaster because teacher expectations and pupil behavior are still very far apart, and ones that tie in with school or school district science goals. Begin your sciencing program with a "small is beautiful" approach, and take your time in moving into more uncertain territory. The time for taking greater risks may be when you have a few successful trials under your belt.

If you have chosen an activity in which live animals are to be brought into the classroom, it is a good idea to introduce the activity to the whole class by setting down some ethical rules for live-animal study. Such considerations should be exercised whatever the animal, since all living things deserve our respectful regard.

Ethical considerations for live-animal study include *at least* the following:

- The animal must have a suitable habitat. This includes both amount and quality of space provided. The habitat should be thoroughly researched and prepared before the animal is brought in. Climate and temperature must also be considered.
- Ongoing care and feeding of the animal is imperative. It is easy to forget, and it is a great responsibility to ensure that animals are well cared for in their confinement.
- Cleaning of the animal's environment is an additional responsibility, one, however distasteful, that cannot be overlooked.
- "Bed and breakfast" arrangements must be made to board animals out during long weekends and other school holidays.
- *Never* should any animal in the children's care be subject to cruel or unusual treatment that would result in that animal's pain, deprivation, or injury.
- In spite of the great care we exercise in looking after and caring for our small guests, some of them may die. Should this unhappy event occur, it may be very valuable (after appropriate attention to children's feelings about such a loss) to approach the demise as scientists, examining the evidence and suggesting hypotheses to explain how the death might have occurred. Such an inquiry may be helpful in preventing similar losses in the future.

Collecting animals from their natural habitat also imposes responsibilities. These are discussed fully in Activity 53. Such responsibilities must also be clearly identified and accepted before sciencing investigations are allowed to proceed.

In spite of the greater responsibilities imposed on teacher and students by gathering and caring for living creatures in the classroom, the benefits so far outweigh the costs as to make such activities very much worth the efforts.

These activities should provide you with a more than ample supply of sciencing opportunities for the entire school year, in a program that includes science every day of the week. They may also serve as models for developing your own activities to reflect the interests and curriculum concerns of your individual class. Whichever activities you choose and use, our experiences tell us that such a sciencing program will not only increase children's conceptual understandings of basic scientific principles but will also elevate levels of thinking and problem-solving capabilities, promote socially responsible behavior, and fill children with the spirit and joy of working as scientific explorers.

CLASSROOM APPLICATIONS

Mary Thornhill is cautiously stepping into beginning sciencing in her grade 3–4 class. Her experience with science is small, and yes, she *is* afraid of spiders! She has studied the three categories of activities and affirms that she will make initial selections from category B. Knowing her children well, she concludes that investigative play with water is best left until later when children can exercise greater responsibility over their own behavior. As a matter of personal choice, she will avoid spiders and squids and other such beasties for now, working all the while to overcome her personal distaste.

This is the first time that these children will engage in cooperative learning, and Mary uses some of the orientation procedures described in Chapter 2 to introduce the group to the program. She explains the procedures clearly and makes her expectations about behavior explicit. She provides ample opportunity for pupils to raise questions about the work and alerts them to expect to begin work on the following day.

The activity she has selected is Studying Flowers (25). Following the "Notes to the Teacher," she prepares an assault on the local supermarket and manages to acquire three tired bunches of posies at minimal cost. She has also prepared five copies of the activity card, since she will be running five working groups.

That evening, she studies her class list and arranges the children into groups. Joey may not be in the same group with Ben, at least at first, because putting them together is likely to spell trouble. Farah needs to work with a group that is more accepting of her special needs. She juggles the names until she is satisfied that the children in each group have the best chance of becoming a cooperative unit.

She schedules the sciencing activity for just after lunch, so that she has a few moments to arrange the tables into centers.

As the children return from lunch, she gives each one a group number and directs them to go to their respective centers. When they have done this, she reiterates the kind of activity it is going to be and the procedures to be followed. She then distributes four different flowers at each center, plus some scissors, several sheets of paper, and an activity card. She tells the children that several magnifying lenses and a small knife are available for communal use, if needed. When the children begin to work on the activity, following the directions on the activity card, Mary moves about the room observing

the pupils' work. Which pupils seem to need more direction? ("I don't understand. What are we supposed to do?") Which pupils seem to get right down to the task? Which children seem to take leadership roles? Which pupils are "fringe members" of their group? Mary's interventions with the groups are directed toward their behavior rather than to the Flower Study, and she recognizes that this is the first step the children are taking in working toward a more responsibly functioning collective. She also knows that *at best,* such responsible cooperative behavior may take several months to emerge, sometimes longer, and that she must work to facilitate this during her movements about the room.

After the pupils have had about 10 minutes on the task, she gives a signal that the activity will conclude in 5 more minutes. When the time is up, she reminds the children about cleanup. Waste is collected, and whatever notes and diagrams the children have made are brought with them to the Debriefing. The children help return the tables to their original positions and then return to their own seats for Debriefing. Mary has made notes of some of the questions that she will ask during the Debriefing session. She will also try to attend to each pupil's ideas and to concentrate on using the reflective type of response (see Chapter 3).

Sample Debriefing Scenario

TEACHER: What observations did you make about flowers?
> Asking that observations be shared

KYLE: They all had long green stems. Some of them had leaves on the stems.

TEACHER: So flowers had stems and some had leaves.
> Reflecting pupil's idea

KYLE: Yeah.

TEACHER: What other observations were made?
> Asking for more observations to be shared

JOHANNA: The flowers were different colors.

TEACHER: So you noticed the differences in the colors of the flowers.
> Reflecting pupil's idea

JOHANNA: Yes. And some of them had nice smells. Some smelled phooey.

TEACHER: There was a difference in the way they smelled.
> Reflecting pupil's idea

JOHANNA: Yeah.

TEACHER: Did you make some other observations?
> Asking for more observations

SARAH: The leaves had different shapes.

TEACHER: You noticed how different the leaves were.
> Reflecting pupil's idea

Will you describe some of the differences you saw?
> Asking pupils to compare

SARAH: *(Describes the varieties of leaves.)*

TEACHER: Thank you, Sarah.

Appreciates pupil's contribution

Does anyone else want to make some observations?

Asking for more observations

BEN: The petals had different shapes too. Some flowers were big and some were little.

TEACHER: You saw the differences in size and also the differences in the shapes of the petals.

Reflecting pupil's idea

BEN: Yeah.

TEACHER: I was wondering if there was a way to group these flowers. Would you see any way of arranging them in groups?

Asking for classifying to be done

GUY: Well, I'd put the ones that smell nice in one group.

TEACHER: Perhaps you'd have a name for that group?

Asking for the identification of an attribute-alike category

GUY: I don't know. Nice-smellers. *(Laughs.)*

Mary proceeds in this fashion using selected higher-order questions and many reflective responses to debrief the initial play session with flowers. She does not attempt the more difficult challenging questions at this time. They will be used later, after Replay.

There is, of course, the initial discomfort Mary feels about such an open-ended inquiry. No "right" answers are being sought here. Pupils are not being asked to name the flowers and label their parts. All of this is very discrepant with Mary's old style of teaching, and she may even have some lingering doubts and hesitations about the ultimate value of this emphasis on inquiry rather than on specific information. Her awareness of these feelings helps her to manage them, and she keeps thinking about strategies she might use to liberate her from her old ways. She is on a growing and learning path—one that is sometimes uphill.

In drawing the sciencing session to a close, Mary engages the pupils in an evaluation of the activity so that she can get some ideas about their responses to this way of working. "What did you like about it?" "How did it go for you?" "Were there things about it that you'd like to see improved?" "What were some things you learned?" She uses this information in building her next day's plans. Tomorrow, there will be Replay of the Flower Study. Her working groups may require some adjustment. On the third day of Replay, she will bring in different flowers to observe and compare. By then the children may be ready to handle some of the more challenging questions in the Debriefing sessions. Perhaps by the fifth day the children will be ready for one or more of the Creating tasks, and Mary is thinking about the possibility of having the children make artificial flowers with colored tissue paper and pipe cleaners. Having gotten this first field trial under her belt, Mary may be ready to tackle Activity 40, Magnets, in the next round of sciencing.

Now that you have read the introductory materials, examine the activities, then take the plunge and begin sciencing.

CATEGORY A: WET, WETTER, WETTEST

Activities that involve investigative play with water

Activity 1: Water Fountains

Activity 2: Rain

Activity 3: Sinking and Floating

Activity 4: Sound and Pitch

Activity 5: Siphoning

Activity 6: Absorbency

Activity 7: Solutions

Activity 8: Bubbles

Activity 9: Ice

Activity 10: Suction

Activity 11: Life in Water

Activity 1: Water Fountains

In this center the children work with the equipment provided and make some observations about water flow. They are asked to record their observations.

Activity Card

- Use the materials in this center to make some observations about how water flows through the openings of the containers.
- Try as many investigations as you can think of.
- Discuss your ideas with each other.
- Then make a record of what you observed.

You may have some other ideas about how these materials can be used. Try your ideas and see what happens.

Materials

Clear plastic bottles with removable lids, with holes of various sizes punched in the sides—some in a vertical line, some in a horizontal line; yogurt containers, some with vertically punched holes and some with horizontally punched holes, also with removable lids; water; large basin, to collect water

Thinking Operations Emphasized

Observing and recording; comparing; suggesting hypotheses; examining assumptions; making decisions; interpreting data; applying principles to new situations

Big Ideas

The rate at which water flows through an outlet depends on the size of the outlet, height of the water above the outlet, air pressure on the surface of the water.

Notes to the Teacher

- Reminders about cleanup procedures may be advisable before starting this activity.
- A soldering gun is an efficient tool for making holes in plastic.
- Caution: Heating plastic may produce small amounts of toxic fumes, so do this in a well-ventilated place.

Debriefing

Questions of the following types may promote reflection during Debriefing sessions. They should be used selectively.

- What observations did you make about the way the water flowed out of the holes?
- What differences, if any, did you observe in the water flow?
- Why do you suppose that happened?
- If we tried that with another bottle (container), what do you think might happen?

Extending

After the children have had ample opportunity to carry out investigative play with the "water fountains," you may wish to extend the inquiries in one or more of the following ways:

1. By adding new materials to the center, such as containers with different shapes, also with removable lids; containers with holes irregularly dispersed; different kinds of liquids, such as a mixture of oil and water
2. By introducing new activity cards; by calling for ways of measuring waterflow
3. By asking more challenging questions in later Debriefing sessions, for example:

   - How do you account for the difference in the water flow when the lid is on and when it is off? How do you explain it?
   - If you wanted to change the water flow, how might you do it? Why do you think that would work?
   - What observations did you make about the relationship of the water flow to the size, (shape, position) of the holes? How do you account for this?

4. By introducing questions that call for examination of value issues relating to the topic, for example:

- Should we be careful about wasting water? What do you think? What are your ideas about it?
- Where do you suppose our water comes from? What are your thoughts about it?
- What happens when the water supply is low? What contributes to the decrease in water levels? What are your ideas about it?
- Should we be concerned about conserving water? Tell about your ideas.

Creating

When the children appear to be approaching the limits of their interest in the "water fountain" study, they might be asked to do one or more of the following:

1. Work with a friend. Make a "water fountain" using some of the materials found in class. Make sure that it has a "stop and go" action.
2. With a pencil and paper, design a "water fountain" for a rabbit or other pet. Make sure that it has a "stop and go" action and that the pet will be able to learn how to use it.

Activity 2: Rain

In this activity the children spend some time outdoors on a rainy day and make observations about rain. They are asked to record their observations.

Activity Card

- Work with a partner. Make sure that you have your raincoats, hats, and boots on before going outside.
- Go out into the schoolyard and make some observations about the rain. Use the materials in the Rain Center to help you with your observations.
- Discuss your observations with each other.
- Then come back to the classroom and record your observations.

You may have some other ideas about studying rain. Try out some of your ideas and see what happens.

Materials

Rulers, yardsticks, paper towels, plastic containers, umbrellas, plastic sheeting, plastic bags, marking pens, sticks

Thinking Operations Emphasized

Observing; gathering and recording data; making decisions; suggesting hypotheses; examining assumptions

Big Ideas

Humidity and temperature are two conditions that help determine whether rain will fall. Rain water may contain certain pollutants.

Notes to the Teacher

- Prior to undertaking this activity it would be important to ensure that pupils have appropriate dress and can be protected from getting excessively wet during their rain studies.
- Some climates and times of year are more conducive to rain studies than others. If a rainy day is a rarity in your area, you may wish to have an introductory session on rain before pupils go out.
- In areas where rain is more frequent, these activities may be spread out over a longer period of time.

Debriefing

Questions of the following types may be used during Debriefing sessions to promote reflection about the rain studies. They should be used selectively.

- What observations can be made on a rainy day?
- How is rain different from snow?
- How could you tell if it was raining hard? How did you determine this?
- How can you measure how much rain is falling? What are your ideas?
- Where is the rain coming from? What makes you think that is true?
- How can you tell if it is going to rain? What are your ideas?

Extending

After the initial investigative play period, the children's inquiries may be extended in one or more of the following ways:

1. By introducing new materials to the rain studies, such as thermometers, different kinds of fabrics (feathers, fur, plastic), magnifying glasses, microscopes
2. By adding new activity cards; by inventing ways to measure rainfall
3. By raising more challenging questions in later debriefing sessions, for example:

    - What makes it rain? How do you know that?
    - What's in a raindrop? What observations did you make that allowed you to know that?

- What makes rain warm? What makes it cold? What hypotheses can you think of that would explain the differences in the temperature of the rain?
- What observations did you make about the effect of rain on different types of materials? How do you account for those differences?

4. By raising questions that call for students to examine some value issues related to the topic, for example:

- What do you suppose "acid rain" is? How does it become acid? What are your ideas?
- What do you suppose happens when acid rain falls? What are your ideas?
- What actions should adults take about acid rain? What actions might children take? What are your opinions? What do you see as some consequences of the actions you propose? What are your thoughts on it?

Creating

Some of the following may serve as culminating activities for the rain studies:

1. Have the children work in groups of four or five. Ask them to try to invent a way to measure how much rain will fall in a given period (maybe one hour) on a given day. When the children have collected their data, ask that the data from each group be compared.

2. Have the children work in small groups. Ask them to compare the quantity of rain that falls in different parts of the schoolyard during one rainfall. Ask them to list all the reasons they can think of to account for the differences.

3. Ask for a "rain crew" to carry out observations and studies on each rainy day for a month. Suggest that pupils record their observations and report to the class once a week.

4. Ask the children to write poetry about rain. You might wish to suggest some titles, e.g.:

- "Don't Rain on My Parade"
- "Raindrops Falling on My Head"
- "Thunderstorms"
- "Chasing Rainbows"

5. Ask the children to work with a partner. Ask them to invent a rain-making machine. Ask them to draw a diagram of their invention.

Activity 3: Sinking and Floating

In this activity the children work with water and the objects provided and make observations about things that float and things that sink. The children are also asked to record their observations.

Activity Card

> - Use the materials in the center to make some observations about things that sink and things that float.
> - Try as many investigations as you can think of. Talk with each other about your ideas.
> - Then make a record of what you observed.
>
> Are there other ways to use the materials in this center? Try some new investigations and see what happens.

Materials

Water, either at a water table or in basins; assorted objects for study, such as a sponge, chalk, Ping-Pong balls, modeling clay, tin foil, containers with removable lids, bits of wood, clothespins, stones, Styrofoam chips, plastic dishes and cups, nails, paper cups, paper towels

Thinking Operations Emphasized

Observing and recording; gathering and classifying data; comparing; suggesting hypotheses; designing investigations; applying principles in new situations; imagining and inventing

Big Ideas

Water has buoyancy that allows certain objects to float on the surface. Objects float or sink depending on the amount of water they displace.

Notes to the Teacher

- Before children begin work in this center it might be helpful to remind them about procedures to be used in case of a water spill. Sponges, paper towels, and newspapers should be available.
- You may want to introduce just a few objects for the first Play sessions and add more as later investigations get under way.
- Children will also enjoy bringing objects from home for this center, and they may be encouraged to do so.

Debriefing

Here are some questions that might be raised during Debriefing sessions to promote inquiry about sinking and floating properties:

- Tell about some of the observations you made while working in this center. What observations did you make about objects that floated? What observations did you make about objects that sank?
- In what ways were the objects that floated alike? How were they different?
- How might you compare sinking and floating objects?

Extending

After adequate opportunity for initial investigative play, the children's inquiries may be extended in one or more of the following ways:

1. By adding to the materials in the sinking-and-floating center
2. By introducing other activity cards that give specific focus to the inquiries, for example:

    - Conduct some investigations to turn some of your "sinkers" into "floaters."
    - Conduct some investigations to turn some of your "floaters" into "sinkers."
    - Keep a record of the results of your investigations about sinking and floating objects.
    - Classify the objects you worked with in this center. Establish some groups, and show how each object belongs to a group.

Creating

When the investigative play seems to have run its course, you may wish to extend the pupils' inquiries into more creative problem-solving tasks. For example, ask the children to:

1. Work with a friend. Construct a boat that will float while carrying the weight of at least three "sinkers."
2. Work with a friend. Design a floating bathtub. Draw an illustration of your design.
3. Work with a friend. Design an apparatus that will keep an elephant afloat in the ocean. Draw a picture of your design.

Activity 4: Sound and Pitch

In this activity the children work with the materials to create sounds and to explore the ways in which sounds are made and pitch is raised and lowered.

Activity Card

- Use the materials in the center to see what kinds of sounds you can make.
- Try as many investigations with the materials as you can think of.
- Discuss your observations with each other.
- Then write about what you observed.

Can these materials be used in other ways? Do you have some new ideas for some new investigations? Try them and see what happens.

Materials

Between 8 and 12 glasses or glass jars; a metal spoon; a chopstick; a pitcher of water

Thinking Operations Emphasized

Observing and recording; comparing; classifying; suggesting hypotheses; examining assumptions; summarizing; creating and inventing

Big Ideas

Sounds can be created by striking objects together to make them vibrate. The pitch of a sound can be raised or lowered by modifying the struck object.

Notes to the Teacher

- It's a good idea to remind the children of what to do if a jar or glass breaks and to have a small broom, dustpan, newspapers, sponges, and paper towels on hand.

Debriefing

Here are some questions that might be raised during Debriefing sessions. They should be used selectively.

- What observations did you make about how sounds are made?
- What did you do to find that out?
- How do you explain how that happened? What are your ideas about it?
- Why do you suppose that worked? What are your ideas about it?

Extending

After the children have had adequate opportunity to carry out initial investigative play, you may wish to extend the sciencing in one or more of the following ways:

1. By introducing a wider variety of materials to the center, such as different sets of jars and glasses; tin cans; different liquids, such as mineral oil or water mixed with sand; a xylophone; a pitchpipe; a tuning fork
2. By introducing other activity cards; by asking that ways be found to measure sound
3. By asking more challenging questions in later Debriefing sessions, for example:

   - What did you observe about the amount of water in the jar and the sound produced? How do you explain that? What are your ideas about it?
   - What did you do to change the sounds? How did that work?
   - In what ways may sounds be changed?
   - Can you explain how that works?
   - How are the sounds that come from the jars or glasses similar to and different from the sounds on the xylophone? Sounds on the pitchpipe?
   - What differences did you observe in the sounds made by the different liquids? How do you explain them?

4. By raising questions that ask pupils to examine some value issues related to the topic, for example:

   - Are there some sounds that are pleasant to hear? What are your opinions?
   - Are there some sounds that are hurtful? Do you have some ideas about this?
   - Suppose someone is producing noise or sound that you find objectionable. What should you do about it? What are your ideas?
   - What do you suppose might occur if you did take some action to oppose noise? What might be some consequences of your actions? What are your thoughts?

Creating

When the students have come to the end of their enthusiasm for investigative play with "water music," they might enjoy participating in one or more of the following culminating activities:

1. Have the students work with a friend and make up a simple tune that they can play on their musical jars. Ask them to perform it for the class. Have them figure out a way to record the music so that someone else might be able to learn to play it.
2. Have the students compare their musical instrument made of jars to some other musical instrument, like a piano or a guitar. Have them work with a friend to make a list of as many similarities and differences as they can think of.
3. Have the students, each working with a friend, choose another instrument (for example, a piano or a guitar), either one found in the classroom or one that they have at home, and try to tune their musical jars so that at least eight of the keys match the instrument in pitch.

Activity 5: Siphoning

In this center the children work with water and with clear plastic tubing to explore how siphons work. The children are asked to record their observations.

Activity Card

- Use the materials in this center to carry out some investigations of how water can be made to flow from one bucket into another.
- Try as many investigations as you can think of.
- Observe carefully what occurs, and talk about your ideas with each other.
- Then write about what you found.

You may have thought of some other ways to use these materials. Try out your new ideas and see what happens.

Materials

Buckets or pails of water; transparent (glass or plastic) containers of different sizes; clear plastic tubing; funnels

Thinking Operations Emphasized

Observing and recording; gathering and organizing data; summarizing; designing investigations; suggesting hypotheses; examining assumptions; inventing and creating

Big Ideas

Air pressure and its absence (vacuum) can be used to move liquid between containers.

Notes to the Teacher

- This activity is definitely very wet! It is a good idea to prepare for this in advance by placing plastic sheeting on the floor around the center and by giving pupils clear and explicit instructions for cleanup after the activity is over. Clear plastic tubing, if not available in your school, can be purchased inexpensively at a pet shop that sells tropical fish supplies.

Debriefing

Here are some questions that might be raised during Debriefing sessions. They should be used selectively.

- What investigations did you carry out today? What observations did you make about how the siphons worked?
- What did you do to make that work?
- How do you explain that? What are your ideas about it?

Extending

When the children have had ample time for their initial investigations, the inquiry may be extended in one or more of the following ways:

1. By adding new materials to the center, such as water bottles with stoppers, with places to attach the tubing; spray bottles; squirt guns; bottles with holes drilled in tops and bottoms
2. By introducing new activity cards
3. By asking more challenging questions in later debriefing sessions, for example:

   - What did you observe about how water flows from one level to another?
   - In what other ways can you make water move upward? What are your ideas on that?
   - What other examples can you give of water moving upward? Where else do you see this happen? What ideas do you have about how this works?

Creating

When the children are coming to the end of their interest in working in the siphoning center, you may wish to extend their inquiries by having them do one or both of the following activities:

1. Work with a friend. Draw a picture showing how you would design a system that would carry water from a low level to a house that was built very high up on a hill.
2. Work with a friend. Talk together to come up with at least ten ways that siphoning may be used in everyday situations.

Activity 6: Absorbency

In this activity the children work with eyedroppers and water to make observations about what happens when water is dropped on different types of surfaces.

Activity Card

> - Use the materials in this center to carry out some investigations to see what happens when water is dropped on different surfaces.
> - Try as many investigations as you can think of.
> - Talk with each other about your observations.
> - Then write about your discoveries.
>
> There may be other investigations you can do with these materials. Think of some and try them out to see what happens.

Materials

Pieces of brick, stone, fired and unglazed clay, glass, assorted types of fabrics with different fibers and textures, different kinds of paper (newsprint, construction paper, tissue, waxed paper, bond), different kinds of wood (balsa, plywood, pine), synthetics (plastic, Formica), feathers, crayons, eyedroppers, water, magnifying glasses

Thinking Operations Emphasized

Observing and recording; suggesting hypotheses; comparing; classifying; designing investigations; making decisions

Big Ideas

Different materials have characteristic patterns and rates of absorption.

Notes to the Teacher

- The various materials may be placed on the tabletop and the eyedroppers, in a small container of water, placed in the center of the table. An activity card, perhaps reading "What happens to the water as it comes in contact with each of these different materials? Conduct some investigations to find this out," may be used to give the inquiry another focus.

Debriefing

Here are some questions that might be raised during Debriefing sessions to promote reflection:

- What observations did you make about what happened when water was dropped on these different materials?

- What similarities did you find in the way the water affected the materials? What differences did you find?
- In what ways might these materials be classified? What groups could be set up? In which group would each of the materials belong?

Extending

After the children have had ample time for their investigations, you may wish to extend the inquiry in one or more of the following ways:

1. By adding new materials to the center, such as a squirt bottle, pieces of metal, or different types of liquids, such as mineral oil, alcohol, or soda pop
2. By introducing new activity cards; by investigating ways to measure rates of absorption
3. By asking more challenging questions in later Debriefing sessions, for example:

    - What observation did you make about the materials that did not absorb the water? How do you account for this? What are your ideas?
    - What observations did you make about the materials that took longer to absorb the water? How do you account for this?
    - What observations did you make about the materials that absorbed the water quickly? How do you account for this?
    - What differences and similarities did you find in absorption when you used other liquids? How do you explain this? What are your ideas?

4. By raising questions that call for students to examine some values issues related to the topic, for example:

    - Someone has invented a substance that will make your T-shirts waterproof. You buy it in a can and spray it on your shirt, and it will keep your shirt dry in the rain. But the plastic spray may cause some people to break out in a rash. Should this product be allowed or taken off the market? What are your ideas?
    - Should plastic products that are helpful in some ways but harmful in other ways be allowed on the market? What are your thoughts about this? Can you give some examples about such products from your own experience?
    - What actions should children take with respect to finding out about the potential harmful effects of certain products? What are your thoughts?

Creating

When the children's interest in replaying with the materials seems to be waning, you might wish to culminate the studies with one or more of the following. Have the students:

1. Work with a friend. Make a drawing of some of the observations you made in this center.

2. Draw a picture showing your design of the "perfect rainwear outfit"—raincoat, cap, and boots that will keep a person perfectly dry in a rainstorm.
3. Work with a friend. Think about as many materials as you can that do not easily absorb water. Make a list of these materials. Classify them.
4. Work with a friend. Think about as many materials as you can that absorb water very easily. Make a list of these materials. Classify them.

Activity 7: Solutions

In this center the children work with dry ingredients and water to carry out investigative play with solutions. They are asked to record their observations.

Activity Card

- Use the materials in this center to make some investigations of how dry and wet ingredients combine.
- What observations did you make?
- Talk about what you found with each other.
- Then record your findings.

You may have some new ideas for using the materials in this center. Try out your new ideas and see what happens.

Materials

Assorted dry ingredients, such as flour, salt, cornstarch, sugar, sand, rice, bulgur wheat, dry legumes, baking soda, dry milk powder, instant coffee; clear containers; water; spoons; clock or timer

Thinking Operations Emphasized

Comparing; observing and recording; suggesting hypotheses; examining assumptions; classifying; designing investigations

Big Ideas

Some materials dissolve easily in water; materials that do not dissolve easily in water may be soluble in other liquids.

Notes to the Teacher

- Before the children begin to work in this center they might be reminded of ways to avoid an awesome mess. For example, it might be helpful if they were to wipe up after each exploration instead of leaving the entire cleanup for the end. Lots of warm water, cloths, and plastic covering for the floor are very useful. This activity can be very messy, so it might be a good idea to wait until the children have achieved a relatively high degree of personal responsibility for their work before introducing it. A space might also be provided to allow for the overnight keeping of certain solutions for 24-hour observations.

Debriefing

Here are some questions that may be raised during initial Debriefing sessions:

- What were some of the investigations you conducted in this center?
- What observations did you make?
- What explanations do you have for how that worked?

Extending

After the children have had ample opportunity to conduct initial investigations, you may wish to extend their inquiries in one or more of the following ways:

1. By adding new materials to the center, such as different types of liquids (oil, vinegar, alcohol, soda pop) or by adding liquid mixtures (oil and water, alcohol solutions)
2. By introducing new activity cards
3. By introducing more challenging questions in later Debriefing sessions, for example:

    - What are some of the similarities and some of the differences you have seen in the ways dry and wet ingredients combine? What explanations do you have for how this happens?

- What classification systems can you set up, based on your discoveries in this center?
- What materials are more soluble? How do you explain this? What materials are less soluble? How do you explain this?

Creating

When the children's interest in the inquiries seems to be on the wane, you might wish to initiate some other kinds of problems for them to examine, for example:

1. Ask the students what observations can be made when certain solutions are left to stand for long periods of time, such as 24 hours? 48 hours? one week? Ask them to work with a friend to conduct some inquiries to find this out. Then suggest some hypotheses to explain it.
2. Have the students work with a friend. Ask them to make a ball by combining wet and dry ingredients, and to record their procedures.
3. Ask the students to write a story about a "secret formula" that has certain magical properties.

Activity 8: Bubbles

In this center the children work with soapy water to make some observations about bubbles.

Activity Card

> - Use the materials in this center to find out what you can about bubbles.
> - What observations did you make?
> - Talk to each other about what you found.
> - Then write about your observations.
>
> You may wish to use the materials in this center to create some other investigations. Try out your ideas and see what happens.

Materials

A solution made of a few drops of glycerine in a gallon of water, with a capful of liquid detergent, in a plastic bucket or container; straws; flexible wire and cutters; a few funnels of different sizes

Thinking Operations Emphasized

Observing and recording; comparing; suggesting hypotheses; designing investigations; imagining

Big Ideas

Bubbles are thin layers of water kept intact by surface tension.

Notes to the Teacher

- Before children begin work in this center it may be important to remind them about what needs to be done in the event of spills. Sponges, paper towels, and cloths should be available for cleanup. Children might also be reminded that soapy water will hurt if it gets in their eyes and is likely to be slippery if too much of it falls to the floor. Plastic sheeting as a floor cover may be a good idea for this center. Commercially obtained bottles of bubbles may also be used for this center.

Debriefing

Here are some questions that may be raised during initial Debriefing sessions:

- What observations did you make about bubbles?
- What did you observe about their size? shape? color?
- What observations did you make about the "life" of a bubble? Which bubbles lasted longer? How do you explain this?
- What makes a bubble pop more quickly? How do you know that is true?

Extending

When the initial Play periods seem to have lost their productivity, you may wish to extend the inquiry in one or more of the following ways:

1. By adding new materials to the bubble center, such as bubble pipes, sponges, waxed paper with holes of various sizes, paper cones, wire frames of different shapes
2. By introducing new activity cards; investigating how bubbles can be measured
3. By introducing more challenging questions in later Debriefing sessions, for example:

   - Why do you suppose bubbles are almost always round?
   - How do you suppose you could make a square bubble?
   - Why do you suppose bubbles have colors? Where does the coloring come from? What explanations do you have for this?
   - Why do you suppose bubbles pop so quickly? How might you extend the life of a bubble? Conduct some investigations to see how this might be done.
   - What makes the biggest bubble? How do you explain this?

Creating

To bring these studies to a culmination, you may wish to invite the students to carry out one or more of the following creative activities:

1. Work with a friend. Design a house made of bubbles. Draw a picture of it.
2. Write a poem or make up a song about bubbles.
3. Make up a story, "The Bubble That Never Popped."

Activity 9: Ice

In this center the children observe the properties of ice. They are asked to record their observations.

Activity Card

- Use the materials in this center to find out what you can about ice.
- What observations did you make?
- Talk with each other about what you found.
- Then record your findings.

You may have some other ideas about using the materials in this center. Try out some of your ideas and see what happens.

Materials

A bag of ice cubes; newspapers or a plastic tabletop cover; ruler; balance scales; plastic dishes or containers; clock or other timer; hammer; scissors; nails; paper towels; salt

Thinking Operations Emphasized

Observing and recording; comparing; suggesting hypotheses; examining assumptions; designing investigations; applying principles; imagining and creating; making decisions

Big Ideas

Water usually freezes at 32° F. When it melts, the amount of water stays the same. How fast ice melts depends on its shape, amount, and the surrounding temperature.

Notes to the Teacher

- Bags of ice cubes can often be bought at the local gas station or supermarket. One bag should be adequate for one day's activity.

Debriefing

During Debriefing sessions, you may wish to raise some of the following types of questions to encourage reflection about the inquiry:

- What observations did you make about the ice cubes?
- How are ice cubes formed? How do you know that? What assumptions might you be making?
- If you wanted to change the shape of an ice cube, how might you do that? What assumptions might you be making?
- How do you know that would work?
- Why do you suppose ice cubes stick together? How do you explain this?
- Why do ice cubes melt at different rates? How can you explain this? What assumptions might you be making?

Extending

When the pupils have had ample opportunity for initial investigative play, the activity may be extended in one or more of the following ways:

1. By adding some new activity cards to the center to give a different focus to the inquiries, for example:

    - Conduct some investigations to find differences between ice and water.
    - Conduct some investigations to find out how you might slow down the melting of ice. Figure out how to measure and record the different rates of melting.

- Conduct some investigations to find out how you might speed up the melting of ice. Figure out a way of measuring the rate of melting. Record your findings.

2. By raising more challenging questions during later Debriefing sessions, for example:

   - In what ways can the melting of ice be speeded up? What examples can you give to show that that is true?
   - What other types of liquids might be frozen? How do you know that is true?
   - With what other types of liquids may ice be formed? What hypotheses do you have about this? What kinds of tests might you carry out to see if your ideas work?
   - Why do you suppose ice is slippery? How can you explain this?

3. By examining some value issues related to the topic, for example:

   Snowblowers are very effective machines for moving ice and snow. But they use a lot of energy and make a big racket.

   Some people in North City say that snowblowers are essential machines. Others say they should be outlawed because they consume too much energy and make noise pollution! The critics say, "What's wrong with snowshovels?"

   - What are your opinions? How should these issues be decided? Whose side are you on?

Creating

At the end of their inquiries about the properties of ice, you may wish to have the children engage in other extending activities, for example:

1. Have the children make carvings out of ice.
2. Have the groups conduct inquiries to determine the differences in weight and volume between ice and water.
3. Have the children figure out ways to carry large blocks of ice from house to school with a minimum of melting.
4. Have the pupils draw pictures of ice houses.
5. Have the children write stories about how it might feel to live in an ice house, or ask them to imagine what it would be like to live as Eskimos did, in an igloo.

Activity 10: Suction

In this investigation the children play with the materials provided to investigate the concept of suction—what it is and how it works. They are also asked to record their observations.

Activity Card

> - Use the materials in this center to find out what you can about suction.
> - What observations did you make? Try out some investigations and see what happens.
> - Talk about your discoveries with each other.
> - Then write about what you found.
>
> You may have some other ideas about how to use the materials in this center. Try out your ideas and see what happens.

Materials

A basin of water; plastic tubing; straws; eyedroppers; toilet plunger; rubber suction cups; syringes

Thinking Operations Emphasized

Observing; suggesting hypotheses; comparing; examining assumptions; designing investigations; imagining and creating

Big Ideas

When some of the air inside a space is removed, inside air pressure becomes less than outside air pressure. This may result in such effects as contraction and suction.

Notes to the Teacher

- The plastic tubing should be cut into several different lengths so that observations can be made within these variables. Discarded medical syringes may be obtained through the school nurse. Rubber suction cups might be found in a toy or hardware store.

Debriefing

The following types of questions might stimulate reflection about suction. They should be used selectively.

- What observations did you make about how water was raised through the straws? tubing? eyedroppers? syringes?
- How did it happen? How do you explain it?
- Are some assumptions being made here? How do you know?

- How is the process of suction different with the syringe and the straw? How do you explain the differences?

Extending

When the pupils seem to be coming to the end of their interest in the suction investigations, you may wish to extend their inquiries in some of the following ways:

1. By adding new activity cards to give the investigations a different focus
2. By raising some more challenging questions during later Debriefing sessions, for example:

   - What kinds of machines or tools rely on suction to make them work? Are some assumptions being made here? How do you know?
   - Under what conditions does suction fail? How can this be explained?
   - What are some differences between the suction process with the rubber cups and with the plastic pipe? the rubber cups and the straw?

Creating

To culminate the inquiries for this center, you might ask the students to:

1. Work with a friend. Design a machine that uses water and suction to do its job.
2. Work with a friend. Think up and list as many machines or tools as you can that depend on suction to work.
3. Think of a good way to increase suction power. Use the materials in the center to try out your ideas.

Activity 11: Life in Water

In this activity the students carry out investigative play with the materials provided to examine the concept of life in water—what may live in water and how. They are also asked to record their observations.

Activity Card

> - Use the materials in this center to find out what you can about what lives in water.
> - What observations did you make?
> - Try some investigations and see what happens.
> - Talk about your ideas with each other.
> - Then write about what you observed.
>
> You may have some other ideas about how to use the materials in this center. Try out your ideas and see what happens.

Materials

Several cut flowers; glass vase; water; goldfish; goldfish bowl; several types of seeds (lima beans, acorns, rice, barley, sunflower seeds, dry peas, lentils, mung beans, alfalfa seeds, peanuts; lemon, lime, grapefruit, apple, and orange seeds; melon, squash, and avocado seeds); flat dishes; blotting paper; paper cups; 6 to 8 jars of several sizes; onion, potato, radish, celery stalk, asparagus stalk, green onions; food coloring

Thinking Operations Emphasized

Observing and recording; comparing; suggesting hypotheses; gathering and interpreting data; identifying assumptions; designing investigations; making decisions; imagining and creating

Big Ideas

Water is extremely important for all living things. Plants and animals depend on water to live and grow.

Notes to the Teacher

- This investigative play is helped along by a few advance preparations. For example, begin several days in advance to immerse some of the seeds in water, in a glass jar. Place onion and potato in water, in glass jars. Place celery stalk in water, to which a drop of food coloring has been added. These "starters" should be included in the materials for the center, as well as additional seeds, and vegetables that begin in dry condition. At least one marine animal (e.g., goldfish, brine shrimp, snail) should be included in the materials for this center; these are easily obtained at the local pet shop.

Debriefing

The following types of questions might be helpful in promoting pupils' reflection about their inquiries:

- What observations did you make about what lives in water?
- How did you know that?
- What did you find out about what cannot live in water?
- How did you know that?

Extending

When the investigative play with these materials seems to be losing appeal, you may wish to extend the inquiries in one or more of the following ways:

1. By introducing new materials to the center, for example, other marine animals (guppies, shrimp, mollies), amphibians (turtles, frogs), nonmarine animals (caterpil-

lar, ants, lizard, hamster, gerbil, other insects), salt water, sea plants (seaweed, kelp), other root vegetables (turnips, carrots, parsley), other vegetables (tomatoes, squash), cuttings from green plants

2. By adding new activity cards to give the investigations a different focus
3. By raising more challenging questions during later Debriefing sessions, for example:

   - What kinds of investigations were carried out with salt water? What are some differences between salt and fresh water? What are some differences between what may live in salt and fresh water?
   - What did you find out about animals that live in water? How do "water animals" differ from "land animals"? How did you know that?
   - What did you find out about plants that live in water? How do "water plants" differ from "land plants"? How did you know that?
   - How might the animals (or plants) be classified? What groups might be set up?
   - How is it possible for a fish to live in water? What are your ideas? How is it that a cow (dog, chicken, person, etc.) cannot live in water? What are your ideas?
   - What did you find out about plants' need for water? How did you know that?

4. By raising questions that call for pupils' examination of some value issues related to the topic, for example:

   Occasionally an oil tanker that is transporting crude oil from where it is taken from the ground to the place where it is to be refined has a terrible accident. The tanker breaks up, and the oil spills into the ocean.

   - What are some consequences of these spills on plant and animal life in the ocean? What are your thoughts?
   - What are some consequences of these spills on our own lives? What are your opinions?
   - How do you suppose the oil should be cleaned up? Who should pay for this? What are your opinions?
   - What actions ought to be considered to prevent future spills? What are your ideas about this?
   - Is this a question that children ought to be concerned with? What do you think about it?

Creating

The inquiries may be culminated in one or more of the following creative activities:

1. Take a trip to the aquarium for observations of fresh and salt water marine animals, leading to the construction of papier-mâché aquarium animals for the classroom. These may be hung from the classroom ceiling, giving the effect of animals in water.
2. Have the children earn money to buy a small aquarium for the classroom.
3. Have the children work in pairs to draw or paint a picture of a marine animal. Collect all the pictures in a class book.

4. Have each student draw or paint a picture of an imaginary deep-sea marine animal.
5. Have the children work in pairs to think up and write stories: "My Life in the Sea," by Henry the Whale; "Sea Dangers," by Sally the Seal; "The Mermaid Who Changed into a TV Model"; "The Octopus's Garden."

CATEGORY B: NO FUSS, NO MUSS, NO STICKY MESS

Activities that will not leave too much mess on tables, on the floor, or around the room

Activity 12: Light

Activity 13: Thermometers

Activity 14: Electricity

Activity 15: Air

Activity 16: Balances

Activity 17: Pendulums

Activity 18: Magnifiers

Activity 19: Light and Shadow

Activity 20: Measuring

Activity 21: Growing Plants from Seeds

Activity 22: Seeds from Fruit from Seeds

Activity 23: Molds

Activity 24: Yeast

Activity 25: Flowers

Activity 26: Foods (1): How Foods Change

Activity 27: Foods (2): Composition

Activity 28: Skins

Activity 29: Bones and Shells

Activity 30: Skeletons

Activity 31: Birds

Activity 32: Parachutes

Activity 33: Sounds with Strings

Activity 34: Wind Sounds

Activity 35: Wind Energy

Activity 12: Light

In this center the children work with mirrors to make observations about reflecting surfaces. They are asked to record their observations.

Activity Card

> - Use the materials in this center to make some observations of the reflections you see in mirrors.
> - Try as many different investigations as you can think of.
> - Talk with each other about what you observed.
> - Then write about your observations.
>
> You may have some other ideas for using the materials in this center. Try them out and see what observations you can make.

Materials

Several squares of mirror, with tapes on edges; shaving mirror or other magnifying mirror; dentist's mirrors; full-length mirror; symmetrical and asymmetrical pictures;

illustrations from magazines; large and small print letters; pencils, paper clips, balls of different sizes, books, other objects of different shapes

Thinking Operations Emphasized

Observing and recording; comparing; suggesting hypotheses; examining assumptions; designing investigations; summarizing; imagining and creating

Big Ideas

Reflection requires light. Reflected objects are reversed, as in a mirror.

Notes to the Teacher

- Glass and mirror business establishments will cut an old mirror into squares at a reasonable price, if you explain that this is for school use. Masking tape protects the edges, avoids cuts, and can also be used to hinge two or three pieces of mirror together.
- Mirrors do break occasionally. Clear tape or adhesive backing may hold the broken pieces together.
- It is probably a good idea to remind students of procedures to follow in dealing with broken glass. Have a broom, dustpan, and newspapers available in case of breakage.

Debriefing

Here are some questions that might encourage further inquiry. They should be used selectively during Debriefing.

- What observations did you make about mirrors?
- What did you do to find that out?
- How did that work?
- Do you have some ideas that might explain it?

Extending

After the students have been given ample opportunity to carry out investigative play with the materials in this center, you may wish to extend the inquiries in one or more of the following ways:

1. By providing additional materials in the center, such as old mirrors and scraping tools, a deck of cards, pattern blocks, a flashlight or candle, a kaleidoscope
2. By introducing new activity cards
3. By asking more challenging questions in later Debriefing sessions, for example:

- What happens when you move something closer or farther away from a mirror? What observations have you made about that? Do you have any theories about how that works?
- How can a mirror change the way things look? How does that work? Do you have any ideas that might explain it?
- Try to think of as many ways to use a mirror as you can.

Creating

When the children seem to be coming to an end of their interest in this center, you may ask them to undertake other tasks that emphasize more imagining and creating skills, for example:

1. Work with a partner. Combine two or more mirrors in a way that will allow you to see images around a corner.
2. Work with a friend. Make your own mirror. What materials are better for this? What materials are poor reflectors? How can you explain this?
3. Work with a friend. Play with a flashlight and a mirror. Write or tell about the observations that can be made with these two tools.
4. Write a story, "The Child on the Other Side of the Mirror."
5. Write a poem, "The Mirror of Your Mind."

Activity 13: Thermometers

In this center the children work with thermometers to make observations about temperature and the conditions that cause temperature to change. They are asked to record their observations.

Activity Card

- Use the materials in this center to study temperature.
- Try to find out what temperature is.
- What objects are "hot"? What are the temperatures of "hot" objects?
- What objects are "cold"? What are the temperatures of "cold" objects?
- What objects are "warm"? What are the temperatures of "warm" objects?
- How does temperature change?
- Work together to conduct investigations to see what you can find out. Then write about what you found.

You may have other ideas about investigating temperature. Try out your ideas and see what happens.

Materials

A variety of thermometers (indoor, outdoor, body temperature thermometers); a variety of warm, cold, and room-temperature objects (a basin of warm or hot water, ice cubes, a package of frozen food, a container of milk, modeling clay, etc.)

Thinking Operations Emphasized

Observing; comparing; suggesting hypotheses; designing investigations; examining assumptions; gathering and recording data; applying principles; imagining and creating; making decisions; classifying

Big Ideas

One measure of an object's heat is its temperature. The human body responds to changes in temperature with a variety of physiological processes.

Notes to the Teacher

- You may wish to avoid using any of the breakable types of thermometers, depending on your perception of how carefully the children are able to work with the materials.

Debriefing

Here are some questions that might encourage reflection about temperatures. They should be used selectively in Debriefing sessions.

- What objects are cold? What temperatures do cold objects have? How did you figure this out?
- What objects are warm? What temperatures do warm objects have? How did you figure this out?
- What objects are hot? What temperatures do hot objects have? How did you figure this out?
- What other observations did you make about temperature?
- How do you explain some of the differences in temperature you found among the various objects?
- How does temperature change? How do you know that?
- What makes an object cold? hot? warm? How do you explain this?
- Did you do other kinds of investigations with these materials?

Extending

After the students have had sufficient time to conduct their initial investigations you may wish to extend their inquiries in one or more of the following ways:

1. By introducing new activity cards to the center to give new focus to the inquiries, for example:

- Make a chart of 20 objects and their temperatures. Classify the objects by arranging them into groups.
- Using pans of quite hot, warm, and quite cold water, conduct investigations to find out how certain temperatures feel on your hands. What observations can be made here?
- How can warm be made cold? How can cold be made warm? Conduct some investigations and write about your findings.

2. By raising more challenging questions in later Debriefing sessions, for example:

- How do you account for the fact that different thermometers give different readings for the same object?
- How do you account for the fact that different parts of the body show different temperature readings?
- In what ways can you raise the temperature of your hands?
- In what ways can you lower the temperature of your hands?
- What is the warmest part of the classroom? How do you account for that?
- What is the coolest area of the classroom? How do you account for that?

3. By raising questions that call for students to examine some value issues related to the topic, for example:

- Some people who live in places where it gets quite hot depend on air conditioners to cool off their homes, cars, and places of business. Is this a good way to use energy? What do you think?
- Some people who live in places where it gets quite cold depend on central heating systems, using oil, to heat their homes and places of work. Is this good? What do you think?
- Should we be concerned about the use of energy to heat and cool our homes and places of work? What are your thoughts on this?

Creating

When the children seem to be reaching the limit of their interest in the investigative play activities, you might ask them to do one or more of the following culminating activities:

1. Make a thermometer that shows temperature in Farenheit degrees. Make another one that shows temperature in Celsius degrees.
2. Draw a picture of a thermometer that could take the temperature of a volcano when it's erupting.
3. Work with a friend. Think up and list as many uses as you can for thermometers.
4. Write a story about the hottest day on record.
5. Draw some pictures of what ice crystals might look like.

6. Work with a friend. Think up and list as many things as you can think of that cold temperature is good for. Make a list of as many things as you can think of that hot temperature is good for.

Activity 14: Electricity

In this center the children work with batteries, wires, and low-wattage bulbs to make observations about electrical energy and electric circuitry.

Activity Card

- Work with the materials in this center to make some observations about electricity and how it works.
- Talk with each other about what you observed.
- Then write about your observations.

You may have some different ideas about how to use these materials. Try out your ideas and see what happens.

Materials

Low-wattage bulbs (flashlight bulbs, 25-watt bulbs); dry cell batteries; wires and clamps; switches; a telegraph key; a bell or buzzer

Thinking Operations Emphasized

Observing; comparing; designing investigations; generating and testing hypotheses; gathering and recording data; examining assumptions; making decisions; imagining and creating

Big Ideas

Electricity can be produced by a dry cell to make light, sound, motion, or heat.

Notes to the Teacher

- The materials in this center should be in two forms: sets that are already assembled and unassembled materials sufficient to create other sets. One assembled set should provide an example of a simple electrical circuit, working on an on-off switch, to light up a bulb. The other set should demonstrate electrical circuitry for a telegraph key. Materials should also be provided for pupils to assemble their own circuits. Pupils may also be encouraged to disassemble and reassemble the demonstration sets.

Debriefing

Here are some questions that might be used in Debriefing sessions to promote reflection. They should be used selectively.

- What observations did you make about how electricity works?
- What did you do to find that out?
- Do you have some ideas that might explain it?
- How did your electrical model compare with the one that was in the center?
- In what ways are the electric light model and the telegraph key model alike? How are they different?

Extending

After the children have carried out initial investigative play with the materials, the inquiry might be extended in one or more of the following ways:

1. By introducing additional materials to the center, for example, additional electric lights, additional wire, simple electric motors, different types of switches, and dead batteries that can be taken apart
2. By adding new activity cards to give the investigative play a different focus

3. By raising more challenging questions about the inquiries, for example:

- Under what conditions does the model work? When does the model fail to work? How can you explain this? Can you think of a way to test that theory?
- In what ways is your model like (different from) the electric light system in this classroom?
- What are some other electrical systems that are used in this classroom? in this school? How are they like (different from) the models you built?
- Where do you suppose electricity comes from? What ideas do you have about it? How could you test your idea?

4. By raising questions that call for students' examination of values issues related to the topic, for example:

New York City, and the surrounding metropolitan area, needs and uses a great deal of electricity. The more people who live in the area, and the more who work in the city, the

more electricity is needed. The city officials are running out of resources to supply the demand.

Canada, the neighboring country to the north, can supply the United States with more electrical power. But some Canadians have said, "If you weren't so extravagant in your use of electricity, you wouldn't need so much. Why should we give our precious resources to you?"

- Are we wasteful in our use of electricity? Can you give some examples to support your opinion? Should Canada give us this extra power? What are your ideas?

Creating

You may wish to bring these activities to culmination by asking the children to participate in one or more of the following tasks:

1. Work with a friend. Use the battery, wires, light bulbs, and switches to design a game that can be played in this classroom.
2. Make a pencil-and-paper design of an electrical circuit.
3. Work with a friend to design a plan to use electricity to produce sound. Draw a diagram of how your system would work.
4. Work with a friend and list as many uses of electricity as you can think of.
5. Write a story titled "The Day the Lights Went Out." Make it as scary as you can.
6. Put your imagination to work and think of how the very first electric light might have been invented. Write a little play about this event.

Activity 15: Air

In this center the children work with balloons to carry out investigative play with air. They are asked to record their observations.

Activity Card

- Use the materials in this center to find out what you can about air.
- What observations can be made about air?
- What does air look like?
- How can you move it from place to place?
- How heavy or light is it? How do you know it's there?
- Try as many investigations as you can think of to help you to find out about air.
- Then write about what you found.

You may have some other ideas for using the materials in this center. Try some of your ideas and see what happens.

Materials

Many balloons of different shapes and sizes; string; a balance scale; rubber bands; a timer

Thinking Operations Emphasized

Observing; comparing; collecting and recording data; suggesting hypotheses; examining assumptions; designing investigations; decision making; imagining and creating

Big Ideas

Air exerts pressure and has weight; air pressure can be harnessed to do work.

Notes to the Teacher

- This is a very safe activity and one for which the materials are easily obtained. It is also a great deal of fun for the students. An activity of this type may be a good first activity for teachers who wish to begin this kind of sciencing program.

Debriefing

Here are some questions that are likely to promote reflection during Debriefing sessions. They should be used selectively.

- What observations did you make about air?
- What observations did you make about balloons?
- How did balloons help you in your air studies?
- What did you do to find that out?
- Do you have some ideas that might explain it?
- How did you know that there was air in the balloon? How could you tell that for sure?
- When the balloon "popped," what happened? Where did the noise come from? How do you explain it?

Extending

When the pupils have had sufficient time to conduct their investigative play, you may wish to extend the activity in one or more of the following ways:

1. By adding new materials to the center, such as a helium-filled balloon, a pinwheel, and a "parachute" made with handkerchief and string
2. By introducing new activity cards, for example:

    - How many filled balloons does it take to lift a paper clip? a piece of paper? a paper cup? What observations did you make as you did these investigations?
    - How many filled balloons would it take to lift a chair? What are your ideas? Conduct some investigations and try to figure this out.

3. By raising more challenging questions in later Debriefing sessions, for example:

- What might be some good ways to get air into a balloon?
- In what ways do we get air to work for us?
- How do we get the air to stay in a balloon?
- Figure out a good way to see how long you can get the air to stay in a balloon. Test your idea to see how it works.
- How do you weigh air?
- Where does the air go when you let it out of the balloon?

4. By raising questions that call for students to examine some values issues related to the topic, for example:

- Is our air "clean"? What is clean air? How do you know?
- What makes air "dirty"? What in our own community makes our air dirty? How do you know? What examples can you give to support your opinion?
- Should we be concerned about clean or dirty air? What are your ideas?
- What actions should adults be taking on this issue? What actions should we take? What might be some consequences of those actions? What are your ideas?

Creating

Here are some more creative activities that might be used to wind up the investigative play in this center. Ask the students to:

1. Write a story about going to visit a friend in a hot-air balloon. Draw a picture of your balloon.
2. Work with a friend. Try to figure out how large a balloon you would need to lift the both of you off the floor.
3. Work with a friend. Make a list of as many ways as you can think of that we can get air to work for us.
4. Write a story called "The Yellow Balloon."
5. Write a poem called "The Balloon Man."
6. Imagine what it would be like to travel around the world in a balloon. Draw some pictures to describe your adventures.
7. Work with a friend. Use the materials in the center to make your own balloon.

Activity 16: Balances

In this center the children work either in the classroom or on the playground to make observations about the ways in which balances work.

Activity Card

> - Use the materials to carry out some investigations to see how balances work.
> - Try out as many ideas as you can think of to show how things balance.
> - Talk with each other about your investigations.
> - Then write about your observations.
>
> Perhaps there are other ways to use these materials. Do you have some new ideas for using them? Try out your ideas and see what happens.

Materials

See-saw or teeter-totter on the school playground, if available; a 5-foot by 8-inch board; a cement block to serve as a fulcrum; rulers; straight sticks; doweling; children's blocks; assorted objects for balancing

Thinking Operations Emphasized

Observing; collecting and recording data; designing investigations; suggesting hypotheses; testing hypotheses; examing assumptions; interpreting data

Big Ideas

The balance between two objects on opposite sides of a fulcrum is determined by each object's weight and its distance from the fulcrum.

Notes to the Teacher

- The concepts involved in this investigative play are basic to many scientific principles studied at both the primary and intermediate levels. There will be much to investigate with these materials. Therefore, it may be worthwhile to re-create this center several times during the school year.

Debriefing

Here are some questions that may stimulate pupil reflection during Debriefing sessions:

- What observations did you make about balance when you were using the playground equipment?
- When the people (or objects) do not balance, what are some ways you can change the situation?

- How did you make the objects balance?
- How can you explain why that worked?

Extending

After the children have had repeated opportunities to play with the balances inside and outside the classroom, you may wish to extend the inquiry in one or more of the following ways:

1. By adding materials to the center such as balance scales, a variety of weights, Ping-Pong balls, nuts, bolts, nails, bricks, blocks
2. By introducing new activity cards to give the inquiry new focus
3. By asking more challenging questions in later Debriefing sessions, for example:

   - In what ways were you able to construct a balance like the one in the school yard?
   - In what ways were you able to construct small balances?
   - How do you work to balance a very heavy object with a much lighter object? Why does that work? How do you explain it?
   - What do you need to do in order to make things balance?

Creating

When the children's enthusiasm for these activities seems to be waning, you may wish to culminate the Play by asking them to undertake one or more of the following tasks:

1. Work with a friend. Draw a picture of a balance that would evenly balance a dinosaur and a cat. What would it look like? How would it work?
2. Work with a friend. Talk together and make a list of as many ways as you can think of in which balances are used in our lives.
3. Work with the materials in the center to build a balance that would support two books.
4. Draw a picture of a mobile. Then get the materials you need to build it. Make sure that it is fully balanced and hang it in your classroom.

Activity 17: Pendulums

In this center the children work with weights and strings to make observations about how pendulums move. They are asked to record their observations.

Activity Card

- Use the materials in the center to make some pendulums.
- Hang them and make some observations about how they move.
- Try out some investigations. Change the size and weight of the bobs. Change the length of the string. Think of some other things to try. Observe what happens when you make these changes.
- Then write about your observations.

You may think of some entirely new ways to use the materials in this center. Try out your new ideas and see what happens.

Materials

A variety of weights (different-sized nuts, modeling clay, some bobs, tops, rocks, etc.); different lengths of string; scissors; elastic bands; masking tape

Thinking Operations Emphasized

Observing; comparing; suggesting hypotheses; collecting, recording, and interpreting data; designing investigations; examining assumptions; making decisions

Big Ideas

The time it takes for a pendulum to swing back and forth varies with its length. It is independent of the weight of the bob.

Notes to the Teacher

- Pendulums may be hung from light fixtures to achieve the best effects. This may require some assistance from the teacher. They may also be hung from tables. There should be sufficient space around the pendulum for it to swing freely.

Debriefing

The following types of questions may help to promote reflection during the Debriefing sessions. They should be used selectively.

- What observations did you make about pendulums?
- What kinds of investigations did you try?
- How did that work? How can you explain it?
- What are some differences you observed in the pendulums? What are some similarities?

Extending

When the children have had sufficient opportunity to conduct their pendulum inquiries, you may wish to extend the investigations in one or more of the following ways:

1. By adding new materials to the center, such as a stopwatch or a clock with a second hand and chart paper to measure and record the observations
2. By introducing new activity cards
3. By raising more challenging questions in later Debriefing sessions, for example:

   - What observations did you make when you put heavier weights on your pendulum? How do you explain that?
   - What observations did you make when you changed the length of the string? How do you explain that?
   - What observations did you make when you placed two pendulums side by side? How do you explain that?
   - How might you increase the length of swing time of your pendulums? Why do you think that might work?

Creating

When the children seem ready to move away from this investigative play, you might ask them to undertake one or more of the following culminating activities:

1. Work with a friend. Think about pendulums and list as many uses as you can for them.
2. Invent a pendulum that will never stop—one that will keep on swinging forever. Draw a picture of it. Then use the materials in the center to build it and test your plan.
3. Think about the work that a pendulum can do. Figure out a way to use a pendulum to open and close a door. Draw a picture of your invention.

Activity 18: Magnifiers

In this center the children carry out investigative play with magnifying lenses. They are asked to record their observations.

Activity Card

> - Use the materials in this center to make some observations about magnifiers.
> - Try as many investigations as you can think of.
> - Talk with each other about your findings.
> - Then write about your observations.
>
> You may have thought of some other ways to use the materials in this center. Try your ideas and see what happens.

Materials

Different kinds of magnifiers, such as hand magnifiers, lenses from old reading glasses, lenses from old cameras or projectors, a telescope, a microscope; a few tall, clear, straight-sided jars; some magazines, pictures, newspapers; a variety of insects—caterpillars, ants, earthworms, flies, etc. (optional)

Thinking Operations Emphasized

Observing; comparing; classifying and interpreting data; designing investigations; generating hypotheses; examining assumptions; making decisions; summarizing

Big Ideas

Lenses are specially shaped pieces of glass that distort images. They may increase or decrease the size of the image.

Notes to the Teacher

- Using dead insects may be offensive to some teachers, and such materials are optional for this center. Should you wish to include insects for these studies, the children should be cautioned on their handling, since they are fragile, and on their careful return to storage boxes.
- If you wish to capitalize on the use of insects for these studies, you may consider the potential extending activities for further inquiries.

Debriefing

Here are some questions that might be raised during Debriefing sessions to promote pupil reflection. They should be used selectively.

- What observations did you make of objects seen under the magnifying lenses?
- What glasses make the best magnifiers? How do you explain that?
- How do you compare what is seen under the magnifying lenses to what is seen without magnification?
- How does a magnifying glass compare to a window glass? What are some of the similarities? What are some differences?

Extending

After the students have had ample time to carry out investigative play with the materials, you may wish to extend their inquiries in one or more of the following ways:

1. By adding new materials to the center, such as a pair of binoculars and pieces of plain glass
2. By introducing new activity cards to give a new focus to the inquiries, for example:

   - Which is the best magnifier for studying a caterpillar?
   - Observe and record your study of the sky with and without the magnifying lenses.

3. By asking more challenging questions in later Debriefing sessions, for example:

   - How do you suppose a magnifying glass works? How do you explain it?
   - How do you suppose you can make a magnifying glass?
   - How can you make a lens make things look smaller instead of larger?

4. By raising questions that call for examination of some value issues related to the topic, for example:

> The scientist wanted to study the new baby's skin under a microscope. But the baby's father said that it was dangerous for the baby to be examined with the lens and refused permission.

- What are your ideas? Is this a dangerous action for the baby? How do you know? What examples can you give to support your opinion?
- If you think this is dangerous, what do you think might happen?
- If you think it is not dangerous, should the scientist try to convince the baby's father? What are your opinions?

Creating

When the children seem to be coming to an end of their interest in the investigative play, you may wish to ask them to undertake one or more of the following tasks:

1. Study hanging water drops under magnification. This may be done both indoors and outdoors. Draw some pictures of what you have observed.
2. Study ice under magnification. Draw some pictures of what you have observed.
3. Study the skin of an onion under magnification. Draw some pictures of what you have seen.
4. Study one hair from your head under magnification. Draw some pictures of what you have observed.

Activity 19: Light and Shadow

In this center the children work with various light sources to make observations about light and shadow. They are asked to record their observations.

Activity Card

> - Use the materials in the center to make some observations of light and shadow.
> - Try as many investigations as you can think of to see how shadows are made.
> - Talk with each other about what you have found.
> - Then write about your findings.
>
> You may have thought of different investigations that can be tried with these materials. Try your ideas and see what you can discover.

Materials

Flashlights; overhead projector; filmstrip projector; screen; a darkened corner; a white sheet; pieces of black and white construction paper or posterboard

Thinking Operations Emphasized

Observing; comparing; collecting and interpreting data; suggesting hypotheses; examining assumptions; designing investigations; making decisions; summarizing

Big Ideas

When an opaque body stands in the path of a beam of light, a shadow forms. Shadow size depends on the distance between the object, the light, and the screen.

Notes to the Teacher

- A candle is a popular addition to this center. Before the children study the shadow effects produced by candles, you may wish to ensure that appropriate precautions are taken and adult supervision is provided.

Debriefing

Here are examples of questions that may stimulate thinking about the light and shadow studies. They should be used selectively.

- What observations did you make about shadows?
- What observations did you make about how light makes shadows?
- How do you compare light and shadow? What are some differences? What are some similarities?
- What are the best conditions for creating shadows? How do you explain this?
- What are some investigations that you tried? What happened when you did that? How do you explain it?

Extending

After the students have had sufficient time to play with the materials in this center, you may wish to extend the inquiries in one or more of the following ways:

1. By adding new materials to the center, for example, a cardboard box open at each end covered by a sheet on one side, a candle, a sundial
2. By introducing new activity cards to give the inquiry new focus, for example:

    - In what ways are shadows made by candles and shadows made by flashlights different? Try some investigations and see what observations you can make.

3. By asking more challenging questions in later Debriefing sessions, for example:

   - How are shadows made? How do you know that is true?
   - In what ways can the shapes of shadows be changed? How did you find that out?
   - Why do you suppose shadows disappear in a very dark room? How do you explain that?
   - Why do you suppose shadows have no colors? How do you explain that?

4. By providing an opportunity for students to extend their inquiries out-of-doors on a sunny day
5. By raising questions that call for students to examine some value issues related to the topic, for example:

   Some people believe that you can tell your future by the position of the sun and the planets in our solar system. This is called astrology.

   - What are your ideas about this? Where did you get your information? Should everybody believe this? What do you think?

Creating

When the children's interest in the materials of this center seems to be waning, you may wish to culminate the activity in one or more of the following ways:

1. A small group of children may wish to put on a "shadow play" to be shared with the class.
2. Children may make shadow puppets and give a puppet show for the class.
3. Some children may wish to write a story called "Scared of Shadows."
4. Children may draw their full shadows, using materials available in the center.
5. Shadow profiles of faces (silhouettes) may also be made. Can children identify which child is represented by each shadow profile?

Activity 20: Measuring

In this center the children use the materials provided to gain increased understanding of how to measure. They are asked to record their observations.

Activity Card

> - Use the materials in this center to find out what you can about taking measurements.
> - Make some measurements using some of the different materials provided.
> - Make some observations of how the different measures work.
> - Talk with each other about what you found.
> - Then write about your findings.
>
> There may be some other investigations to make with these materials. Try your ideas and see what happens.

Materials

Rulers of various sizes, both metric and nonmetric; tape measures, both metal and cloth; rubber bands; string; Popsicle sticks; strips of paper; blocks; peanuts (in shells); a cutout tracing of a human foot; a cutout tracing of a human hand

Thinking Operations Emphasized

Observing; collecting data; comparing and recording data; making decisions; applying principles; designing investigations; examining assumptions

Big Ideas

Standard units of measurement are an essential part of the mathematical language used to make comparisons, design investigations, and interpret the results.

Notes to the Teacher

In this center it may be helpful to use different activity cards to give more than one focus to the children's inquiries. Activity cards might address the following types of investigations:

- How many "foot" lengths is the width of our classroom? Conduct some investigations to see what you can find out.
- How many "hand" lengths is the width of our classroom?
- How many Popsicle stick lengths is the width of our room?
- How many inches is the width of our classroom? How many meters?

Debriefing

The following types of questions may be used to promote reflection during the Debriefing sessions:

- What are some observations you made about measuring?
- What, in your opinion, was the best way to measure a chair? a table? the room? the door?
- What are your reasons for thinking that that was the best way?
- In what ways is measuring with a ruler and measuring with a Popsicle stick alike? How are the methods different?
- How does it help us to know that the width of the room is a specific number of hands?
- How does it help us to know that the width of the room is a specific number of inches?

Extending

After the children have had sufficient time to carry out investigative play with the materials in this center, you may wish to extend the inquiry in one or more of the following ways:

1. By adding new activity cards, for example:

- What are some good ways to measure a hand? Conduct some investigations to discover good ways.
- What are some good ways to measure a nose? Conduct some investigations to discover good ways.
- What are some good ways to measure a balloon? Conduct some investigations to discover good ways.
- What are some good ways to measure milk or water? Conduct some investigations to discover good ways.

- How many different answers do you get when four children measure the door? Figure out some good ways of deciding who is correct.

2. By asking more challenging questions in later Debriefing sessions, for example:

- What instruments give more reliable measures? How did you figure that out?
- What instruments give less reliable results? How did you figure that out?
- What happens when two people measuring the same surface get two different results? How do we find out which was more accurate? How do we know?

3. By raising questions that call for examination of value issues related to the topic, for example:

- How can you tell if a measurement is accurate when you get a measurement of your blood pressure from the doctor? What are your ideas?
- How can you tell if a measurement is accurate when the carpenters take the measurements for a new garage door? What are your ideas?
- How can you tell if a measurement is accurate if the weatherman tells us that it is 85°F today? What are your ideas?
- Should we believe what the "experts" tell us about their measurements? Where do you think we would need to be very careful about believing certain measurements to be true? What are your thoughts on this?

Creating

Before the measuring activity is concluded, you may wish to have the students engage in one or more of the following tasks:

1. Work with a friend. Try to figure out a way to measure each other's height accurately. Measure and measure again until you are sure that your measurement is accurate.
2. Work with a friend. Try to think of as many different ways to measure things as you can. Make a list of those different measures.
3. Invent a way to measure a bird. Write about your plan, or draw a picture of how you would do it.
4. Invent a way to measure the ocean. Write or draw your ideas.

Activity 21: Growing Plants from Seeds

In this center the children study different seeds, plant them, and make some observations about seeds and how they grow. They are asked to record their observations.

Activity Card

- Use the materials in this center to make some investigations with seeds.
- Make some observations and decide how these seeds might be classified. Set up some categories, and place the seeds into the category where each belongs. Then record your classification.
- Examine two kinds of seeds and compare them. How are they alike? How are they different? Find as many similarities and differences as you can, and record your findings.

You may have some other ideas for conducting investigations with these seeds. Try your ideas and see what discoveries you can make.

Materials

A variety of seeds (fast-growing seeds are preferable, for example, lettuce, lima bean, mung bean, corn, alfalfa, watercress, radish), paper towels or blotting paper, waxed paper or plastic wrap; saucers, water; sand, potting soil; small pots or other containers, such as milk containers, for planting; large spoons for digging

Thinking Operations Emphasized

Observing; comparing; collecting and recording data; examining assumptions; suggesting hypotheses; designing investigations; making decisions; evaluating; summarizing; applying principles

Big Ideas

Most plants we know are germinated from seeds. Warmth and water are the important conditions for germinating plants. There are a huge variety of plants.

Notes to the Teacher

- Plastic sheets, newspapers, dustpan, and broom should be available for cleanup, since even when exercising caution, some dirt may sneak onto the floor.
- It is helpful if the seeds placed in the center are labeled.

Debriefing

The following types of questions may help to promote pupil thinking about the investigations carried out in this center. They should be used selectively during Debriefing.

- What observations did you make about what is in a seed?
- What observations did you make about how seeds grow?
- What differences did you find in the growth of the seeds under different growing conditions? How do you explain this? What are your ideas?
- In what ways were the seeds different? How were they alike?
- What do you suppose are some other things that grow from seeds? How do you know that? What examples can you give to support your assumptions?

Extending

The seed-growing investigative play may be extended in one or more of the following ways:

1. By adding other seeds to the center, for example, flower seeds, herb seeds, vegetable seeds (tomato, green beans, squash, green pepper)
2. By adding growing plants to the center, for example, a potato or sweet potato, the end of a carrot, the top of a pineapple, an onion, a clove of garlic, house plants
3. By adding new activity cards, for example:

    - Take some bean seeds. Place them on a very wet paper towel, each seed on its own dish. Cover the dish with plastic wrap or waxed paper. Place one dish in a warm place and the other in a cool place. Observe what happens for one week. Record your observations. Then suggest some hypotheses to explain any differences you might find.
    - Conduct the same investigation using corn seeds. Compare the corn growth with the bean growth. Record your findings. Suggest some hypotheses to explain any differences you might find.
    - Conduct the same investigation with alfalfa seeds or mung beans. Compare these seeds with the corn and the bean plants. Record your findings. Then suggest some hypotheses to explain any differences you might find.
    - Plant some seeds in soil in pots. Label them. Put them in different places around the room. Study them every day for a month. Record your findings. Then suggest some hypotheses to explain any differences you might find.

4. By raising more challenging questions at later Debriefing sessions, for example:

    - Some plants grow from seeds, like radishes. Other plants grow from pieces of themselves, like potatoes. How do you explain this? What are your ideas?
    - What do plants need to grow? What are your ideas about this? What examples can you give to support your assumptions?
    - Why do plants need light in order to grow? How do you explain this? What hypotheses can you suggest?
    - Where do you suppose seeds come from? What are your ideas?
    - What are some foods that come from plants? Think of as many as you can. Then classify them.

5. By raising questions that call for the examination of value issues related to the topic, for example:

> A scientist has invented a way to destroy the pests that attack corn. Working in his laboratory, he developed a brand-new, genetically engineered microbe, a new form of life that he wants to release into the environment. The scientist claims that this form of life will be perfectly safe for us, that it will only be destructive for cutworms, a common corn pest.
>
> The Environmental Protection Agency has a different opinion. The agency is not sure that this new microbe will be safe. It has told the scientist that he will not be able to release the microbe into the environment. The scientist is very upset. He has spent years and years on his experiments, and a great deal of research money has gone into them.
>
> On the one hand, it is a good idea to fight the pests that attack corn. On the other hand, releasing a new form of life into our environment might have serious consequences.

- Whom should we believe? How should we try to figure this out?
- If you could vote, whose side would you be on? What are your ideas about this?

Creating

One or more of the following types of extending activities may bring these studies to a more creative culmination:

1. The children may build a large wooden planter and plant their own vegetable garden in the corner of the school yard.
2. The children may study the following plants and draw or paint some pictures of them: a cabbage leaf, an eggplant, a mushroom, a stalk of celery, a peanut.
3. The children may work in pairs. They may be asked to find out what they can about raisins. Then they may draw some pictures that show how raisins start from seeds and wind up in cereal bowls.

Activity 22: Seeds from Fruit from Seeds

In this center children collect seeds from different fruits and vegetables, some familiar and some less familiar. They are asked to observe, classify, and interpret data with respect to how plants reproduce and form new plants.

Activity Card

> - Use the materials in this center to find out what you can about seeds. For example, where are seeds found? How do they get there? What do they look like?
> - How are seeds of different fruits and vegetables similar? How are they

different? What are some of their characteristics? What may they be used for?

- Find as many seeds as you can and make some observations of them. Record your findings.
- Make some more observations and decide how these seeds might be classified. Set up some categories and sort the seeds into the categories. Then record your classifications.

You may have some other ideas for conducting investigations with these seeds. Try your ideas and see what discoveries you can make.

Materials

A variety of locally available fruits and vegetables, such as apple, orange, lemon, grapefruit, grapes, cherries, plum, watermelon, banana, string beans, green pepper, avocado, squash, peas in pods, peanuts; containers for planting, such as paper cups, tin cans, milk cartons, egg cartons, plastic pots; soil, water; markers, such as Popsicle sticks or tongue depressors; several knives; paper towels; magnifying lenses; rulers and meter sticks

Thinking Operations Emphasized

Observing; comparing; classifying; suggesting hypotheses; examining assumptions; interpreting data; designing investigations; making decisions

Big Ideas

Seeds are produced in the fruit of plants. New plants are germinated from these seeds. Some fruits of plants (seeds) are edible by humans.

Notes to the Teacher

- This activity would make a good follow-up to Activity 21, Growing Plants from Seeds. Every child working in the center may have his or her own seeds to grow. If sharp knives are to be used in cutting fruits and vegetables, children should be cautioned in advance about their use. In the event that some seeds do not sprout, it is a good idea to examine this in the Debriefing.

Debriefing

Here are some questions that might be used during Debriefing sessions to advance pupil inquiry about plants, fruits, and their seeds. They should be used selectively.

- What observations did you make about the seeds you found?
- In what ways were the seeds alike? How were they different?

- In what ways are vegetable seeds similar to fruit seeds? How are they different?
- Why do you suppose these fruits and vegetables have seeds? What hypotheses can you suggest to explain this?
- How might these seeds be classified? What kinds of categories could be set up?

Extending

After the students have had ample opportunity for investigative play with the seeds, their inquiries may be extended in several ways, for example:

1. By adding other seeds to the center, such as dandelion seed heads, tree seeds (fir cones, chestnuts, "helicopter" seed pods from trees such as the maple), packaged seeds
2. By adding some starter vegetable plants such as tomato, green pepper, or squash
3. By adding new activity cards, for example:

   - Work with a friend. Plant some fruit and vegetable seeds. Label them so that you will have a record of what you planted and where. Observe your plants every day for a month, and keep a record of what you did to help them grow and what happened. What differences do you observe in what is happening to each of your plants?
   - Work with a friend. Make some predictions about what your plants will look like as they begin to grow. Draw some pictures or diagrams that indicate shape, color, texture, and size of your plants.

4. By raising more challenging questions at later Debriefing sessions, for example:

   - What observations did you make about where seeds come from? What examples can you give?
   - What observations did you make about the conditions under which seeds grow? What examples can you give?
   - What observations did you make about the length of time it takes for seeds to germinate? What examples can you give?
   - Some seeds do not grow after they are planted. How do you explain this? What hypotheses can you suggest?
   - What ideas do you have about how fruits and vegetables are grown on a large scale? What, in your studies, led you to those ideas?
   - What did you find out about the best ways for growing seeds? What did you find out about the best ways for planting seeds? What observations did you make about these things?
   - Some plants like oranges are reproduced with seeds from their own fruits. What ideas do you have about how other plants are reproduced, like carrots, lettuce, roses, and English ivy? What investigations could be carried out to test your ideas?

5. By raising questions that call for examination of some value issues related to the topic, for example:

- To what extent should farmers be permitted to use pesticides in controlling the pests that attack fruits and vegetables in their growing stages?
- What might be some consequences to the farmer (the storekeeper, the consumer, children) of pesticide use?
- What might be some consequences to the farmer (the storekeeper, the consumer, children) of a ban on pesticides?
- If you wanted to avoid eating fruits and vegetables that have been sprayed with pesticides, what might you do? What are your ideas about this? What examples do you have that support your opinions?

Creating

When the investigative play with seeds seems to be on the wane, you may wish to open some more creative routes of inquiry for the students, for example:

1. Children may work with partners using seeds gathered from fruits and vegetables to create seed mosaics. This can be done by painting them and gluing them to construction paper to create original designs.
2. Children may work singly or in pairs to create jewelry from seeds. Necklaces, rings, bracelets, headdresses, and belts can be created with string, needle, thread, and painted seeds.
3. Older students might work in pairs or in small groups to design investigations to calculate the rate of success in sprouting purchased seeds compared to dandelion seeds. What percentage of purchased seeds sprout? What percentage of seeds gathered from fruit, vegetables, or weeds? How can this be explained? What are the implications of these findings for the farmer?
4. Children may work together to build a planter (see Activity 21) and grow a vegetable garden. This can be a very "fruitful" activity with rich potential for many additional investigations.
5. Children may work in small groups to plan, prepare, and cook a vegetarian lunch. Such a creative undertaking may be enjoyed by primary and intermediate students.

Activity 23: Molds

In this investigative play the pupils carry out inquiries in the world of the fungus family—specifically, molds. They are asked to record their observations.

Activity Card

- Use the materials in this center to make some observations of mold.
- Try some investigations to see what you can discover about what mold is, how it grows, what it looks like, what it smells like.
- Talk with each other about your observations.
- Then write about what you observed.

You may have some other ideas about using the materials in this center. Try them out and see what happens.

Materials

Slices of bread, some cheese, a half container of plain yogurt; containers or plastic bags to keep samples moist; slices of tomato, string beans, green pepper; magnifying lenses; sugar; water (A flat plastic pan with a layer of soil on which to lay fresh, unmolded samples could also be used for growing molds as soil already contains the spores of molds. To keep the soil moist, the pan should be covered with plastic wrap.)

Thinking Operations Emphasized

Observing and recording; comparing; suggesting hypotheses; identifying assumptions; designing investigations; making decisions; creating and inventing

Big Ideas

Molds are plant-like organisms of the fungus family. They are colonies of single-celled microorganisms that usually need dark and damp conditions to grow.

Notes to the Teacher

- This will need some advance preparation to provide samples of items that have already begun to mold as well as items likely to grow mold during the investigations. To encourage mold formation, keep items moist, as drying inhibits mold. Good candidates for growing mold are foods without preservatives—breads, dairy products, fruits, and vegetables. Place in plastic bags (to keep moisture in), outside of the refrigerator, and mold should begin to form in a few days.

Debriefing

Here are some questions that might be raised during Debriefing sessions to encourage further inquiry. They should be used selectively.

- What observations did you make about mold? What observations did you make about how mold grows?
- What differences did you observe in the different molds? What were some similarities?
- Where do you suppose molds come from? What hypotheses can you suggest? How would you test that idea?
- What kinds of foods are more likely to grow mold? What makes you think that is true?
- What kinds of foods are less likely to grow mold? What makes you think that is true?
- What do you suppose helps mold to grow? What in your studies of mold led you to that idea?
- What do you suppose would prevent mold from growing? What examples could you give that would support that idea?

Extending

The initial investigative play might be extended in one or more of the following ways:

1. By introducing new foods that depend on special varieties of mold for flavor and texture, such as blue cheese, Gorgonzola, and Camembert
2. By introducing several dried foods such as dried mushrooms, tomatoes, prunes, raisins, and apricots
3. By introducing a microscope so that molds can be examined much more closely. Microscopes are usually available among the science supplies of most elementary schools. If not, try borrowing one from a neighboring junior or senior high school science teacher.
4. By introducing new activity cards to the center, for example:

   - Design an investigation that will allow you to observe the effects of moisture and dryness on the growth of molds.
   - Design an investigation that will allow you to observe the effects of darkness and light on the growth of molds.
   - Design an investigation that will allow you to observe the effects of temperature on the growth of molds.
   - Design an investigation that will allow you to observe the life cycle of a mold. Record your observations.

5. By raising more challenging questions in later Debriefing sessions, for example:

   - What observations of mold did you make in the microscope? How did these differ from the observations with the naked eye?
   - How do these organisms compare with plants? How are they alike? What are some differences?
   - How are these organisms affected by the changes in growth conditions? What examples can you give to support your ideas?

- What examples can you give of how organisms are useful to us? How are they harmful to us?
- Why do you suppose the dried foods did not develop mold? What hypotheses can you suggest that would explain this? How could you test that idea?

6. By raising questions that call for examining value issues related to the topic, for example:

> Maximilian opened the cottage cheese container that had been in the refrigerator and saw that the top of the cheese was covered with mold. "Yecchhh!" he yelled, and threw the container into the garbage. "Mold can kill you," he said to his little brother, "so don't go near the garbage."

- What do you think? Is Maximilian right? Can mold kill you? What are your opinions? What examples can you give to support your point of view?

Creating

Some of the following activities may be used to bring these inquiries to a more creative culmination:

1. Children may be asked to find molds at home and bring them to class.
2. Children may work in small groups to design investigations in which mold may be grown more quickly.
3. Children may work cooperatively or alone to illustrate the molds that they have observed through the microscope.
4. Children may work cooperatively or alone to write stories such as "Slime and Mold," "The Mold That Took Over the Breadbox," "The Mold That Nobody Loved," and "The Mold That Was Afraid of Sunlight."

Activity 24: Yeast

In this investigative play pupils carry out inquiries in the world of microorganisms—specifically yeast. They are asked to record their observations.

Activity Card

- Use the materials in this center to find out what you can about this microorganism called yeast.
- Try some investigations to see what you can discover about what yeast is, what it looks like, how it grows, and what it smells like.
- Talk with each other about your observations.
- Then write about what you observed.

Materials

Slices of bread of several different varieties; yeast cakes, packets of dried yeast; sugar, honey, molasses; water, apple juice; containers and bowls of various sizes; flour (whole wheat, white enriched, rye), magnifying lenses

Thinking Operations Emphasized

Observing and recording; comparing; examining assumptions; suggesting hypotheses; making decisions; designing investigations

Big Ideas

Yeast is a microorganism (structure that cannot be seen with the naked eye) that needs a temperate climate (not too hot or too cold) to grow. Yeast feeds on sugar.

Notes to the Teacher

- Cakes of live yeast can generally be purchased at the local bakery shop, although a special request must be made of the baker. While packets of dry yeast are found on the shelves of most supermarkets, it is considerably cheaper to buy dry yeast in bulk, at the neighborhood health food shop. Dry yeast is best kept for long periods in the refrigerator, and it is a good idea to check the "expiration date" on packets, as these tiny organisms do not live forever.

Debriefing

Here are some questions that might be raised during Debriefing sessions to promote pupil inquiry about these concepts. They should be used selectively.

- What observations did you make about yeast?
- What are some differences between the cakes of yeast and dry yeast?
- What are some differences you found in how yeast grows?
- How is yeast like plants? How is it different?
- How is yeast like fungi, such as mold? How is it different?
- How is yeast like other fungi, such as mold? How is it different?

Extending

After the students have had an opportunity to carry out extensive investigative play with yeast, you may wish to extend the inquiries in one or more of the following ways:

1. By adding new materials to the center, especially a microscope (see Activity 23) and some sourdough

2. By introducing new activity cards that call for designing new projects or investigations, for example:

   - Design an investigation that will allow you to observe the best conditions for growing yeast.
   - Design an investigation that will allow you to observe the affect of heat and cold on yeast growth.
   - Design an investigation that will allow you to observe the affect of light and darkness on yeast growth.
   - Design an investigation that will allow you to observe the kinds of foods yeast eats.
   - Design an investigation that will allow you to observe the life cycle of yeast.
   - Design an investigation that will allow you to observe the way yeast works in our food.
   - Design an investigation that will allow you to observe the gas bubbles produced by growing yeast.

3. By asking more challenging questions at later Debriefing sessions, for example:

   - What observations did you make about the best conditions for growing yeast? What examples can you give to support these ideas?
   - What observations did you make about the affect of heat and cold on yeast growth? What hypotheses can you suggest to explain why yeast does not grow in cold water?
   - Under what conditions does yeast die? How do you know that is true?
   - How is the life cycle of yeast different from and similar to the life cycle of plants?
   - How is it possible for yeast to be brought back to life from its dry state? What are your ideas?
   - What other living things can be dried and reconstituted? What examples can you think of?
   - What do we have to know about yeast in order to make it work for us in our food?

4. By raising questions that call for examination of value issues related to the topic, for example:

   Yeast is a wonderful organism. It can be dried out, preserved for a long time, and then reconstituted. One day, there may be a way to dry out other forms of life and reconstitute them later on.

   - Should we try to do this? If so, what forms of life would benefit from this treatment? What forms of life should be exempt? What are your thoughts on this? What might be some consequences of your proposals?

Creating

When the children's interest in the investigative play with yeast seems to be nearing an end, you may wish to culminate the inquiries with one or more of the following activities:

1. Baking bread is a natural! If the children begin early in the day, you can have warm bread for lunch. See *The Tassajara Bread Book* by Edward Espe Brown (Shambala, 1970) or Bernard Clayton's *Complete Bread Book* (Simon and Schuster, 1973) for dozens of excellent recipes.
2. The students can make their own sourdough. Most bread books include a sourdough starter recipe. Starters can also be purchased (dry) from health food stores, but it is probably more interesting for children to discover that these spores already exist in the air.
3. The students can make sourdough pancakes.
4. The students can bake unyeasted bread and compare it to yeasted bread.
5. The students can write stories: "My Microorganism Garden," "The Yeast That Saved the World," "Yeasties, Beasties, and Other Critters."

Activity 25: Flowers

In this center the children examine flowers and study their parts and their structures.

Activity Card

- Study the flowers you see in this center.
- Talk with each other about what you see.
- Make a list of all the observations you can make about the flowers.

You may have some ideas for carrying out investigations with these flowers. Try your ideas and see what happens.

Materials

At least four different kinds of flowers (for example, daisy, chrysanthemum, carnation, rose—whatever can be easily acquired in your neighborhood market or garden); several pairs of scissors; a knife; several magnifying lenses; white paper

Thinking Operations Emphasized

Observing and recording; comparing; classifying and interpreting data; imagining and creating; making decisions; identifying assumptions

Big Ideas

Flowers are parts of plants and come in a variety of shapes, colors, and smells. Flowers become fruit bodies that produce the seeds used to create new plants.

Notes to the Teacher

- Inexpensive bunches of assorted flowers may be found in many supermarkets. Supermarket managers may be willing to unload yesterday's wilted posies at reduced rates for school use.

Debriefing

Here are some questions that may be raised during Debriefing sessions. They should be used selectively.

- What observations did you make about flowers?
- What observations did you make about the different parts of flowers?
- What were some of the differences you observed about the different flowers?
- What were some of the similarities?
- In what ways might these flowers be classified? What kinds of categories might be set up?

Extending

There are many ways in which the flower study may be extended, for example:

1. Other flowers can be brought in and examined and compared.
2. Flowers can be compared with nonflowering plants. Similarities and differences can be recorded.
3. Scents of flowers can be compared and recorded.
4. Flowers can be classified. Pupils can set up categories according to their own criteria.
5. More challenging questions may be raised in later Debriefing sessions, for example:

   - Why do you suppose some flowers have a pleasant smell and others have no smell?
   - Where do flowers get their smell? What do you suppose makes the smell?
   - Why do you suppose some plants have flowers and others do not have flowers? How do you explain this?
   - Suppose that you wanted to grow a flower. How might you do that? What are some ways?
   - Which flowers do you like best? What are some reasons for your choice of those flowers?
   - Which flowers would you like to plant in your own garden? What are some reasons for choosing those flowers?

6. Questions that call for pupils to examine value issues related to the topic may also be included, for example:

   - Is it more important to use our land to grow flowers or food? What are your thoughts?
   - Why do you think flowers are important? What are your ideas about this?

   The local park is trying to raise money to build a large flower garden. Some people are saying that the park is for playing and that if there is some land to spare, it should be turned into tennis courts. Other people say that flowers are so beautiful, a big flower garden should be created for everyone's enjoyment.

   - Where do you stand on this issue? What are your opinions?

Creating

As the children move from their investigative play into more creative activities, they may be asked to try one or more of the following:

- Growing flowers from seeds, including building or finding materials to serve as flowerpots; purchasing or otherwise acquiring seeds; planting seeds; providing hospitable growing conditions, including sunlight, water, and warmth; observing and recording growth; hypothesizing about the lack of germination of some seeds
- Drying and pressing flowers
- Collecting pictures of flowers and classifying them
- Drawing pictures of flowers and labeling parts
- Writing poems about flowers
- Making artificial flowers with colored tissue paper and pipe cleaners
- Visiting a nursery or greenhouse to study mass production of flowers

Activity 26: Foods (1): How Foods Change

In this center the children study food, especially the conditions under which food changes and how the changes occur. They are asked to record their observations.

Activity Card

> - Use the materials in this center to conduct some investigations to see how foods change.
> - Make some observations of what happens to certain foods over certain intervals of time.
> - Talk with each other about your observations.
> - Then write about what you found.
>
> You may have some other ideas for investigating the changes that take place in foods. Try out your ideas and see what discoveries you can make.

Materials

Small quantities of some of the following foods: butter, apple, salt, egg, milk, bread, potato, tomato, orange, sugar, corn flakes, peanuts, dry legumes, rice, crackers, flour, tea, coffee beans, hot dogs, raw chopped meat, cheese; pot or pan; hot plate; scales; magnifying lens; spoons; jars

Thinking Operations Emphasized

Observing and recording; classifying; comparing; designing investigations; making decisions; summarizing; evaluating; imagining and creating; suggesting hypotheses; identifying assumptions

Big Ideas

Certain foods undergo change when they are heated, dried, processed, preserved, combined (with other foods), cooked, fermented, allowed to decay.

Notes to the Teacher

• No specific food is mandatory for this inquiry—practically whatever is easily available in your refrigerator or cupboard may be used. Several food groups should, however, be represented. There might be a small amount of mess in handling the food, and newspaper on the tables is a good precaution. Children should also be cautioned about proper use of the hot plate and warned not to ingest any of the food samples.

Debriefing

Several types of questions may be helpful in promoting thoughtful reflection about the changes seen in foods, for example:

• What observations did you make about the foods?
• What observations did you make about how the foods could change? How did some of the changes occur?
• What kinds of changes did you see in the apple? potato? orange?
• How were these changes alike? How were they different?
• How do you explain these changes? What hypotheses can you suggest that might explain them?
• What kinds of changes did you see in the rice? beans? How do you explain this?
• In what ways could you change the egg? the salt? the flour? the bread? the tea? the sugar? What are your ideas about this?
• What observations did you make about some of the conditions that change foods? How do you explain how that works?
• Why do you suppose an apple, left overnight on the table, changes but rice does not? How do you explain this? What hypotheses can you suggest?

Extending

The children's inquiry into the conditions under which foods change may be extended in one of several ways, for example:

1. By adding new foods to the center: yogurt, bean sprouts, mushrooms, yeast, fish, tofu, lettuce, smoked meat, banana, onion

2. By introducing new activity cards, for example:

   - What happens to bread (apple, potato, egg, fish, etc.) if left on a plate for three days? Observe and record your findings. How do you explain what happened? How do you explain the differences seen among the foods you studied?
   - What happens to bread (apple, potato, egg, fish, etc.) if left on a plate in the refrigerator for three days? Observe and record your findings. How do you explain what happened? How do you account for the differences between the changes in the food outside and inside the refrigerator?
   - In how many ways does bread change? Conduct some investigations and record your findings.
   - Figure out as many ways as you can to change the composition of these foods. Conduct inquiries to test some of your ideas.
   - What happens to bread (apple, potato, egg, fish, etc.) when it is heated or cooked? Conduct some inquiries and record your findings.

3. By raising more challenging questions in later Debriefing sessions, for example:

   - What observations did you make about foods that change rapidly? What theories can you suggest that might explain these rapid changes?
   - What observations did you make about foods that change slowly? What theories can you suggest that might explain the slowness of the changes?
   - What observations did you make about foods that hardly changed at all? What theories can you suggest that might explain this?
   - What different kinds of changes did you observe? How do these changes occur?
   - In what ways could these foods be grouped? What categories could be set up? What other foods might be added to each of the groups in your classification?
   - In what ways could changes in food be speeded up? How might they be slowed down? What are your ideas about this?
   - What do you suppose causes the brown spots in banana? apple? potato? What hypotheses can you suggest?
   - What makes mold? Where does it come from? What is it made of? What are your ideas?
   - What makes food smell bad? What are your ideas about how this happens?
   - What other things change, besides food? What examples can you give of other changes?

4. By raising questions that call for examination of value issues related to the topic, for example:

   Some foods are packaged so that they will have a longer shelf life in the markets. That means that certain chemicals are added to the food to preserve them for longer periods. Many processed foods contain small amounts of these chemical additives.

Some people believe that these additives are bad for you and that you should stay away from them. Other people claim that the amounts of chemical additives in the packaged foods are so small that you couldn't really be hurt by eating them.

- Where do you stand on this issue? What foods do you eat that contain chemical additives? What foods contain no additives?
- What are your beliefs about what kinds of foods are good for you? What examples support your opinions?

Creating

The following types of creative activities emphasize the changing of foods. The children may undertake one or more of these to culminate the foods inquiry:

- Making butter
- Making peanut butter
- Making noodles
- Making bread
- Making popcorn
- Making ice cream

Activity 27: Foods (2): Composition

In this center the children observe the composition of some foods. They are asked to record their findings.

Activity Card

- Use the materials in this center to conduct some investigations of these foods.
- What can you observe about their colors, weight, texture, and taste?
- Discuss your observations with each other, and write about what you found.
- Set up some categories for the foods in this center. Classify each item of food by placing it in the category where it belongs. Record your classifications.

You may have some other ideas for conducting investigations with these foods. Try them out and see what you can discover.

Materials

Small quantities of some of the following foods: butter, potato chips, potato, orange, egg, peanuts, crackers, fish, meat, dried legumes, onion, sugar, apple, milk, rice, tomato, lettuce, cheese, bean sprouts, mushrooms, lemon, bread; scales; small knives

Thinking Operations Emphasized

Observing and recording; collecting, comparing, and classifying data; examining assumptions; suggesting hypotheses; making decisions; evaluating

Big Ideas

Humans consume a variety of foods and food products, both animal and vegetable. Different foods appeal through appearance, taste, smell, texture. The nutritional value of a food may be high or low, depending on its content.

Notes to the Teacher

- No specific food is mandatory for this center. Foods should, however, represent several food groups and should be in condition for children to taste.

Debriefing

The following types of questions may be raised in Debriefing sessions to help promote more thoughtful inquiry about food composition. They should be used selectively.

- What observations did you make about these foods? about their colors? about their weight? about seeds? about texture? about consistency? about taste?
- How do you suppose butter is made? What is there about the butter that allows you to make that assumption?
- How does the taste of (one food) compare with the taste of (another food)? How are they alike? How are they different?
- How do you suppose bread is made? What do you suppose it is made of? What is there about bread that allows you to make those assumptions?
- Why do you suppose a pound of potato chips takes up more room than a pound of potatoes? How do you explain this? What are your ideas?
- What do you suppose a tomato is made of? How could you test that idea to see if it is true?
- What do you suppose an apple is made of? How could you test that idea to see if it is true?
- In what ways might the foods in the center be classified? What kinds of categories could be set up?

Extending

The studies of the composition of foods may be extended in one or more of the following ways:

1. By adding new foods to study, for example: dried spaghetti or macaroni, hot dogs, breakfast cereal, peanut butter, soda pop, mushrooms, honey, a candy bar, canned fruit, dried figs or dates, chewing gum, gelatin powders, fruit juice, parsley
2. By adding new activity cards, for example:

   - How might you group these foods by taste? What kinds of categories could be set up? Conduct some investigations and record your findings.
   - How might you group these foods according to what is good for you to eat? What kinds of categories could be set up? Conduct some investigations and record your findings.
   - Make some investigations of the weights and volumes of some of the foods. Make a chart and record your findings.
   - Study (a particular food). Try to figure out what is in this food. Record your findings.
   - Which foods do you like best? What is there about these foods that appeals to you? Which foods do you like least? What is there about them that makes you dislike them?

3. By raising more challenging questions at later Debriefing sessions, for example:

   - How do you know (a specific food) is good for you to eat? How can you tell? What examples can you give to support your assumption?
   - What are some good ways to keep some foods fresh? How does that work? What are your ideas?
   - What are some differences between eating potato chips (or other prepared, packaged food) and eating peanuts? Think of as many differences as you can.
   - What ingredients go into spaghetti? What do you think? How might you check that out to know if it is true?
   - What ingredients go into soda pop? What do you think? How might you check that out to know if it is true?
   - In what ways are sugar and honey alike? How are they different?
   - What tastes in foods do you enjoy most? What ingredients create those tastes?
   - What tastes in foods do you dislike? What ingredients create those flavors?

4. By raising questions that call for examination of some value issues related to the topic, for example:

   The Trim-Line Company has just invented a way to cut down on the bulk size of certain foods. Using a new process of dehydration, they have been able to reduce the size of such products as lettuce, tomatoes, apples, watermelon, and others without losing any of the important nutrients of the foods. You can buy these "trim" foods in plastic packages. A head of lettuce is now able to fit into a package the size of an envelope; an apple is now the size of a peanut; a tomato can be reduced to the size of a pea. Of course, these things don't look like lettuce or apple or tomato. And they don't taste like lettuce or apple or tomato. But they are just as good for you.

- What are your opinions about this kind of food? Would you eat it? Should everybody? Think of all the space they would save on the supermarket shelves! What are your ideas?

Creating

The studies of the composition of foods may be extended further through one or more of the following culminating activities:

1. The children may plan a menu and cook breakfast for the class. Or they could make peanut butter, bake bread, make their own pasta.
2. The children may sprout mung beans or lima beans, seeds like orange and grapefruit pips or apple seeds, or root vegetables like potatoes, sweet potatoes, or carrots.
3. The children may draw pictures of foods based on their observations.

Activity 28: Skins

In this center the children carry out investigative play with a variety of skins in order to make observations of their properties and functions.

Activity Card

> - Use the materials in this center to conduct some investigations about skin.
> - In what ways are the skins alike? How are they different?
> - Make some observations about strength, texture, hardness or softness, edibility, color, shape, smell, and function.
> - Talk with each other about your observations.
> - Then write about what you found.
>
> You may have some other ideas about how these skins may be examined. Try out your ideas and see what discoveries you can make.

Materials

A variety of skins, including fruit skins (apple, banana, orange, grape, mango, coconut, pear, melon), vegetable skins (potato, onion, carrot, squash, tomato), nut skins (peanuts, almonds, sunflower seeds, filberts), and animal skins (pieces of leather, molted reptile skins, pieces of fur); small knives; magnifying lenses; microscope

Thinking Operations Emphasized

Observing; comparing; classifying and interpreting data; examining assumptions; suggesting hypotheses; designing investigations; making decisions; evaluating

Big Ideas

Animal skins function primarily for protection. Skin is a growing organ. It has color (pigmentation) and comes in layers; it may have hair, feathers, or scales.

Notes to the Teacher

- A few simple precautions will avoid any messy residue from this activity. Newspaper spread on the table prior to investigative play should be all that is needed. Discarded food skins can be stored in a large plastic container for use in Replay activities, though it may be the worse for wear. Acquiring molted reptile skins may prove more difficult, unless your school is in or near a desert area, where such molting is a fairly common occurrence. The high school science teacher might be able to help you out. Failing such acquisition, the investigative play will not seriously suffer.

Debriefing

Here are examples of questions that might be asked during Debriefing to keep the inquiry in process. They should be used selectively.

- What observations did you make about skin in general?
- More specifically, what observations did you make about the strength of skin? the texture? its hardness or softness? its color? its edibility? its shape? its smell?
- What kinds of living things have skin? Can you give some examples?
- What living things have no skin? Can you give some examples?
- In what ways might these skins be grouped?
- What do you suppose skin is good for? What hypotheses can you suggest?
- What are some differences between animal skins and plant skins?
- Why do you suppose some animals shed their skins? How is this done? What are your ideas about it?
- Which skins are more attractive? What is there about them that makes them attractive? What are your ideas about this?

Extending

The investigative play with skins might be extended in one or more of the following ways:

1. By adding new material to the center, for example, feathers; hair; fish skins (smelly!); chicken skin, chicken feet (available in Chinese markets where chickens are sold), chicken necks; crab, shrimp, oyster or mussel shells
2. By introducing new activity cards, for example:

- Compare feathers and leathers. How are they alike? How are they different? Record your ideas.
- Conduct some investigations to see what the relationship is between hair and skin.
- Compare the shells of marine animals with skin. How are these coverings alike? How are they different?
- Conduct some investigations to see how your skin is different from or similar to chicken skin, banana skin, and onion skin. Record your findings.

3. By raising more challenging questions during later Debriefing sessions, for example:

- What do you suppose skin is made of? What examples can you give to support your theory?
- Why do you suppose you find moisture on skin? How do you explain how it gets there?
- Why do you suppose human and animal skin has hair? What theories do yo have about this?
- Why do you suppose human skins come in different colors? How do you explain this? What are your ideas?
- What makes skin wrinkle? How do you explain this? What are your ideas?
- How does skin heal itself when it is cut? How do you explain this? What are your ideas?

4. By raising questions that allow for the examination of value issues related to the topic, for example:

Some merchants carry out a very lucrative business trading in animal skins. They find out which skins are the most desirable—that is, which skins will be worth the most money—and then they find ways to acquire those skins. Some of this trading is illegal, but much of it is legal business. Look at some of the smart shops in town. You will see shoes made of alligator skins, purses made of eel skins, coats made of fox skins, and jackets made of seal skins.

- Every one of these articles of apparel costs an animal a life. Is it worth it? Where do you stand on this issue?
- What clothing of your own comes from animal skins?
- Are there alternatives? What would be some consequences if we decided not to use animal skins to keep us warm? What are your ideas?

Creating

Here are some suggestions for ways in which the investigations with skin might be creatively concluded:

1. Ask the children to work in pairs and to think of 20 good uses for animal skins.

2. Ask the children to work in pairs to draw pictures of the skin of an alligator (lizard, snake).
3. Ask the children to write some stories about skin: "You're Under My Skin!" "Shivering Skins!" "I'd Like to Change My Skin."
4. Ask the children to work in pairs to create ten metaphors about skin, like "a skin as smooth as silk" or "a skin as wrinkled as an old eggplant."

Activity 29: Bones and Shells

In this center the children carry out investigative play with bones and shells to observe and compare the properties and structures of internal and external skeletal structures.

Activity Card

> - Use the materials in this center to make some observations about bones and shells.
> - What differences do you see in the bone samples? What similarities?
> - What differences do you see between the bones and the shells? What similarities?
> - Conduct some investigations to find out about the differences in hardness, texture, smoothness, flexibility, weight, strength, breakability, and size.
> - Talk with each other about what you have found.
> - Then write about your observations.
>
> You may have some other ideas for investigations with these bones and shells. Try out your ideas and see what discoveries you can make.

Materials

A variety of bone samples (chicken, fish, beef, pork, lamb); models of skeletal structures (dog, cat, lizard, etc.); photographs or models of human skeletons; a variety of shells from assorted shellfish (crab, lobster, clam, oyster, scallops, mussels); a turtle shell

Thinking Operations Emphasized

Observing and recording; comparing; suggesting hypotheses; gathering and interpreting data; designing investigations; making decisions; evaluating; identifying assumptions

Big Ideas

The function of an internal skeleton is to maintain structure and stability, and provide for motility. External skeletons function to protect the animal as well.

Notes to the Teacher

- Collecting an assortment of bones and shells may require some thought, advance planning, and legwork. Try the local butcher for animal bones (beef, lamb, and pork). Or simply save the bones from a meat or fish meal. If you do not live in a coastal area, mollusks and crustaceans are perhaps better acquired through the good offices of a fishmonger. (Think of the feasts you'll have before giving the bones and shells up for study!) Hospitals may be willing to donate outdated X-ray pictures, and the local or school library may be a source of photographs of human and animal skeletons. Try your high school biology teacher for bone loans. As a last resort, you can purchase these items from biological supply companies, if your school has the budget for such extravagance.

Debriefing

The following types of questions may contribute to more thoughtful examinations of skeletal structures. They should, however, be used selectively.

- What observations did you make of these bones and these shells?
- What observations did you make about the properties of bones (hardness, texture, flexibility, weight, size, etc.)?
- What differences did you observe between bones and shells? What similarities?
- What differences did you observe among the bone samples?
- What observations did you make about the properties of shells?
- What observations did you make about how bones are connected? about how shells are connected?
- What do you suppose are some functions of bones? of shells? How do you know that?

Extending

After the students have had sufficient opportunities to engage in investigative play with these materials, you may wish to extend the inquiries in one or more of the following ways:

1. By adding new material to the center, such as photographs of skeletons (see especially the Teacher's Guide for *Bones: Elementary Science Study,* Webster Division, McGraw-Hill, St. Louis). Photographs of crustaceans and mollusks in natural habitats may also be included.
2. By introducing new activity cards
3. By raising more challenging questions in later Debriefing sessions, for example:

- In what ways might these bones and shells be classified?
- How might you tell about the kind of animal this was? What evidence are you using to figure that out?
- How do bones mend themselves when they are broken? What are some theories that you can think of to explain this?
- What kinds of animals have no bones? In what ways are they different from animals with bones?
- How are bones like (different from) the skeletal frameworks of buildings?

4. By raising questions that call for students to examine some value issues related to the topic, for example:

Margaret wears a bone from a rabbit's foot around her neck. She says that it is her good luck piece, that whenever she wears it she is bound to have good luck follow her. What's more, if she should forget her lucky rabbit's foot bone, she is bound to get into trouble.

- What are your ideas about this? Are bones good for lucky pieces? Do you have other ideas about lucky pieces?
- What is your opinion of how good luck comes to you? What examples can you give to support your ideas?

Creating

There are several ways of bringing this investigative play to a creative culmination. The following ideas are offered as suggestions. (See also the suggestions in Activity 30.)

1. Whole fish skeletons, in particular, make very good rubbings, and children can work in pairs to do this art activity. Rubbings can be made by placing lightweight paper over a well-cleaned fish skeleton, then rubbing gently with charcoal or very soft pencil.
2. Students may work in teams to draw pictures of the skeletons of cats, rabbits, frogs, snakes, and other animals.
3. Students may work together to draw pictures of the external skeletal structures of lobsters, crabs, shrimps, and crayfish.
4. Students may learn the song "Dry Bones" ("Toe bone connected to the foot bone") and/or write a parody of it.
5. Students may write stories or plays: "The Skeleton in My Closet," "My Broken Bone," "The Case of the Missing Bone."

Activity 30: Skeletons

In this center the children work with fish skeletons to make some observations about skeletal structures.

Activity Card

> - Use the materials in this center to make some observations about skeletons.
> - Look sharply. Try to notice everything you can about these bones.
> - Talk with each other about what you observe.
> - Then write about your observations.
>
> You may have other ideas for investigations with these materials. Try your ideas and see what you can discover.

Materials

Three or four whole fish skeletons (salmon, flounder, carp, sole—any available local fish is appropriate); parts of fish skeletons; newspaper; paper towels

Thinking Operations Emphasized

Observing; comparing; classifying and interpreting data; summarizing; applying principles; making decisions; imagining and creating; suggesting hypotheses

Big Ideas

Internal skeletons are made up of arrangements of bones that vary among different animals. They maintain structure and stability, and help us move.

Notes to the Teacher

- Acquiring fish skeletons requires personal ingenuity and the cooperation of fish-eating friends. Ask your local fish store for the discards of filleted fish. Soaking the bones in a mild soap-and-water solution dilutes strong odors.

Debriefing

The following types of questions may contribute to more thoughtful reflection about skeletons during initial Debriefing sessions. They should, of course, be used selectively.

- What observations did you make about skeletons?
- What observations did you make about the location of the larger bones?
- What observations did you make about the location of the smaller bones?
- What observations did you make about how bones are connected?
- How is one particular skeletal structure like or different from another?

- What observations did you make about the texture of the bones?
- What do you suppose bones are made of?

Extending

After the children have had sufficient time to work with the materials in this center, you may wish to extend the inquiry in one or more of the following ways:

1. By adding new materials to the center, such as other kinds of skeletal structures (for example, chicken or duck) or photographs of skeletal structures
2. By introducing new activity cards
3. By raising more challenging questions in later Debriefing sessions, for example:

    - What kinds of animals have skeletal structures? How do you know this?
    - What kinds of animals do not have skeletal structures? How do you know this?
    - In what ways might bones be classified? What kinds of categories could be set up?
    - How do bones help us move?
    - How do animals that do not have bones move?
    - How do bones break? How do they mend? How do you know this?

Creating

When interest in investigative play seems to be diminishing it might be advantageous to integrate this study with other areas of the curriculum, for example:

1. Buy and eat a fish and a chicken for an impromptu class lunch. After boiling all the bones with bleach for a few hours and drying them thoroughly, have the children work in groups to try to reconstruct the skeletons.
2. Have some children use clay to create a skeletal structure for an imaginary animal. Ask them to write a description of this animal or draw some pictures of it.
3. Ask the children to try to feel the bones in their arms, legs, and heads. Ask them to try to draw some pictures of the bones inside them.
4. Ask the children to try to feel the way their fingers move and to try to draw some pictures of how the bones are connected in their hands.
5. Ask the children to try to imagine what their own skeletons might look like. They may be asked to draw some pictures of how they envision their own skeletons.
6. Ask the children to write a song about bones.

Activity 31: Birds

The investigative play in this center emphasizes extensive observations of birds in their natural habitat, and the recording of those observations. To do this requires the construction of a bird feeder and so this activity actually has two parts.

Activity Card (1)

- Use the materials in this center to design and build a bird feeder that can hang outside your classroom window. When the feeder is finished and hung in place with a supply of birdseed, you will be able to observe and study the birds that come to feed.
- You will need to decide what type of feeder will allow you to see the birds easily, the birds to feed easily, and you to take it down when necessary to replenish the birdseed.

Activity Card (2)

- Place your feeder in a position so that you may see the birds easily.
- Work together to watch the feeder for a long time. What observations can you make about the birds that come? their distinctive markings? how they feed? when they come? their individual and group behavior? the shape of head and beak? their sizes? their different sounds? how they communicate with each other? when they come to the feeder?
- Talk to each other about your observations.
- Keep a record of what you have observed.

Materials

Several good-size pieces of wood (redwood, cedar, pine—or whatever is easily available and not too hard for the children to cut through); nails, hammer, saw, pliers, screwdriver; thin wire; sturdy cord or rope; three or four lengths of ½-inch doweling; illustrations of bird feeders; binoculars; birdseed

Thinking Operations Emphasized

Designing projects; making decisions; observing; comparing; classifying data; collecting and organizing data; suggesting hypotheses; evaluating; making decisions; creating and imagining

Big Ideas

Birds are generally characterized by their wings, feathers, two feet, and ability to fly. There are many different types of birds; they differ in color, shape, size, and ways of flight. Birds may live on land or water.

Notes to the Teacher

- At first glance this activity is likely to seem more suited to suburban or rural school settings, where a greater variety of birds is likely to be found. But there are birds in cities too, and there is a good chance that they will come to the feeder once they have learned of its existence. This may take some time.
- Note that the activity is carried out in two parts. There is the hands-on science involved in the construction of the feeder. You may wish to include a library book in the center showing different types of feeders. Children may, of course, wish to create their own designs, and this should be encouraged. There is much to be learned from any creative attempt.
- There is also the observational part of the activity. Binoculars are important but not imperative. Once birds start to come, there will be much for pupils to do in observing and recording what they see.
- Birdseed, available in hardware stores, pet shops, and five-and-tens, is cheap. Have pupils earn money to buy it.
- Once the birds have discovered the feeder, it is important that the children continue to stock it with feed, as the birds may become dependent on it, especially in very cold seasons.

Debriefing

The following types of questions are offered as examples of what may be asked during the Debriefing sessions to promote more thoughtful inquiry. These questions address both the building and observational stages of this activity and should be used selectively.

- What kind of feeder did you decide to build? Why did you think that was a good design for a feeder?
- Where will it be placed? What makes that a good location?
- How will it be refilled when it is empty? What plans are being made for that?
- How will birds get access to the feeder? How will that work?
- What kinds of birds have you observed?
- What observations have you made about their colors? their size? their feathers? the shape of their heads? their beaks? the way they feed? their sounds? their individual and group behavior?
- Which birds feed together? How do you know?
- How do birds communicate with each other? What theories do you have about this?
- What are some differences you have observed in birds of different species?
- What observations have you made about how they see? hear?
- What observations have you made about how they fly?
- How do you suppose they found out about the feeder? What hypotheses can you suggest to explain this?

Extending

The study of birds may be extended in one or more of the following ways:

1. By introducing a caged bird (canary, mynah, parakeet, finch) to the class for observation and comparison
2. By introducing new activity cards that extend the study of birds to outside the school
3. By raising more challenging questions in later Debriefing sessions, for example:

   - Are birds smart? How do you know?
   - What are birds good for? How do you know this? Can you give some examples?
   - In what ways are birds like bees? How are they different?
   - How do birds learn to fly? What are your ideas about this?
   - How do birds learn to build a nest? How do you explain this?
   - Do birds have feelings? How do you know? What examples can you give?
   - How are birds born? How do you know? How are they looked after when they are very young? How do you know that?
   - Is it better for birds to be pets, in cages, or to be in the wild? What are your ideas? Tell why you have those beliefs.
   - When do birds sing? What theories do you have about that?
   - What different kinds of foods do different birds eat? How do you know this? What accounts for those differences? What hypotheses can you suggest that would explain them?

4. By raising questions that allow for the examination of some value issues related to the topic, for example:

   The zoo in Honolulu has a bald eagle, America's national bird, in a cage, on view for all visitors. The eagle has had its wings clipped, so that it may not fly. In any case, it would not be able to fly in the cage because it is too small.

   - What are your views on birds in cages? Should we keep birds in cages so that we may have the pleasure of seeing them? Or shall we let them go free to fly as they wish? What is your opinion on this? What data support your opinions? Do you have examples to give?

Creating

There are many creative and intriguing ways of culminating the study of birds. For example, the children may:

1. Draw illustrations of the birds that have come to the feeder and put these together in a class bird book.
2. Gather and classify pictures of birds.
3. Make papier-mâché birds mounted on string and suspend them from the ceiling of the classroom.

4. Make a large construction of bird wings of paper and doweling.
5. Gather feathers for study.
6. Learn to imitate bird sounds.

Activity 32: Parachutes

In this center the children work with fabric, string, and weights to make their own parachutes and observe how air exerts pressure to keep parachutes afloat.

Activity Card

> - Use the materials in the center to make some parachutes.
> - Play with the parachutes and conduct some investigations with them.
> - Make some observations of how they work.
> - Talk with each other about what you see.
> - Then write about what you observed.
>
> You may have some other ideas for using the materials in this center. Try out your ideas and see what happens.

Materials

An assortment of fabrics (plastic, old bedsheets, gauze, burlap, etc.) cut into squares of various sizes; an assortment of "weights" (clothespins, pieces of wood, nuts and bolts); string; scissors

Thinking Operations Emphasized

Observing; collecting and recording data; comparing and interpreting data; suggesting hypotheses; designing investigations; identifying assumptions; applying principles; making decisions; imagining and creating

Big Ideas

Air is a substance that surrounds us and takes up space. Air exerts pressure, which creates resistance on the undersurface of a parachute to slow its descent.

Notes to the Teacher

- It may be a good idea to spend some time scouting out a safe, high place from which parachutes may be dropped. You will probably want to discuss some safety rules and to remind the children of these before they begin their work.

Debriefing

Here are some questions that might be raised to promote more thoughtful reflection during the Debriefing sessions. They should be used selectively.

- What observations did you make about parachutes?
- How did you discover that?
- What observations did you make about the parachutes that stayed up in the air longer?
- How do you account for that?
- What observations did you make about the parachutes that fell more quickly? How do you explain that?
- What did you observe about the air in the parachute? How did that work?

Extending

When the children have had sufficient opportunities to conduct their inquiries, the inquiry might be extended in one or more of the following ways:

1. By providing new materials in the center, such as much larger pieces of cloth, much larger "weights," cloths of heavier weight (such as cottons, muslins, plastic sheeting)
2. By introducing new activity cards, for example:

   - Conduct some investigations to see which fabrics make the best parachutes. Record your findings.
   - What kind of work can parachutes do? Try some investigations and see how many things you can discover.

3. By raising more challenging types of questions in later Debriefing sessions, for example:

   - What fabric, in your opinion, makes for better parachutes? How can you tell that?
   - What fabric, in your observation, makes for less successful parachutes? How can you tell?
   - Suppose you wanted to make a parachute to hold a very heavy weight. What would you have to do? How do you know that would work?
   - What makes a parachute work? Where did you get that idea from? How do you know that is true?
   - your work in this center, what are some new discoveries you made about air? How did you find that out? How do you know that is true?
   - What other tools work like parachutes? What examples can you give of how they work?

Creating

When the children have exhausted their Replay activities in this center, you may wish to bring the inquiries to conclusion by having them undertake one or more of the following activities:

1. Work with a friend. Try to think of as many ways as you can to show how air pressure helps us to do work. List the ways.
2. Use a ½-inch dowel, a piece of sturdy paper, and a straight pin to make a pinwheel. Compare the way your pinwheel works to the way a parachute works.
3. Write a story, "My First Parachute Drop." Imagine how it would feel and write it.

Activity 33: Sounds with Strings

In this center the children work with string and other materials to make observations about vibration and sound.

Activity Card

> - Use the materials in this center to make some stringed instruments.
> - What different kinds of instruments can be made?
> - How are the sounds made on each?
> - Try out your ideas and make some observations of what happens.
> - Then talk together and write about what you observed.
>
> There may be many other ways to use the materials in this center. Do you have some other ideas? Try them out and see what happens.

Materials

Rubber bands, string, scissors, fine wire, wire cutters, a few cans, several sturdy cardboard containers, wood strips (approximately ¼ by 1¼ inches), stapler

Thinking Operations Emphasized

Observing; comparing and interpreting data; suggesting hypotheses; examining assumptions; making decisions; creating and imagining; designing investigations

Big Ideas

Vibrating objects produce sound. Changing the vibrations by using different objects and/or changing their dimensions changes the sound.

Notes to the Teacher

- This is a very safe activity, one that might be implemented at the very beginning of your sciencing program. If wood strips cannot be obtained easily, a 12-inch ruler may be substituted for the sound board to which string or rubber bands may be attached with a stapler.

Debriefing

Here are some questions that might be used during the Debriefing sessions to promote pupil reflection:

- What kinds of instruments did you make in this center?
- What observations did you make about the way each of your instruments produced sound?
- In what ways did the sounds obtained from the rubber-band instruments and the sounds from the stringed instruments compare? How were the sounds alike? How were they different?
- In what ways were the sounds produced by the wire instruments like the other instruments? How were these sounds different?
- What observations did you make about how the sounds could be changed?

Extending

When the students have had sufficient time to carry out initial investigative play, you might wish to extend the play in one or more of the following ways:

1. By adding to the materials in the center, for example, adding actual musical instruments: dulcimer, autoharp, guitar, ukelele
2. By introducing new activity cards, for example:

   - Use your instrument to play a song.
   - Conduct some investigations to show how you might change the sounds that your instrument makes.
   - Conduct some investigations to try to figure out how the sounds are made.

3. By raising more challenging questions in later Debriefing sessions, for example:

   - Which of these materials, in your opinion, makes a more beautiful sound? What materials help to produce this sound? How do you explain that?
   - Compare two of the instruments that were made in this center. In what ways are they alike? How are they different?
   - Compare one of the instruments you made with one of the "real" instruments. How are these alike? How are they different?
   - What observations were made about how pitch is raised or lowered? What observations were made about how volume is raised or lowered?

- What observations were made about what happens to the string, wire, or rubber band when the instrument is played?

4. By raising questions that allow students to examine some value issues related to the topic, for example:

   You have a choice to make. You have a chance to learn to play a brand-new instrument—to take lessons and learn to play it well.

   - What instrument would you choose to learn? What is there about it that would appeal to you?
   - What kind of sounds would you like to make with this instrument? What are your ideas?

Creating

When the children's interest in investigative play seems to be exhausted, you may wish to have them undertake one or more of the following tasks:

1. Use one or more of the instruments made in this center. Make up a song. Play it for the class.
2. Form a "band" in which each student uses a different instrument. Make up a song together and play it for the class.
3. Make up some words to one or more of your original songs.
4. Select a song that you have learned in your class. Try to figure out how to play it on your instruments.

Activity 34: Wind Sounds

In this center the children work with the materials and, using their breath, try to create and vary sounds.

Activity Card

- Use the materials in the center to make some musical instruments.
- Try to make instruments that make different kinds of sounds when you use your breath.
- See how many different kinds of sounds your instruments can make.

You may have some other ideas for using the materials in this center. Try out your ideas and see what happens.

Materials

Cardboard tubing from various paper products; narrow-necked bottles, such as pop bottles, vinegar bottles, syrup bottles, salad dressing bottles; straws, both paper and plastic

Thinking Operations Emphasized

Observing; comparing; classifying and interpreting data; suggesting hypotheses; applying principles; designing investigations; making decisions; evaluating; inventing and creating

Big Ideas

Vibrations produce sound. You can make vibrations in a column of air. The sound can be varied by changing the size and shape of the air column.

Notes to the Teacher

• This is a very safe activity, but the investigative play will, of course, be rather noisy. You may wish to be prepared for the possibility of much noisy play coming from this center and schedule this activity accordingly.

Debriefing

The following types of questions might be raised during initial Debriefing sessions to promote pupil reflection. They should be used selectively.

• What observations did you make about the instruments you created?
• What observations did you make about how sounds were created?
• In what ways did your instruments compare with each other? How were your instruments alike? How were they different?
• How would you group the instruments you made? What categories might be set up? Where would each of the instruments belong?
• What observations did you make about how you could vary the sounds on your instruments? What observations did you make about how pitch could be changed? Volume?

Extending

After the children have had ample opportunity to conduct their initial investigations, you may wish to extend the inquiry in one or more of the following ways:

1. By adding materials to the center, for example, real wind instruments such as simple whistles, flutophones, recorders, flutes. Any wind instrument that may be obtained easily can be added to this center.

2. By adding new activity cards
3. By raising more challenging questions in later Debriefing sessions, for example:

- How are the sounds produced? How do you explain this?
- What materials contribute to the production of the sound? How do you know?
- What materials make better sounds? How do you know?
- How do these wind instruments compare with stringed instruments? How are they alike? How are they different?
- How are the "real" instruments like (different from) the ones you made in the center?

Creating

When the children seem to have come to the end of their enthusiasm for these materials, you may wish to ask the students to undertake one or more of the following tasks:

1. Work with one or two friends. Using some instruments made in the center, form a band. Prepare a piece of music to perform for the class.
2. Work with one or two friends. Sing a song that you have learned in school. Then try to play that song on your instruments.
3. Listen to a record or a tape of an orchestral piece. Try to listen for the wind instruments. See if you can figure out a way to identify them.
4. What do you think the very first musical instrument looked like? Imagine it and draw a picture of it.

Activity 35: Wind Energy

In this center the children make pinwheels and study and observe how pinwheels are made to work.

Activity Card

- Use the materials in the center to make some pinwheels.
- Conduct some investigations to find out how pinwheels work.
- How does the design of the pinwheel make it work better? Talk with each other about your ideas.
- Then write about what you observed.

You may have some other ideas for using these materials to observe how wind works. Try your ideas and see what happens.

Materials

Heavy bond paper, cut in squares measuring 8 by 8 and 12 by 12 inches; ¼-inch dowels cut into 12-inch lengths or pencils with eraser tops; crayons; scissors; straight pins; a model of a pinwheel

Thinking Operations Emphasized

Observing; comparing and interpreting data; applying principles; suggesting hypotheses; examining assumptions; summarizing; making decisions; imagining and creating

Big Ideas

Air is a substance that surrounds us and takes up space. When air moves, we feel it as wind. Wind may be used as a source of energy.

Notes to the Teacher

- This is an activity in which limited teacher effort yields major results in promoting conceptual understanding. It is safe, clean, and very enjoyable.
- Pupils may use the crayons provided to make more colorful pinwheels. You may wish to make several different pinwheels to serve as models for this center.

Debriefing

Questions such as the following might be raised at initial Debriefing sessions to promote further reflection about wind power:

- What observations did you make about how to make a pinwheel turn?
- What observations did you make about the direction in which the pinwheel turned? How do you explain this?
- Suppose you wanted to make it turn in the other direction. How might you arrange for that to happen?
- What observations did you make about the shape of the pinwheel?
- What other shape could it have and still turn?

Extending

There are several ways in which the pupil inquiry about wind power may be extended, for example:

1. By introducing new activity cards, for example:

- How does the shape of a pinwheel make it turn? Try out different shapes and make some observations of what happens.
- How does the size of the pinwheel help it turn? Try out different sizes and observe and record what happens.

- How does the strength of the wind affect the way the pinwheel turns? Try out different wind strengths and observe and record what happens.
- In what other ways does wind power work for us? Working in pairs, list the ways in which wind power is used in our lives.
- In what ways can the pinwheel be made to help something else to work? Invent ways to show how the pinwheel's action may contribute to the working of another machine.

2. By raising more challenging questions in later Debriefing sessions, for example:

- What other examples can be thought of to show how wind can be used as a source of energy?
- Where do you suppose wind comes from? Where did you get that idea?
- There may be times when the power of the wind can be a destructive force. What examples can you give of this?

3. By raising questions that allow for the examination of value issues relating to the topic, for example:

Wind can exert a powerful force, and this power can be used to generate energy. Some people have been using wind power as an alternative to fossil fuels.

- What are your views on such an alternative?
- If wind power is so good and so cheap, why don't more people use it?
- What are some of its limitations, in your opinion? What are some of its good features? What data back up your opinions?

Creating

Before leaving this inquiry, you may wish to give pupils opportunities for more inventive tasks, such as these:

1. Design and build a large windmill that will use wind power to do some other work.
2. Design and build a kite that uses wind power to fly.
3. Invent a wind-making machine—a machine that will create a force of wind when the natural wind dies down. Draw a picture of it.
4. Design and build a sailboat to show how wind power works to move boats.
5. Write a poem about the terrifying power of the wind.
6. Write a story, using your imagination, to tell where the sound of the wind comes from.

Activity 36: Static Electricity

In this center the children work with the materials provided to make observations about static electricity. They are asked to record their observations.

Activity Card

> - Use the materials in this center to conduct some investigations about how materials stick together.
> - How can you get these materials to stick together?
> - Which materials are better at this?
> - Which are less good?
> - What observations can you make about how this works?
> - Talk with each other about what you have found.
> - Then write about your observations.
>
> You may have some other ideas for using these materials. Try your ideas and see what happens.

Materials

Small pieces of tissue paper; a rubber comb or a resin rod; a few pieces of fabric (wool, nylon, other synthetics, cotton, silk, fur); balloons

Thinking Operations Emphasized

Observing; comparing; classifying; interpreting data; designing investigations; suggesting hypotheses; examining assumptions; applying principles; making decisions; imagining and inventing; evaluating

Big Ideas

Friction produced by rubbing two objects together may create a static charge. Different combinations of materials produce a greater or smaller static charge.

Notes to the Teacher

- This is a safe, clean, and dry activity with a productive yield in terms of pupil learning. Materials needed are easily found, and teachers who are just beginning their sciencing programs may wish to consider this among their first choices.

Debriefing

Here are some questions that might be raised at initial Debriefing sessions to promote reflection about the inquiry. They should be used selectively.

- What observations did you make about the materials in this center?
- What observations did you make about the materials that stuck together? How do you explain that? What are your ideas?

- What observations did you make about any noises you heard? How do you explain those noises? What are your ideas?
- What observations did you make about what you felt when a noise was heard? How do you explain this? What are your ideas?
- What differences did you observe in the ways the materials stuck together? How do you explain this? What are your ideas?

Extending

The static electricity study may be extended in several ways, for example:

1. By introducing additional materials, such as a dish of flour and a dish of water
2. By introducing other activity cards, for example:

   - What happens when you rub a piece of wool against an inflated balloon and then place the balloon next to a wall? How do you explain this? Does it always work? How do you explain that? Observe and record what happens.
   - What happens when you rub a comb with a piece of wool and then place your hand over the comb? How do you explain this? Does it always work? How do you explain that? Observe and record what happens.

3. By raising more challenging questions in later Debriefing sessions, for example:

   - What are some observations you made about static electricity?
   - What can you do to make static electricity?
   - What kinds of materials help to make static electricity? How do you explain this?
   - What kinds of materials do not help to make static electricity? How do you explain this?
   - How do you explain the magnetic attraction of the balloon when it is charged? What are your ideas?

Creating

As the children move from their investigations into more creating types of activities, they might like to try one or more of the following tasks:

1. Make a drawing showing how static electricity was produced in your investigations.
2. Design an investigation to show that static electricity can repel as well as attract.
3. Design an investigation to demonstrate that there is electricity built up in the materials.
4. Write a story called "The Charged Cat."

Activity 37: Kites

In this center the children build kites and make some observations of how they are made to fly. They are asked to record their observations.

Activity Card

> - Use the materials in this center to design and build your own kite.
> - Ask your teacher's permission to take your kites outside to fly. Conduct some investigations and make some observations of how kites fly.
> - What helps a kite to fly better?
> - Talk about what you observed and then write your ideas.

Materials

Strips of balsa wood or wooden dowels of two lengths (some of 2 feet, others of 1½ feet); large sheets of colored tissue paper or light plastic sheeting; string; stapler; glue

Thinking Operations Emphasized

Observing; collecting and recording data; comparing and interpreting data; examining assumptions; suggesting hypotheses; applying principles; making decisions; creating and inventing

Big Ideas

Many children's toys demonstrate basic scientific principles. Kites, for example, make use of the wind as an aerodynamic force.

Notes to the Teacher

- Thin strips of wood or dowels can be purchased inexpensively at a local lumberyard and cut to your specifications.
- The glue used should be the firmer-bonding kind rather than the rubber cement or white paste normally found in school supplies.
- One or two models of kites may be made or commercially obtained and placed in the center as examples.
- Children should, of course, have the opportunity of taking their kites outside to fly and to observe and record what occurs. This activity may be best done during a windier season.

Debriefing

During initial Debriefing sessions, the following types of questions might be raised to promote reflection about kite construction and kite flying:

- What are some observations you made about building kites?
- What observations were made about the kinds of shapes that kites have? What did you observe about the materials used in kite building?
- What observations were made about the relationship between the shape of a kite and the way it flies?
- What do you suppose keeps a kite up in the air? How do you explain this?
- What do you suppose makes a kite fall? How do you explain this?

Extending

When the children have completed their kite building and have had some chance to fly the kites, the inquiry may be extended in one or more of the following ways:

1. By introducing kites of other shapes (box kites, Japanese wind-sock kites, fish kites) and observing how these fly
2. By introducing other wind-powered toys (paper airplanes, pinwheels, sailboats, balloon-borne baskets) for making comparisons
3. By raising more challenging questions, following more extensive investigative play, for example:

   - Why do you suppose some kites fly better with tails and others do not? How do you explain this?
   - What observations did you make about the purpose of a tail on a kite?
   - How might you measure how high your kite can fly? What are your ideas?
   - How much weight might your kite carry? What are your predictions? How might you test your ideas?
   - How are kites different from (similar to) pinwheels? windmills? sailboats? airplanes?

4. By raising questions that allow for the examination of value issues related to the topic, for example:

   - Are kites safe toys? What makes them safe or unsafe? What are your ideas about this? What data back up your opinions? Can you give some examples that support your opinions?

Creating

When the children have exhausted their interest in investigative play with kites, you may wish to culminate the kite activity in one or more of the following ways:

1. Hold a kite flying contest.
2. Make a classroom or hall display of children's kites.
3. Have the children design a machine to determine the force or speed of the wind.
4. Have the children design and build a wind vane.

5. Have the children study clouds. Ask them to draw pictures or write stories or poems about clouds.

Activity 38: Bouncing Balls

In this center the children carry out investigative play with a variety of balls. They are asked to record their findings.

Activity Card

- Use the materials in the center to conduct some investigations about bouncing balls.
- How high do the balls bounce?
- Which balls bounce higher?
- Make some observations and record your findings.

You may have some other ideas about conducting investigations with these balls. Try out your ideas and see what you can learn.

Materials

A collection of balls of different sizes, weights, and compositions, for example, rubber balls, clay balls, ball bearings, volleyballs, polyethylene balls, a ball of yarn, rubber-band balls, tennis balls, Ping-Pong balls, footballs, basketballs, plastic balls, a ball of string, a golf ball, a billiard ball, a marble, a balloon; different surfaces on which to bounce the balls, for example, pieces of wood, tile, foam rubber, pieces of metal sheeting, sand, a pan of water, corrugated paper, plastic sheeting, Styrofoam chips

Thinking Operations Emphasized

Observing; comparing; classifying and interpreting data; designing investigations; applying principles; making decisions; summarizing; evaluating; suggesting hypotheses; identifying assumptions; imagining and inventing

Big Ideas

Elasticity of balls causes them to bounce. The extent to which a ball can bounce against a hard surface is a measure of its elasticity.

Notes to the Teacher

- Balls may, of course, be found in the school's recreational equipment storage area. Children may also be encouraged to bring balls from home to add variety to the materials in the center.

Debriefing

During initial Debriefing sessions, children's thinking about the inquiry may be further stimulated by asking some of the following types of questions:

- What observations did you make about bouncing balls?
- What differences did you notice? What were some similarities?
- If you wanted to classify these balls, what kinds of groups could you set up? In what group would each ball belong?
- What observations did you make about dropping balls on different surfaces? How do you explain what happened? What are your ideas?
- What ways did you invent to measure how high balls bounce? How did you decide that that would be a good way to do it?
- Which balls bounce higher? How do you explain that?

Extending

When the children have had sufficient chance to carry out their initial investigative play with the balls, you may wish to extend their inquiries in one or more of the following ways:

1. By adding some new activity cards to the center, for example:

   - What are some good ways to measure the bounce? Conduct some investigations and record your findings.
   - What happens when you drop a ball from different heights? Conduct some investigations and record your findings.
   - What happens when you drop a ball on different surfaces? Conduct some inquiries and record your findings.
   - What are some of the differences you have observed in the different balls? Set up a classification system and place each ball in the group where it belongs.
   - What can you do to change the way a ball bounces? Conduct some investigations and record your findings.
   - What other things bounce? Conduct some investigations and record your findings.
   - What things do not bounce? Conduct some investigations and record your findings.
   - Make a chart to show how different balls bounce.

2. By raising more challenging questions following more extensive investigative play, for example:

   - What theories can you suggest to explain why some things bounce and others do not? How could you test those theories?
   - What theories can you suggest to explain why some balls bounce better on some surfaces than on other surfaces?
   - What theories can you suggest to explain why some balls bounce higher?

Creating

Before leaving the investigative play on bouncing balls, you may wish to have the students carry out one or more of the following culminating activities:

1. Work with a friend. Invent a brand-new game, using a small and a large ball. Invent a scoring system for your game.
2. Work with a friend. Figure out a good way to measure the path a ball takes when you throw it. Write about your ideas.
3. Make a pencil-and-paper design using circles of different colors.
4. Work with a friend. Think of 20 different uses for balls. Make a list of your ideas.
5. Write the story "The Magic Ball."

Activity 39: Friction and Inertia

In this center the children carry out investigative play with tops, yo-yos, gyroscopes, and flywheels. They are asked to record their observations.

Activity Card

> - Use the materials in the center to study how these toys work.
> - What makes the tops spin? What makes them stop?
> - What makes the yo-yos work? What makes them stop?
> - How do the other toys work? What makes them stop?
> - Conduct some investigations and make some careful observations.
> - Talk with each other and then write your observations.
>
> You may have some other ideas for using these materials. Try out your ideas and make some observations.

Materials

Several tops of different sizes and shapes; several yo-yos; one or two gyroscopes; one or two flywheels; one or two Frisbees

Thinking Operations Emphasized

Observing and recording; comparing; classifying and interpreting data; suggesting hypotheses; examining assumptions; designing investigations; making decisions; imagining and creating; evaluating and criticizing

Big Ideas

Things in motion tend to stay in motion as long as no external force interferes. Friction causes things to slow and stop. Things at rest tend to stay at rest. These tendencies are known as inertia.

Notes to the Teacher

- The tops in this center should be both the whip-spun kind and the twirled kind. They may be commercially obtained or homemade.
- Children may also be asked to bring some of these items from home.

Debriefing

The following types of questions may promote reflection about the ways these toys work:

- What observations did you make about how tops spin? About what makes them stop spinning?
- In what ways are tops like yo-yos? How are they different?
- What observations did you make about gyroscopes? How are these like tops?
- What keeps a top spinning? How do you explain this? What makes it stop spinning? How do you explain that?

Extending

You may wish to extend the children's thinking on this inquiry in some of the following ways:

1. By adding new toys to the center, such as a ball, a wheel or set of wheels, toy cars
2. By adding new activity cards, for example:

- How long can you make a top spin? Conduct some investigations and record your findings.
- How long can you make a gyroscope spin? Conduct some investigations and record your findings.
- Study tops and yo-yos. Find as many similarities and differences as you can. Record your findings.
- Carry out some investigations with the Frisbee. Record your observations.

3. By raising more challenging questions in later Debriefing sessions, for example:

- What are the properties of a good top? Why do you think that will work better?
- How are Frisbees like tops or yo-yos? How are they different?
- What other kinds of toys operate on the same principles as tops and yo-yos? What makes you think so?
- What kinds of toys depend on a gyroscope for their action? What makes you think so?
- If you wanted to keep a top spinning for a very long time, what might you do? What makes you think that would work?

4. By raising questions that allow for examination of some value issues related to the topic, for example:

Alexander saved his allowance for one month to buy a toy that was advertised on television. He wanted it very much, and he just couldn't wait to get it. When he finally got the money together, he bought it, took it home, and began to play with it immediately. He hadn't had it for more than 30 minutes when it broke. He was *so* angry! He felt cheated. What kind of material was used in making this toy that it would break so quickly? And what kind of people would make toys that break so fast?

- Have you had similar experiences? What examples can you give of toys that break quickly? What kinds of materials are they made of? Do some materials break down faster? What materials last longer?
- Should there be some laws regulating the kinds of toys that manufacturers make for children? What kinds of laws should there be? What are your ideas?

Creating

The students may be asked to undertake one or more of the following activities to culminate their investigative play with these concepts:

1. Work with a friend. Use lollipop sticks or toothpicks and cardboard to make some tops.
2. Work with a friend. Make up a game using yo-yos.
3. Work with a friend. Using the materials in the center, build a small model swing. Describe how swings, tops, and yo-yos are alike.
4. Work with a friend. Make a list of as many toys as you can think of. Set up some groups to show how these may be classified.
5. Using whatever materials are available, make your own gyroscope.

Activity 40: Magnets

In this center children carry out investigative play with magnets. They are asked to record their observations.

Activity Card

> - Use the materials in the center to conduct some investigations with magnets.
> - What can magnets do?
> - What materials work best with magnets?
> - Try some investigations and see what you can find.
> - Talk with each other about your ideas.
> - Then write about your observations.
>
> You may have some other ideas for investigations with magnets. Try them and see what discoveries you can make.

Materials

Different kinds of magnets (horseshoe magnets and bar magnets of different sizes and strengths); various small objects containing metal (straight pins, paper clips, metal filings, thumbtacks, staples, nails, screws, picture hooks, coins); various larger objects containing metal (scissors, stapler, hammer, screwdriver, pliers, wrench, can opener, spoon, fork); various nonmetal objects (plastic spoons, Styrofoam cups, plastic pens, paper products, glass objects, ceramic objects, cloth, cork objects)

Thinking Operations Emphasized

Observing and recording; comparing; classifying data; interpreting data; applying principles; making decisions; designing investigations; suggesting hypotheses; examining assumptions; summarizing; imagining and inventing

Big Ideas

Some materials have magnetic properties. Magnets attract or repel each other, depending on their positions.

Notes to the Teacher

- If possible, try to obtain metal objects containing cobalt, nickel, and iron, as these are strongly attracted to magnets. A Canadian nickel should be included, if possible, as well as a U.S. nickel. Iron filings are usually available in science equipment storage areas. If not available in your school, try the local high school physics department.

Debriefing

The following types of questions might be raised during initial Debriefing sessions to promote reflection about magnetism. They should be used selectively.

- What observations did you make about the materials in this center?
- What observations did you make about the objects that were attracted by the magnets? How do you explain this phenomenon?
- What observations did you make about the objects that were not attracted by the magnets? How do you explain this lack of attraction?
- What differences did you observe between the horseshoe and the bar magnets? What similarities did you observe?
- What observations did you make about the ends of the bar magnet? How do you explain this effect? What are your ideas?

Extending

When the children appear ready to have their investigative play extended, consider the following options:

1. Adding new materials to the center, for example, small place pins stuck in corks in a small basin of water, bar magnets hung from a frame, and objects that contain combinations of metal and nonmetal parts
2. Introducing new activity cards, for example:

   - How can these objects be classified? Set up some categories and place each item in the category in which it belongs.
   - What work can magnets do? Try some investigations and record your findings.

3. Raising more challenging questions in later Debriefing sessions, for example:

   - How do you use a magnet to make an object move? How do you explain how it works?
   - How could you group the objects in this center? How would you decide in which group each object belonged?

- What theories can you suggest to explain why some items are attracted to the magnets and some are not?
- What theories can you suggest to explain how a magnet gets its power?
- How do you make a magnet? What are your ideas?
- What are magnets good for? What are your ideas?

Creating

To culminate the investigative play, you may wish to have the children undertake one or more of the following tasks:

1. Work with a friend. Make a magnet.
2. Work with a friend. Figure out a way to find out the strength of a magnet. Conduct some investigations and record your findings.
3. Work with a friend. Place a bar magnet under a piece of paper. Sprinkle some iron filings on the paper. Observe what happens. Draw some pictures of what you see. Then suggest some hypotheses to explain it.
4. Try to imagine what kind of magnet you would need to lift a car. Draw a picture of it.
5. Write a story, "The Magnet That Wouldn't Let Go."

Activity 41: Wheels and Axles

In this center the children carry out investigative play with wheels and axles to make observations about simple machines. They are asked to record their observations.

Activity Card

> - Use the materials in this center to conduct some investigations with wheels.
> - What observations can you make about wheels?
> - What observations can you make about how wheels are made to turn?
> - What observations can you make about how wheels make our work easier?
> - Talk with each other about your ideas.
> - Then write about your observations.
>
> You may have some other ideas for using the materials in this center. Try them out and see what you can learn.

Materials

A supply of wheels of various sizes and constructions (for example, plastic wheels from children's toy trucks and cars, wagon wheels, rubber wheels from children's toys, an old automobile tire, metal wheels with axles, a bicycle wheel, a steering wheel); wheels from household appliances (for example, pencil sharpener, meat grinder, egg beater); spring scale; bricks, concrete blocks, large pieces of timber, and/or other weights; large plastic tubs or large cartons

Thinking Operations Emphasized

Observing and recording; comparing; interpreting data; suggesting hypotheses; examining assumptions; designing investigations; making decisions; evaluating; applying principles; imagining and inventing

Big Ideas

A wheel is a simple machine with several different functions. In one function it allows us to move things more easily. Wheels are found in many children's toys.

Notes to the Teacher

- In acquiring a collection of wheels, begin first with what is available in the science storage room. Then try your own basement, attic, kitchen, storage closet, or garage. If your collection is still meager, visit "junk stores" in your neighborhood. Ask the children to bring in broken toys with wheels. Finally, there is the old, reliable hardware store if you feel financially flush.

Debriefing

More thoughtful inquiry about the concepts underlying how wheels work may be generated with the following types of questions during initial Debriefing sessions:

- What observations did you make about wheels?
- What observations did you make about how wheels are made to turn?
- In what ways do wheels help us do work?
- Sometimes wheels make our work easier. How do you explain this? What are your ideas?

Extending

If you wish to extend pupil inquiry about wheels, some of the following ideas may be tried:

1. Adding a doorknob and a screwdriver to the center and introducing new activity cards that focus inquiry on these new materials, for example:

- Where is the wheel function in these tools? How are these like other wheels? Conduct some investigations and record your findings.
- Use a scale and figure out how much force is required to turn wheels of different sizes. Conduct some investigations and record your findings.
- Use a scale to figure out how much force is required to move a concrete block with and without wheels. Conduct some investigations and record your findings.

2. Raising more challenging questions in later Debriefing sessions, for example:

- Think of some ways in which wheels are used to do work for you. What examples can you give?
- What can make a wheel move more easily? What can make a wheel move more slowly? What can make it more difficult for a wheel to move? What examples can you give?
- In what different ways can wheels be made to move? What examples can you give?

3. Raising questions that allow for the examination of value issues related to the topic, for example:

- It takes energy to drive wheels, but wheels make life easier for us. If you had to conserve energy, what wheel-driven machines would you be able to do without? What are your thoughts on this?
- What wheel-driven machines would you not be able to give up? What are your views?

Creating

The students may be asked to participate in some of the following culminating tasks to round out the work in this center:

1. Work with a friend. Take a trip throughout the school. Observe the many ways in which wheels are used in this school to do work. Record your observations.
2. Work with a friend. Using any material available in the room, construct a machine that operates with one or more wheels.
3. Invent a machine that uses wheels to dial a telephone. Draw a picture of it.
4. Invent a machine that uses wheels to give an elephant a bath. Draw a picture of it.
5. Write a story about the day the wheel was invented.

Activity 42: Levers

In this center the children carry out investigative play with a variety of levers, inclined planes, and weights. They are asked to record their observations.

Activity Card

> - Use the materials in this center to find out what you can about how levers work.
> - How can the levers be used to lift heavy things?
> - What is the difference when you lift heavy weights with and without a lever? Make some observations and record your findings.
>
> Try some other investigations with these materials. Make up your own investigations and see what discoveries you can make.

Materials

A variety of small boards (for example, a ruler, a yardstick or meterstick, several shelves of different lengths and widths); a variety of bricks, concrete blocks and other bars that may serve as a fulcrum; materials of different weights (for example, metal weights, heavy books, bricks, firewood, bag of soil, concrete); a spring scale

Thinking Operations Emphasized

Observing and recording; comparing; classifying and interpreting data; examining assumptions; suggesting hypotheses; designing investigations; applying principles; evaluating; making decisions; summarizing; imagining and inventing

Big Ideas

Levers are simple machines that make work easier. They allow us to lift heavy loads. The human forearm is sometimes used as a lever.

Notes to the Teacher

- The school storage room or basement may turn up discarded or unusable shelves that would make ideal material for the lever center.
- There should be several objects of quite heavy weights (25 to 50 pounds) along with objects that weigh less.

Debriefing

Here are some questions that might be raised during initial Debriefing sessions to promote reflection about how levers work:

- What observations have you made about how levers work?
- How can you explain how they work? What are your ideas?
- In what ways is a lever like your arm? How is it different? In what ways does your arm work like a lever? In what ways does your foot work like a lever?
- What observations have you made about how levers and inclined planes help us in our work?

Extending

The investigative play in the levers center may be extended in one or more of the following ways:

1. By adding new materials to the center, for example, nutcrackers, wheelbarrow, bottle opener, crowbar, ice tongs, tweezers, scissors
2. By adding some new activity cards to give a different focus to the inquiries, for example:

   - Design some investigations to show how you use a lever to lift some very heavy weights. Record your findings.
   - Design some investigations to show how you would balance light weights against heavy weights. Record your findings.
   - Design some investigations to show how much force you need to use to lift a 25-pound weight. You will need a spring scale for this. Record your findings.
   - Design some investigations to show how the amount of force necessary to move an object up an inclined plane changes with the slope of the incline. Record your findings.

3. By raising more challenging questions in later Debriefing sessions, for example:

   - What are some differences between an inclined plane and a lever? What are some similarities?
   - In what ways is a wheelbarrow like a nutcracker? How are they different?
   - How much force does it take to lift a 25-pound weight without a lever? How much with a lever? How do you explain the difference?
   - What observations did you make about how the lever works when you move the fulcrum to different positions?

Creating

Some of the following may be presented to the students as culminating activities for the lever studies:

1. Work with a friend. Think up and list as many ways as you can to show how your arm works as a lever.
2. Work with a friend. Draw a diagram to show how two people would use an inclined

plane or a lever (or both) to move a piano into an apartment on the top floor of a building that has no elevator.

3. Work with a friend. Design an investigation to find out how much energy it takes to climb a flight of stairs or go up a ramp, each going the same distance from the main floor to the second floor. Figure out a way to measure your findings.

Activity 43: Pulleys

In this center the children carry out investigative play with pulleys, observing and recording how they function.

Activity Card

> - Use the materials in this center to conduct some investigations with pulleys.
> - What can pulleys do?
> - How do they work?
> - How can a pulley make your work easier?
> - Try out some investigations and make some observations about pulleys.
> - Then write about what you found.
>
> You may have some other ideas for using these materials. Try out your ideas and see what you can learn.

Materials

Three or four pulleys of different sizes; heavy string or rope; weights and/or blocks of wood, for lifting; bricks, concrete blocks, lumber

Thinking Operations Emphasized

Observing and recording; comparing and interpreting data; suggesting hypotheses; examining assumptions; designing investigations; making decisions; applying principles; evaluating; imagining and creating

Big Ideas

Pulleys are simple machines that help us to lift weights.

Notes to the Teacher

- Pulleys are generally found in the storage area containing general science materials. They may also be acquired inexpensively in secondhand shops or more expensively in hardware stores.
- Blocks of wood, with hooks, should be provided so that pulleys may be attached in movable positions. There should be at least one concrete block or block of wood that weighs at least 50 pounds so that students are able to experience the work of pulleys in more realistic situations.

Debriefing

Some of the following types of questions might be asked during Debriefing sessions to promote reflection about the work with pulleys:

- What observations did you make about pulleys?
- What differences did you observe about the ways pulleys work?
- What makes a pulley work? How do you explain this?
- What might be some uses for pulleys? What are your ideas?

Extending

The investigative play with pulleys may be extended in one or more of the following ways:

1. By adding to the materials in the center, for example, a spring scale and other very heavy weights
2. By adding new activity cards, for example:

    - How much will you have to pull on the spring balance in order to raise the 10-pound weight? the 25-pound weight? the 5-pound weight? Conduct some investigations and record your observations. Suggest some hypotheses that might explain how this works.
    - How much will you have to pull on the spring balance to raise the weights without the pulley? Conduct some investigations and record your observations. Suggest some hypotheses that might explain the differences you found.

3. By raising more challenging questions in later Debriefing sessions, for example:

    - In what places in or around the school can pulleys be seen working? What observations can be made about the work they do?
    - What might happen if you used two pulleys to raise a 50-pound weight? What makes you think that would happen?
    - If you didn't have a pulley and needed to raise a very heavy weight, how could you do it? What other ways might work?

4. By raising some questions that call for examination of value issues related to the topic, for example:

> Some people hold the idea that hard work is good for you. If pulleys can make your work easier, perhaps we shouldn't use them.

> - What are your ideas about this? What do you think? Can you give some examples to support your opinions?

Creating

Before collapsing the pulley center, you might ask the pupils to undertake one or more of the following culminating activities:

1. Work with a friend. Make a pulley using whatever materials are available in the classroom. Test it to see how much weight it can lift.
2. Work with a friend. Draw a picture of a pulley system that could be used to lift an elephant in a large cage aboard a ship.
3. Imagine the day long ago when a pulley was first invented. How did this happen? What kind of a person could have invented this concept? What was life like at that time? Think about it and write about it in a short story.

Activity 44: Sounds Around Us

In this center the children do investigative play with the materials provided to make observations about sound—how it is made, how it is carried, its intensity, and its effect on people. They are asked to record their observations.

Activity Card

> - Use the materials in this center to conduct some investigations about sounds.
> - What kinds of sounds can be made?
> - What do you have to do to create sounds?
> - What do you have to do to change sounds?
> - Try some investigations and see what you can find out.
> - Talk with each other about your ideas. Then figure out a way to classify these sounds. Make a chart showing your categories.
>
> You may have some of your own ideas for conducting investigations about sound. Try your ideas and see what you can learn.

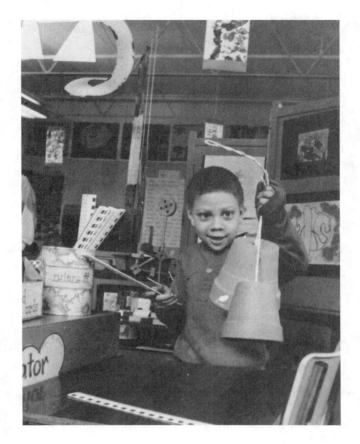

Materials

String, rubber bands, nails, staples, blocks of wood, rocks, bottles, sticks, ruler, yardstick, whistles, tuning fork, drums, xylophones, mallets, harmonica, piece of old garden hose (or other tubing), paper cups, tin cans, funnel, metal fork and spoon, stethoscope

Thinking Operations Emphasized

Observing and recording; comparing; classifying and interpreting data; examining assumptions; suggesting hypotheses; designing investigations; making decisions; summarizing; evaluating; imagining and creating

Big Ideas

Sound is produced by vibrating objects. The quality of a sound depends on the properties of the vibrating objects. Different kinds of vibrations produce harmonic (beautiful) and discordant (ugly) sounds.

Notes to the Teacher

- Investigative play in this center will tend to be quite noisy, so if you choose this activity, be prepared for it. One cannot study sounds without making noise.
- The sound activities may be varied by introducing other activity cards, for example:
  — What kinds of sounds can be made with these materials? Try some investigations and record your findings.
  — How are sounds made? Conduct some investigations and record your findings.
  — What produces pleasant sounds? What produces ugly sounds? Conduct some investigations and record your findings.
  — What sounds can you hear farther away? What sounds travel longer distances? Conduct some investigations and record your findings.

Debriefing

The following types of questions may be used selectively to promote reflection about sounds during initial Debriefing sessions:

- What observations did you make about sounds?
- In what ways might the sounds you made be classified? What kinds of groups did you set up?
- In what ways can sounds be changed? How can this be done? How can you explain how that works?
- What might you do to transmit sound? How does this work?
- What instruments make the loudest sounds? the softest sounds? the highest sounds? the lowest? How do you explain this?
- Which made the most beautiful sounds? What was there about that sound that made it beautiful?
- What's the difference between noise and sound? What are your ideas about it?

Extending

The investigative play with sounds may be extended in one or more of the following ways:

1. By introducing more challenging activity cards to promote new inquiries, for example:

   - Study the sounds in this classroom. Make a list of them. Then classify the sounds you heard.
   - Use the materials in the center to invent an instrument that will transmit sound. Test it to see how far the sound will carry on your instrument. Record your findings.
   - Study the sounds you hear just outside the school. Record your observations by making a list of all the sounds. Then classify the sounds.

- Make a list of all the things you can think of that make sounds. Set up categories and classify the items on your list.
- Conduct some investigations with the telephone. See if you can suggest some hypotheses to explain how it works. Record your observations and your hypotheses.
- Compare the telephone with the instrument you made. How are they alike? How are they different? Record your findings.
- What happens when sound is made in water? Conduct some investigations and record your findings.

2. By raising more challenging questions during later Debriefing sessions, for example:

- How does very loud sound "feel" to your ears? How does soft sound feel? How does harsh sound feel? How does beautiful sound feel?
- How does hearing those sound make *you* feel? Is there a relationship between sounds and how you feel? How do you explain your reactions to the sounds?
- In what ways can sounds be measured? What are your ideas about this?
- In what ways can sounds be increased? How does this work? What are your ideas?
- How does quiet feel to your ears? How does quiet make you feel? How do you explain those feelings? What are your ideas?

3. By raising questions that call for examination of value issues related to the topic, for example:

Brian is angry. Every time he goes to the shopping mall, there is loud music coming out of speakers in almost every store. There is so much loud music everywhere that his ears begin to hurt. Brian hates this music. He thinks that people are entitled to a little peace and quiet. He is getting ready to take some action against the loud music playing in the shopping malls.

- Where do you stand on this issue? Are there times when loud music hurts your ears? Is this something that we should be concerned about?
- What kind of action might Brian take? What might be some consequences of what you are proposing?

Creating

You may wish to have the students engage in some of the following activities to culminate the investigative play with sounds:

1. Work with a friend. Figure out a way to measure sounds. Write about your ideas.
2. Work with a friend. Try some investigations using your voices to make sounds. See how many sounds you can make and how the vocal sounds may be changed.
3. Work with a friend. Try some investigations making echoes. Write about your discoveries.

4. Work with a friend. Stand on a busy street corner for about 15 minutes. Keep a record of all the sounds you hear, the kinds of sounds, and how loud they are. Then work together to draw a picture describing your experience.

5. Work with a friend. Go to a very quiet place, such as a library, garden, seashore, forest, or park. Stay there for at least 15 minutes and keep a record of the kinds of sounds you hear. Then work together to draw a picture of your experience.

6. Work with a friend. Use the materials in the center to make musical sounds. In what ways are musical sounds and other sounds alike? How are they different? Write about your findings.

7. Gather some materials from the sound center that you think will make some unusual instruments to make new music with. Get some help from one or two friends and make up a song using these new instruments.

Activity 45: Tools

In this center the children do investigative play with tools, examining how they work and what work they are able to do. They are asked to record their observations.

Activity Card

- Use the materials in the center to see what you can find out about tools and how they work.
- Conduct some investigations to see how these tools do work.
- Make some observations and write about what you observed.
- How could these tools be classified? Set up categories and arrange the tools in those groups. Keep a record of how you grouped them.

You may have some other ideas for using the materials in this center. Try out your ideas and see what you can find out.

Materials

A variety of tools of many kinds: ruler, stapler, staple remover, funnel, straw, strainer, eggbeater, forceps, medicine dropper, needle, eraser, tape, scissors, pins, paper clips, nails, fasteners, ballpoint pens, thread, string, wire, old clock or watch, candles, cork, hammer, saw, screwdriver, pliers, stethoscope, extension cord, wedge, sandpaper, thermometer, spring balance, magnet, gears, steel wool, glass, camera, compass, sponge, microscope, atomizer, flashlight, mousetrap, air pump

Thinking Operations Emphasized

Observing and recording; classifying, comparing, and interpreting data; suggesting hypotheses; examining assumptions; applying principles; designing investigations; making decisions; imagining and creating

Big Ideas

Many tools are examples of simple machines that help us to do work. Simple machines are often combined to make more complex machines.

Notes to the Teacher

- Tools in this inquiry are thought of in their broadest sense of anything that can be used to perform a specific function. Such tools may be collected from many different sources, for example, the classroom, the science cabinet, the school office, and your own kitchen, basement, attic, toolshed, or study.

Debriefing

In the initial Debriefing sessions, some of the following types of questions may help to promote reflection about tools:

- What observations did you make about (specific tool)? What did you find out about how that tool works? What did you find out about what kinds of work that tool does? What are your ideas about it?
- What were some of the ways in which you classified the tools? In what other ways might they be classified?
- In what ways are (two specific tools) alike? How are they different?
- What observations did you make about how (specific tool) works? How do you explain it?

Extending

The investigative play with tools may be extended in one or more of the following ways:

1. By introducing new tools to the center, for example, paper cutter, jack, wrench, calipers, egg timer, pencil sharpener, tuning fork, wheel, chain, tape measure, protractor
2. By introducing more challenging activity cards, for example:

    - In what ways are screwdrivers and forceps alike? Conduct some investigations and find as many differences and similarities as you can. Record your findings.
    - How does an atomizer work? Conduct some investigations and make some observations. Record your findings.
    - Take a clock apart. Make some observations of how it works. Write about your findings.
    - In what ways are thermometers and tape measures alike? How are they different? Conduct some investigations and record your findings.

3. By raising more challenging questions during later Debriefing sessions, for example:

- What is a tool? How did you arrive at that definition?
- What are some differences between tools and machines? How did you figure that out?
- Which tools do you think are absolutely necessary to your life? Why do you think so? What would your life be like without them? Try to imagine and describe it.
- How did people invent tools? Which tools, do you suppose, were among the very first to be invented? What makes you think so?

4. By raising questions that call for examination of value issues related to the topic, for example:

Some tools are quite dangerous to use, and if we are not very careful, we might get hurt. Yet if we are going to use these tools carefully, at some age, we are going to have to learn how to use them.

- At what age do you think children should learn to use a saw? scissors? a paper cutter? an ice pick? an electric drill? What are your opinions on this issue?
- Which tools do you think should be left entirely out of the reach of children? Can you give some examples that would support your opinions?

Creating

The following are examples of some activities the children might engage in to bring the investigative play with tools to a more inventive culmination:

1. Work with a friend. Use only natural materials to create tools.
2. Work with a friend. Draw pictures of what you think were some of the very first tools used by early people.
3. Work with a friend. Use your imagination to create a play about the discovery of paper. Have class members perform your play for the rest of the class.

Activity 46: Time

In this center the children carry out investigations around the concept of time, using clocks and other timing devices. They are asked to record their observations.

Activity Card

- Use the materials in this center to make some studies of time.
- How is time measured?
- How do clocks measure time?
- What kinds of instruments measure time?
- How are clocks and other timers alike? How are they different?

> • Conduct some investigations and see what you can find out. Then write about your findings.
>
> You may have some other ideas for conducting investigations about time. Try your ideas and see what happens.

Materials

Two or three clocks (for example, a wind-up wristwatch, a quartz watch, a digital clock, a wall clock, an alarm clock, a clock radio, a clock with a sweep second hand) and several timers (for example, stopwatch, hourglass, egg timer)

Thinking Operations Emphasized

Observing and recording; comparing and interpreting data; suggesting hypotheses; identifying assumptions; designing investigations; making decisions; applying principles; evaluating and criticizing; classifying; imagining and creating

Big Ideas

Clocks are used in the accurate measurement of time. Certain tasks take a longer time to do; other tasks take a shorter time.

Notes to the Teacher

The materials in this center may be somewhat more difficult to acquire without relying on personal resources. However, the pupil inquiry that results may be worth the extra effort involved in obtaining the materials. Here are some ideas for getting the materials:

- Ask the parents to donate materials. Make sure they understand that the materials may not necessarily be returned in the same condition. (Thus it is not a good idea to donate the priceless grandfather's clock stored in the attic.)
- Ask personal friends and teaching colleagues for donations of old clocks. They may be happy to unload relics that are just taking up storage space, knowing that the materials will be put to good use.
- Check the local secondhand store or flea market. These resources might net just enough materials to get you started. Make sure, however, that at least one of the clocks may be taken apart.

Debriefing

Here are some examples of types of questions that might be used during initial Debriefing sessions to promote reflection about time and timing devices:

- What observations did you make about how clocks work?
- In what ways are digital clocks like analog clocks? How are they different?
- What are some assumptions that are being made when we time an activity? What are your ideas?
- How are timers like clocks? How are they different? What are your ideas?
- What inaccuracies did you observe among the clocks and timers? How do you explain them? What are your ideas?

Extending

The investigative play in this center may be extended in one or more of the following ways:

1. By adding new activity cards, for example:

   - How long does it take to tie a shoelace? make a paper airplane? blow up a balloon? jump 100 times? fill a glass of water? fill a gallon bucket? bounce a ball 100 times? grow a tooth? read a page of a book? walk to school? write your name? eat your lunch? grow a flower? bake a cake? sew a button on a shirt? Conduct investigations and make observations about the time it takes to do some of these things. Record your findings.

2. By raising more challenging questions during later Debriefing sessions, for example:

   - How long did it take (child) to do 100 bounces? How long did it take (other child)? How do you explain that difference?
   - How long does it take (child) to walk to school? How long does it take (other child)? How do you explain that difference?
   - How long does it take to grow a new tooth? What's your prediction? Why do you think that is true?
   - Why do you suppose it takes longer to grow a flower than it does to bake a cake? How do you explain this?
   - When (child) said it took him 15 minutes to jump 100 times, what assumptions were being made about the timing of this activity?
   - What do you suppose it means when people say that "time flies"? What are your ideas about this?

3. By raising questions that call for examination of some value issues related to the topic, for example:

   Susan's mother tells her that she "wastes her time." Susan likes to spend time sitting in her room by herself. Her mother thinks Susan should be using her time "more productively."

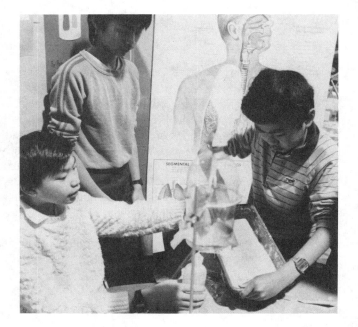

- What are your opinions about "wasting time"? How is time "wasted"? How is time used "productively"? Should we try to be "productively" engaged whenever we can? What are your opinions about this? Can you support your ideas with some examples?

Creating

Before leaving the time study, you may wish to culminate the inquiries by asking the students to undertake one or more of the following tasks:

1. Work with a friend. Make a timing device using a glass of water.
2. Work with a friend. Make a timing device using the sun.
3. Work with a friend. Make a timer using a candle.
4. Write a poem about how you feel when time "drags its feet" or when "time flies."
5. Draw a picture of how it might look when "time flies."

Activity 47: Ourselves (1): Eyes, Ears, Noses, and Tongues

In this center the children carry out investigative play to make observations about individual characteristics and the range of differences among members of the group.

Activity Card

> - Use the materials in this center to make some observations about some of your sense organs.
> - Make some observations of your eyes. Study them and record your findings. Compare your eyes with the eyes of others in your group.
> - Make some observations of your ears. Study them and record what you found. Compare your ears with the ears of others in your group.
> - Make some observations of your nose. Study your nose and record your findings. Compare your nose with the noses of others in your group.
> - Make some observations of your tongue. Study it and record what you observed. Compare your tongue with the tongues of others in your group.
> - How are eyes, ears, noses, and tongues alike? How are they different?
> - Write about your findings.

Materials

Small hand mirrors; shaving mirrors, ceramic or plastic models of eyes and ears, if available; tongue depressors; crayons, colored pencils; large magnifying glass

Thinking Operations Emphasized

Observing and recording; comparing; identifying assumptions; suggesting hypotheses; interpreting data; designing investigations; making decisions; evaluating; summarizing; applying principles; imagining and inventing

Big Ideas

Eyes, nose, tongue, ears, and skin are all human organs. They protect the human organism from harm, alerting it to danger, as well as to pleasure. These organs function differently in different people. Each organ has a range of functioning.

Notes to the Teacher

- This is a safe activity for which few materials need to be gathered. It is a good starter activity for the teacher who is just beginning a sciencing program.
- Before beginning the investigative play, the children should be cautioned about not inserting foreign objects into eyes, ears, and nose in their enthusiasm for inquiry.

Debriefing

The following types of questions may help to promote reflection during initial Debriefing sessions. They should be used selectively.

- What observations did you make about eyes? In what ways are (child's) eyes different from (other child's)? How are they alike? How do you explain the differences?
- What observations did you make about ears? In what ways are (child's) ears different from (other child's)? How are they alike? How do you explain the differences?
- What observations did you make about noses? In what ways is (child's) nose different from yours? How are your noses alike? How do you explain the differences?
- What observations did you make about tongues? In what ways is (child's) tongue different from yours? How are the tongues alike? How do you explain the differences?
- Why do you suppose some people have blue eyes and others have gray or brown? How do you explain this?
- Why do you suppose people's noses have different shapes? How do you explain this?

Extending

The investigative play in this center may be extended in one or more of the following ways:

1. By adding more challenging activity cards, for example:

- What are some things that eyes can do? Conduct some investigations and record your findings.
- What are some things that ears can do? Conduct some investigations and record your findings.
- What are some things that noses can do? Conduct some investigations and record your findings.
- What are some things that tongues can do? Conduct some investigations and record your findings.
- What differences can you observe in these sense organs among the children in your group? How are these differences particularly helpful to each child? Record your findings.
- What child in the group has the best hearing? Conduct some investigations to find this out.

2. By raising more challenging questions in later Debriefing sessions, for example:

- What are some factors that help us see better? What are some things that impair our vision? What are your ideas? How do you know that is true?
- What are some things that help us hear better? What impairs our hearing? What are your ideas? How do you know that is true?
- What helps us smell better? Why do you suppose the sense of smell is important to us? What are your ideas?

- How does the tongue help us taste? How does this work? What are your ideas? How do you know that is true?

3. By raising questions that call for examination of some value issues related to the topic, for example:

Some people have a habit of mocking others who are different. For example, we might try to make fun of people who have visual handicaps. We might call them names like "four eyes" to let the other person know that he or she is being mocked.

- Where do you stand on this kind of behavior? How does it make the person who is doing the name calling feel? How does it make the other person feel?
- What would you do if everyone in your group of boys or girls was ridiculing a child for being different? Would you join in? Would you stand alone? What are your beliefs about this?

Creating

If you wish to extend the inquiries further, you may present students with one or more of the following types of activities:

1. Work with a friend. Draw a picture of each other's eyes, ears, and nose.
2. Work with a friend. Gather data about the eyes of all the children in your class. Make an eye chart showing your findings.
3. Write a story about how your ears got you in trouble.
4. Make some clay models of these important sense organs.

Activity 48: Ourselves (2): Hands and Feet

In this center the children examine their own and each other's hands and feet and make some observations about themselves and the differences observed in the group. They are asked to record their findings.

Activity Card

- Use the materials in this center to study your hands and feet.
- What observations can you make about your hands? Study them and write about what you see.
- Compare each other's hands. How are they alike? How are they different? Record your findings.
- What observations can you make about your feet? Study them and write about what you see.
- Compare each other's feet. How are they alike? How are they different? Record your findings.

Materials

White paper, magnifying glass, mirrors, crayons, pencils, large sheets of paper

Thinking Operations Emphasized

Observing and recording; comparing, collecting, classifying, and interpreting data; suggesting hypotheses; identifying assumptions; designing investigations; making decisions; applying principles; evaluating and criticizing; imagining and creating

Big Ideas

Human hands and feet serve important functions in the human organism. There is a wide range of difference among hands and feet. Handprints and footprints are unique.

Notes to the Teacher

- If you choose to extend this activity into the realm of handprinting and footprinting, the investigative play can become quite messy. Prints are very likely to stray off the paper. So it is probably a good idea to anticipate this, to chat with the children beforehand about carrying out simple precautionary procedures, and to provide sponge, soap, water, and paper towels in the center. If you can overcome your resistance to the creation of a small mess, the activity involving footprinting and handprinting can be both delightful and scientifically rich.

Debriefing

The following types of questions might be raised to promote reflection about the concepts discussed in initial Debriefing sessions. They should be used selectively.

- What observations were made about your hands? What observations were made about your feet?
- In what ways are hands different among people in your group? How do you explain those differences? What are some advantages of such differences?
- In what ways are feet different among people in your group? How do you explain those differences? What are some advantages of such differences?

Extending

The investigative play with hands and feet may be extended in one or more of the following ways:

1. By adding new materials to the center (this is the messy part), for example, ink pads, watercolor paints, and additional paper for fingerprinting, handprinting, footprinting

2. By adding new activity cards, for example:

- Study the fingerprints of all the people in the group. Record your observations.
- Study the footprints of all the people in the group. Record your observations.
- Compare each other's fingerprints, handprints, and footprints. What similarities can be found? What differences? Record your findings.

3. By raising more challenging questions at later Debriefing sessions, for example:

- Why do you suppose everyone has a distinctly different set of fingerprints? handprints? footprints? How do you explain this?
- In what ways are hands like feet? How are they different?
- In what ways are human hands and feet different from and similar to the feet of a monkey? a rabbit? a cat?
- Why do you suppose fingernails and toenails can grow back when they are cut but fingers and toes cannot? How do you explain this? What are your ideas?

4. By raising questions that call for examination of some value issues related to the topic, for example:

People are different in very many ways. Some of them are very small, and some grow to be quite large. Some have very large hands and feet, and some have very small limbs. Some are quite thin; others are not so thin. Some have curly hair, some straight hair, and some have no hair at all!

- Have you heard people mock the appearance of others? Have you heard people call each other rude names to highlight the way in which they are different? What are your opinions about this?
- Should such behavior be approved? ignored? punished?
- When might such behavior be acceptable?
- If you saw this going on in your group, what action might you be willing to take? Where do you stand on this issue?

Creating

Several types of activities may bring this study of hands and feet to culmination, for example:

1. The children may do a handprint or a footprint collage.
2. The hands of all the children in class may be studied and a chart made with the information gathered.
3. The hands of a person over 60 years old may be studied and pictures drawn of the hands.
4. Stories may be written about hands and/or feet, for example, "The Six-fingered Lady," "The Telltale Thumbnail," "The Footprint in the Sand," "The Grotesque Toe," "The Girl with the Purple Nails"

Activity 49: Ourselves (3): Pulse and Heartbeat

In this center the children carry out investigations with pulses and heartbeats and make some observations about the relationship of heartbeat to activity level. They are asked to record their findings.

Activity Card

- Use the materials in the center to conduct some investigations about each other's heartbeat.
- Conduct some investigations to find out about each other's pulse.
- Make a chart and record your observations about the heartbeats of the children in your group.
- Conduct some investigations to find out under what conditions the heartbeat and pulse change. How does it change? Record your findings.

Materials

One or two stethoscopes, graph paper, a watch with a sweep second hand

Thinking Operations Emphasized

Observing and recording; comparing, classifying, and interpreting data; collecting and organizing data; suggesting hypotheses; examining assumptions; summarizing; applying principles; evaluating; making decisions; designing investigations

Big Ideas

Pulse is created by the heart pumping blood through the arteries and can be found in different parts of the body. Exercise and rest can change heartbeat (and pulse).

Notes to the Teacher

- This activity cannot be carried out without the use of stethoscopes, but children's toy stethoscopes are perfectly adequate for the purposes of the inquiry. The school nurse may also be willing to lend a stethoscope for the investigative play.

Debriefing

Questions in the initial Debriefing sessions may follow closely along the lines of the activity card, for example:

- What observations did you make about your own heartbeat?
- What were some similarities you noticed among the members of the group? What were some differences?
- What observations did you make about your pulse? What were some similarities you observed among members of the group? What were some differences?
- What observations did you make about how the beat increased or decreased? How do you explain these changes?
- What observations did you make about the loudness or softness of the sound of the beat? How do you explain those changes?
- What is the connection between what you feel in the pulse and what you hear in the heartbeat? What makes you think that is true?

Extending

The heartbeat and pulse investigative play may be extended in one or more of the following ways:

1. By introducing new activity cards, for example:

   - Jump up and down 20 times. What observations can you make about the change in your heartbeat before and after the jumping exercise? Make a chart or graph showing this information for all the people in your group.
   - Jump up and down 20 times. What observations can you make about the changes in your pulse before and after the jumping? Make a chart or graph showing this information for all the people in your group.
   - Design three exercises. Check your heartbeat and pulse before and after each exercise. Record your findings on a chart or graph showing this information for all the people in your group.

2. By raising more challenging questions at later Debriefing sessions, for example:

   - What observations did you make about the effect of exercise on heartbeat? on pulse? How do you explain this? What are your ideas?
   - What is the relationship of the heartbeat to the pulse? What are your ideas? What information in your charts helps you make this observation?
   - What do you suppose might happen to the heartbeat and pulse during a long sleep? What are your ideas? What information do you have that allows you to make that assumption?
   - Where do you suppose the noise comes from when you hear your heartbeat? What are your ideas?
   - What do you suppose makes the heart work? What are your ideas?
   - What do you suppose happens when a person gets a heart transplant? What might be some effects? What are your ideas?

3. By raising questions that call for examination of some value issues related to the topic, for example:

Joey's father has a "bad" heart. He has had one heart attack, and his doctor has told him that he must be very careful from now on. He must stop smoking, and he must be very careful about the food that he eats. The doctor has said that if Mr. Keith does not follow the doctor's orders, he may be in serious trouble. Joey's father is having a very hard time following the doctor's orders. He is having a particularly hard time giving up smoking. Joey is very distressed. He is afraid that if his father keeps smoking, he will die.

- What should Joey do? Do you have any ideas about this? Is this a serious concern? Should Joey just mind his own business and let his father do as he likes?

Creating

The heartbeat and pulse studies may be culminated in one or more of the following ways:

1. Ask the children to work with a friend. Ask them to draw a picture of how they think the heart works.
2. Ask the children to write a poem about a person with a "loving heart."
3. Ask the children to work with a partner. Ask them to write a mystery story called "The Heart Machine."
4. Ask the children to work with partners. Ask them to use whatever materials are available in class to make a model of a human heart. Ask them to try to figure out a way to show how the heart works.

Activity 50: Ourselves (4): Humans and the Environment

In this center the children carry on investigations to examine the effects of certain environmental conditions on aspects of personal well-being. They are asked to record their findings.

Activity Card

- Use the materials in the center to find out how certain environmental conditions affect the way we feel.
- Carry out some investigations that show how certain sounds affect you.
- Carry out some investigations that show how light and darkness affect you.
- Carry out some investigations that show how the space that you are in affects you.
- Talk with each other about what you experienced and what you found. Then record your ideas.

You may have some other ideas for conducting investigations about how environmental conditions affect your well-being. Try them out and see what discoveries you can make.

Materials

Hammer, nails, chalk, small blackboard, saw, scraps of fabric, scissors, tape recorder, tapes of several different kinds of music, earphones, electric motor, flashlight, 150-watt light bulb, lamp, eyeshades, dark glasses, pillows, carton large enough for a small child to fit inside, primary chair, small stool, one or two timers

Thinking Operations Emphasized

Designing investigations; observing and recording; collecting and interpreting data; examining assumptions; suggesting hypotheses; applying principles; making decisions; evaluating and criticizing; summarizing; imagining and inventing

Big Ideas

Environmental conditions affect living organisms. Living organisms in turn affect the environment. The study of this relationship is called ecology.

Notes to the Teacher

- This activity is probably more suitable for pupils who have had some background with the Play-Debrief-Replay sciencing program, since it calls for a higher degree of independent functioning in the center.
- It is conceivable that pupils may attempt investigations that are potentially hazardous in this center (for example, music of excessively loud volume is physically harmful to hearing), so teachers should exercise care that safety procedures and rules about what investigations may or may not be carried out are strictly enforced.

Debriefing

The following types of questions raised during initial Debriefing sessions may stimulate reflection as well as richer Replay activity. They should be used selectively.

- What observations did you make of the effect of sounds on how you feel?
- What sounds made you feel comfortable? What hypotheses might explain that?
- What sounds made you feel uncomfortable? How would you explain that?
- What observations did you make of the effect of light and darkness on how you feel? What conditions made you feel comfortable or uncomfortable? How do you explain these effects? What hypotheses can you suggest?
- What role does time play in the effects of these conditions on how you feel? What examples can you give to support your ideas?
- What observations did you make of the effect of space on how you feel? What space conditions made you feel comfortable or uncomfortable? How do you explain these effects? What hypotheses can you suggest?
- What other environmental conditions affect your sense of well-being? What examples can you give of how this works? How do you explain it?

Extending

When students' interest in their inquiries with light, space, and sound appear to be diminishing, you may wish to extend the ecological investigations in some of the following ways:

1. By adding certain new materials to the center that would lead to new investigations, for example, items with pleasing and noxious smells (flowers, perfumes, certain spices and alcohol, gasoline or cleaning fluid, decaying fish or eggs), "beautiful" and "ugly" examples of art, items with extreme temperatures (such as ice-cold and very hot water)
2. By introducing new activity cards that invite investigations with these new materials
3. By raising more challenging questions in later Debriefing sessions, for example:

- What observations have you made about the kinds of environmental conditions that affect the way we feel? What list of conditions can be generated? How might these be classified?
- How do these conditions affect the way we live? What examples can you give to support your ideas?
- How do we in turn affect the environment? What observations have you made about how this occurs? What examples can you give? What list may be generated? How might these be classified?
- In what ways are we affected by temperature? sound? light? aesthetics? food? the air we breathe? How do you know this? What examples can you give to support your ideas?
- What kind of an environment do we need in order to live comfortably? safely? How do you know this? What examples can you give to support your ideas?
- In what ways do we change our environment? What examples can you give? What are some consequences of this? How do you know?

4. By raising questions that call for examination of some value issues related to the topic, for example:

   Arthur received a portable tape recorder and earphones for his birthday. He likes to turn the volume way up on his set and listen to the music at the loudest volume. He thinks that this is great fun. His mother has told him many times that this is very likely to hurt his ears and may result in his becoming deaf. But Arthur's mother does not always know when he is listening or how loud the music is.

   - What might be done here? If you were Arthur's friend, what action might you take?
   - Do you agree with Arthur's mother? Is this something that we should care about? Or should we ignore it and let Arthur listen to music as loud as he wishes? What are your views on this issue?

Creating

You may wish to have your students undertake some of the following activities to culminate the ecology investigations:

1. Work with a partner. Together, design and draw an illustration of the "perfect environment to learn in." Explain how this perfect space makes for more comfortable learning.
2. Work with a partner. Imagine a town in which the water was no longer fit to drink. Write a story about it. How did it happen? What was the effect of such a condition on the lives of the people?
3. Work with a partner. Create a plan for improving the school environment. Share your plan with the others in your class, and find out what you would need to do to put it into operation.

CATEGORY C: WHO'S AFRAID OF SPIDERS?

Activities for the intrepid teacher, involving greater mess, greater risk, or a greater management of personal distaste

Activity 51: Squids

Activity 52: Spiders

Activity 53: Minibeasts

Activity 54: Live Animals

Activity 55: Earthworms

Activity 56: Eggs

Activity 57: Colors

Activity 58: Metals

Activity 59: Plastic

Activity 60: Garbage

Activity 51: Squids

In this activity the children examine squids and make some observations about this marine animal. They are asked to record their observations.

Activity Card

- Use the materials in this center to make some observations of squids.
- What can you observe about the shape of the squid?
- What observations can you make about some of its parts?
- How do you suppose the different parts are used?
- Talk with each other and discuss your ideas about this.
- Then make some illustrations showing what you found.

Materials

One squid for each pair of children working in the center; scissors, magnifying lenses, paper towels, newspapers to cover tables

Thinking Operations Emphasized

Observing and recording; collecting, comparing, classifying, and interpreting data; suggesting hypotheses; examining assumptions; designing investigations; making decisions; imagining and creating

Big Ideas

Squids are sea animals. Eight of the ten tentacles surround the mouth. The skeleton is like a shell, but located inside the body.

Notes to the Teacher

- This is an activity in which you might have to control some initial impulse to show revulsion. Gentle and benign creatures of the deep, squids may be purchased fresh, if you live in coastal California, or frozen, in many fish stores or large, well-equipped supermarkets. They are an inexpensive source of protein and make for quite wonderful sciencing activities.
- Instead of scissors, sharper dissecting tools may be used. This will depend on your judgment of student responsibility to work with these more advanced tools.

Debriefing

After the children have had ample opportunity to dissect and study squids, you may wish to raise the following types of questions in Debriefing sessions:

- What observations did you make about the shape of the squid?
- What observations did you make about some of its parts?
- What observations did you make about the inner parts of the animal?
- What do you suppose is the function of that part of the animal?
- How are squids different from fish? How are they like fish?

Extending

It is entirely likely that the squid supply will be exhausted well before the children's enthusiasm for this dissection has waned. You might wish to extend the sciencing activity in one or more of the following ways:

1. By introducing other marine animals for dissection and comparison, for example, shellfish, mollusks, and fish with backbones
2. By creating new activity cards reflecting the newly introduced materials
3. By raising more challenging questions in later Debriefing sessions, for example:

   - What observations did you make about the squids that suggest how this animal moves in the water?

- What observations did you make about the squids that suggest how this animal might take in food? what food it might take in? how it is born? how it lives in the water?
- What other animals that live in the sea are like the squid? What are some similarities? What other sea animals are very different? What are some differences?

4. By introducing other animal parts for dissecting, for example, beef hearts, kidneys, nonviscerated chickens
5. By raising questions that call for examination of some value issues related to the topic, for example:

"Squids are just dumb animals," said Mickey. "It doesn't matter if we cut them up. They don't feel anything anyway."

- What is your view on this? Is Mickey right? How do you know? What examples can you give to support your opinions?

Creating

As a culmination to the squid dissections, you might have the pupils undertake one or more of the following activities:

1. Find out some good ways of cooking squid. Collect the materials you need and make a "squid feast" for the class.
2. Work with a friend. Draw some pictures of squids.
3. Work with a friend. Make a model of a squid from paper or clay.
4. Write a poem, "The Lonely Squid."
5. Write a story, "The Squid That Nobody Loved."

Activity 52: Spiders

In this center the students are asked to collect spiders as their contribution to setting up the center. They will then observe the spiders and record their observations.

Activity Card

- Spend some time observing the spiders in the jars.
- What observations can you make about spiders?
- What do they look like?
- What kinds of parts does a spider's body have?

- What are these parts used for?
- What observations can you make about what the spiders do?
- Talk with each other about your observations. Then write about what you have found.

You may have made other observations. Write about what you have learned, or draw some pictures.

Materials

A few large glass jars or an aquarium to house the spiders so that they may be easily observed; smaller containers, either plastic or glass, for the children's spider hunt; magnifying lenses

Thinking Operations Emphasized

Observing and recording; collecting, comparing, classifying, and interpreting data; suggesting hypotheses; examining assumptions; making decisions; designing investigations; summarizing; imagining and creating

Big Ideas

There are many different kinds of spiders, but all spiders have similar body parts and structures that contribute to their being able to get food and reproduce. Most spiders must eat other living things to survive.

Notes to the Teacher

- Prior to beginning work on this center, it may be helpful to reacquaint yourself with the introductory material that deals with ethical concerns about using living things in the classroom. It may be helpful, too, to review the discussion about collecting and caring for living creatures found in the "Notes to the Teacher" section of Activity 53.
- You may be asking, "How do I tell children where to find spiders?" The answer to that is, "Everywhere." In a nonurban location, the possibilities are endless. In more urban settings, the children may look in and around flowerbeds, in parks, in and around trees and gardens, and in the corners of homes and the school.
- What makes containers suitable for collecting live trophies should be explained to the children. For example, they should have ample room and secure lids, so that spiders will not wander off to more hospitable territory.
- Spiders are very fragile and can easily be damaged if children do not exercise extreme caution in collecting and containing them. Collected spiders may be transferred to

large glass jars or a large aquarium complete with "furnishings." Spiders can be fed flies and must have a supply of water, or else they will die.

Debriefing

After some initial observations and recording, the following types of questions may be raised in early Debriefing sessions to give added focus to the inquiries. They should, however, be used selectively.

- What observations have you made about spiders?
- What observations did you make about the shape of spiders? What did you notice about the structure of the spider's body?
- What did you observe about this animal's behavior?
- In what ways are spiders like flies? ants? caterpillars? How are they different?
- In what ways were the spiders you collected alike? How were they different?

Extending

The children's interest in spiders may be extended in one or more of the following ways:

1. By introducing new activity cards, for example:

- What observations can be made about how and what a spider eats? Study the spiders and record your findings.
- What observations can be made about the behavior of different kinds of spiders? Study the spiders and record your findings.
- What observations can be made when two or more spiders are in the same habitat? Observe the spiders and record your findings.
- How does the spider know there is danger present? Make some observations and write about some examples that support your ideas.

2. By raising more challenging questions in later Debriefing sessions, for example:

- What observations can be made about how and what a spider eats? Why do you suppose that food is particularly good for a spider?
- How does a spider spin a web? What are your ideas on this?
- What are webs made of? What do you think?
- What do you suppose is the purpose of a web? What are your hypotheses?
- What happens when a web gets a hole in it? What do you think?
- What similarities and differences do you find in spider webs? How do you explain these?
- In what ways are spiders like humans? How are they different?
- How do spiders protect themselves? What examples can you give from your observations?
- Why are people afraid of spiders? What are your ideas about this?

3. By raising questions that call for examination of value issues related to the topic, for example:

> Every time Jack sees a spider, he stomps on it. When Bruno asked him why he did that, he said, "They're poisonous animals and they can kill you. It's better if we kill them first."

- How do you suppose Jack got those ideas? Is he right? Do you believe this too?
- Where did your ideas about spiders come from? What data do you have that support your ideas?
- If Bruno disagrees with Jack, what action should he take?
- If Jack managed to kill all the spiders in his garden, what do you suppose might be some consequences? What are your ideas on this?

Creating

You may wish to culminate the sciencing activity on spiders in one or more of the following ways:

1. Ask the children to make a book that tells the most interesting things learned about spiders. Each child may write or draw one page in this book.
2. Ask children to look for spiders in their natural habitat. Ask them to observe the spiders, without disturbing them, and to record, either in writing or drawing, their observations.
3. Ask the children to find some spider webs to study. Ask them to record their findings.
4. Ask the children to work with a partner. Ask each pair to design and build a spider web, using whatever materials are found in class.
5. Ask the children to write a poem called "The Giant Spider."
6. Ask the children to work in pairs to plan a program that would help people overcome their fear of spiders. What would have to be done? How do they know this would work?

Activity 53: Minibeasts

In this center the children collect minibeasts (insects) of all kinds, bring them to the center, observe them, and record their findings.

Activity Card

- Spend some time observing the insects in the jars.
- What observations can you make about these insects?
- What observations can you make about their size? their shape? their colors? the way they move? how they eat? what they eat?

- How do they protect themselves? What observations can you make about the ways in which different insects do this?
- Study two different insects closely. How are they alike? What kinds of differences do you find? Write about what you have found.

You may wish to make some other observations. Study the insects and see what you can learn.

Materials

For collecting: small strainers, small plastic containers for carrying the animals back to school; for keeping in the classroom: some large glass jars with cheesecloth covering or an aquarium, leaves and twigs to form a "natural" habitat

Thinking Operations Emphasized

Observing and recording; collecting, comparing, classifying, and interpreting data; examining assumptions; suggesting hypotheses; summarizing; making decisions; evaluating; applying principles; imagining and creating

Big Ideas

There is great biological diversity in the insect world. Insects have a large variety of body parts and internal structures that help them make or find food and reproduce.

Notes to the Teacher

Before beginning work in this center the children will first be involved in the collection of insects for study. Certain procedures should be made explicit for this part of the activity, for example:

1. *Where to look for minibeasts:* If the school is in a suburban or rural area, minibeasts will be abundant—in ditches, ponds, fields, woods, orchards, and the like. If the school is in an urban area, the children may look in corners of attics and basements, in parks and gardens, on beaches or riverbanks, at construction sites, in trees, and under rocks.
2. *Safety precautions:* If the children are to be looking near deep water, instructions about water safety are very important. If the children are to be looking in and around ponds of stagnant water, thorough hand washing is essential.[3] Consider, too, the use of plastic gloves that can be purchased inexpensively in large quantities.
3. *Precautions that should be taken in the collection of live animals:* Some guidelines may be established that would help children develop a sensitivity to the need to give living things proper care and respect, for example:

   - A good collector searches carefully.
   - A good collector does not destroy the insect's environment.

- A good collector handles the animals carefully, taking care not to hurt or damage them.
- A good collector replaces any part of the animals' environment that he or she has disturbed.
- Good collectors do not collect animals indiscriminately. They take only what they need for study.
- Good collectors do not aim for the biggest collection. They collect carefully and selectively.

4. *Guidelines for keeping living things healthfully and safely in the classroom:* These guidelines would include the following:

- Minibeasts need "homes" where they can live comfortably, with adequate food, air, and water.
- Minibeasts need homes in which they can be observed with a minimum of disruption to their lives.
- Insect homes should be secure so that they are discouraged from departing on their own.[4]

Debriefing

The following types of questions may help to give added focus to pupils' inquiries. They should be used selectively.

- What observations did you make about these insects?
- What observations did you make about shapes? sizes? colors? the way they move? what they eat? their behavior?
- In what ways are these insects alike? How are they different?
- How might they be classified? What kinds of categories might be set up?
- How do you suppose insects see? How do they hear? What makes you think so?
- How do insects protect themselves from danger? How do you know? What examples can you give?

Extending

Pupils' interest in the minibeast inquiry may be extended in one or more of the following ways:

1. By adding new minibeasts to the center, for example, caterpillars, earthworms, slugs, moths, beetles, flies, wasps, ants, grasshoppers
2. By introducing new activity cards
3. By raising more challenging questions in later Debriefing sessions, for example:

- What do you suppose this animal's natural "home" is like? What makes you think that is true?
- How do you think this animal is born? What are your ideas about this? What makes you think that is true?

- How does this animal communicate with others of its species? What are your ideas on this?
- What do you suppose the antennae are for? Why do you think that?
- What do you suppose this animal is useful for? What are your ideas?
- How do you suppose this animal reproduces? What are your ideas on this?

4. By raising questions that call for examination of value issues related to the topic, for example:

> Alice was in her garden observing some ants. She had put a piece of apple out. First, one ant found it. Then, in a short while, there were swarms of ants on the apple. Alice thought that there had to be some way in which the first ant told the other ants in the colony about the apple. This confirmed Alice's belief that ants, even though lowly animals, had "intelligence."

- Where do you stand on this issue? Do ants have intelligence?
- Where do your ideas on this come from? What supporting data have you gathered? What examples do you have to support your point of view?

Creating

There are many ways to extend this minibeast inquiry into more creative activities. Here are some examples of activities that the students might undertake:

1. Work with a friend. Choose one animal and study it carefully. Then draw some illustrations of it.
2. Work with a friend. Make a large model of any animal in your collection, out of papier-mâché.
3. Write a story, "The Bug That Nobody Liked."
4. Work with a friend. Find out how to build a wormarium. Gather the materials you need and build it.

Activity 54: Live Animals

In this center the children make extensive observations of the behavior of a live animal, in captivity. They are asked to record their findings.

Activity Card

> - Study the animal for a long period of time.
> - What observations can you make about: its shape? its color? its skin or fur? its legs? its tail? the way it moves? its hearing? how it sees? how it makes sounds?
> - What observations can you make about how this animal protects itself from danger? What examples can be seen of this behavior?

- Talk to each other about your observations. Then write about what you found.

You may have other ideas for studying this animal. Make your observations and write or tell about what you learned.

Materials

One or more animals that can easily be kept in a cage in the classroom, for example, guinea pig, rabbit, lizard, hamster, snake, white mouse, bird, tropical fish; an appropriate cage or tank; food and water supply; other materials to create a "natural" habitat for the animal selected

Thinking Operations Emphasized

Observing and recording; collecting, comparing, classifying, and interpreting data; suggesting hypotheses; identifying assumptions; designing investigations; making decisions; summarizing; applying principles; evaluating; imagining and creating

Big Ideas

Some animals are alike in the way they live and in the things they do. Others are very different from one another. Animals have certain features that help them live in different environments.

Notes to the Teacher

- Live animals should not come into the classroom until the children have developed sufficiently responsible behavior about their care and protection. Although guinea pigs, rabbits, and hamsters are the more usual classroom guests, you may find much more fun in having Sam the Snake or Leapin' Lizard as a classroom guest.
- These pets are generally found in a local pet shop, where instruction for their care and feeding are part of the purchase.
- Animals from the wild should not be brought in for study unless you can be absolutely sure about their health and about their responses to children. (Will they bite? Do they carry diseases?)
- Children should be involved in the care and feeding of the animal, cleaning the cage, and other responsibilities as part of this study. Guidelines for carrying out these duties should be explicit.
- Ethical considerations for the care and keeping of live animals in the classroom should be carefully reviewed. These are found in the introductory section of this chapter.

Debriefing

The following types of questions may be helpful in promoting reflection about animal behavior and should be used selectively during initial Debriefing sessions:

- What observations did you make about the animal? What observations did you make about the animal's sleeping and waking behavior? its exercise? its feeding habits? how it sets up a burrow? how it responds when children interact with it?
- What observations did you make about the structure of the animal? its skin or fur? its legs? its tail? the way it moves? how it breathes? how it sees? how it hears? how it makes sounds?
- In what ways is this animal like other animals of that species? How is it different?
- Why do you suppose this animal would make a good pet? What are your ideas? What are the attributes of a good pet?
- How do you suppose this animal lives outside of captivity? What are your ideas?
- How does the animal protect itself from danger? How do you know? What examples can you give from your observations?
- How do you suppose the animal feels about living in this classroom? What makes you think that? What behavior did you see that supports that assumption?

Extending

The live animal study may be extended in one or more of the following ways:

1. By introducing another animal, of a different species, into the classroom, for example, chicks, parakeet, or turtle
2. By introducing new activity cards that reflect the extensions of the center
3. By raising more challenging questions in later Debriefing sessions, for example:

   - In what ways is this animal like (another animal)? How are they different?
   - What other animals may be grouped along with this animal? Why do you think they should be grouped together?
   - How smart is this animal? How do you know? What did you see in the animal's behavior that supports that assumption?
   - What kinds of feelings did the animal show in its behavior? What examples support that assumption?
   - How is this animal born? What are your ideas about that? How are its young like human babies? How are they different?
   - If you wanted to teach this animal something, how might you do that? In what ways is your teaching method different from or similar to the teaching you see at school?
   - Is it better for an animal to live in the wild or to live in a protected environment in the care of humans? What are your ideas on this? What makes you think that is good?

4. By raising questions that call for examination of some value issues related to the topic, for example:

- Do animals have feelings? What are your thoughts about this? Where did you get your ideas? What supporting data can you give?
- Can animals be trained to communicate with humans? What are your thoughts about this? Where did you get your ideas? What examples can you give to support your ideas?
- Do animals have intelligence? What are your thoughts about this? Where did you get your ideas? What examples can you give to support your point of view?
- Should humans be "in charge" of animals? For example, if an animal population has become too large, should humans attempt to control that population by systematically killing off the animals, as in the case of the wolves in northern Canada? What are your views on this? Where do you stand on this issue?

Creating

You may wish to bring the live-animal study to culmination by having the pupils undertake one or more of the following activities:

1. Ask the children to work in pairs. Have them collect pictures of animals, set up a classification system for their collection, and put their pictures in a scrapbook organized by category.
2. Ask the children to work with a friend to make papier-mâché models of any animals of their choice.
3. Ask the children to write poetry about a favorite animal.
4. Ask the children to write about what it would be like to live the life of a raccoon in the wild or an eagle.
5. Ask the children to write about what it would be like to live the life of a tiger in a zoo.
6. Ask the children to write about an animal that is scary for them.

Activity 55: Earthworms

In this center the children work with the common earthworm and with a number of different surfaces—hard and soft, dark and light, smooth and rough, wet and dry—to determine the effects of environment on behavior. They are asked to make observations and record their findings.

Activity Card

> - Study the earthworms for a long time.
> - Then, one by one, using the materials in the center, change the surfaces on which you place the earthworms.
> - What observations can be made about the effect of changing the environment on the earthworm's behavior?
> - Talk with each other about your observations.
> - Then write about what you found.

Materials

Earthworms (found in the school yard or a park or, if necessary, purchased from a biological supply house); a variety of items with flat surfaces, such as pieces of cloth with different textures, wood, aluminum foil, plastic wrap; some earth, some sand, water, sandpaper; several magnifying lenses

Thinking Operations Emphasized

Observing and recording; collecting, comparing, classifying, and interpreting data; suggesting hypotheses; examining assumptions; evaluating and criticizing; making decisions; designing investigations; imagining and inventing

Big Ideas

Earthworms are simple animals that live in the soil. They help aerate the soil and aid plant growth. Changing their environment results in a change of behavior.

Notes to the Teacher

- Water should be used only to dampen the surfaces of the soil or sand. Earthworms can drown! Several magnifying lenses are essential for this center, since such close study will yield considerably more data and aid in generating hypotheses.
- Worms can be kept in a plastic pan filled with about 3 to 4 inches of soil, kept moist but not sodden. Children may feed worms by sprinkling fine cuttings of grass, lettuce, or other greens on top of the soil and covering with a fresh layer of soil. This procedure should be repeated every two or three days.

Debriefing

During initial Debriefing sessions, questions such as the following may be helpful in promoting reflection. They should, however, be used selectively.

- What observations did you make about the body of the earthworm?
- What observations did you make about the motion of the earthworm as it moves across a surface?
- What differences in moving behavior were you able to notice and to record?
- Which kinds of surfaces seem to be the preferred environments of the earthworms? How did you determine this? What hypotheses might explain this?
- What other surfaces might be tried? Why do you think that surface would be good to try?

Extending

When the children have had ample time to investigate in detail the characteristics of the earthworms and their behavior under several different environmental conditions, you may wish to extend their inquiries in some of the following ways:

1. By adding new materials to the center, for example, materials with different surfaces. Other materials that would create new environmental effects might also be considered; for example, a large light bulb could be introduced to create differences in brightness and warmth on one side of the living area, leaving the other side untreated, or a bag of ice cubes might be used to cool down one area, while leaving another area untreated.
2. By introducing new activity cards to reflect any new material added to the center
3. By including more challenging questions in later Debriefing sessions, for example:

    - What hypotheses can you suggest for the observed effects of different conditions?
    - What other environmental conditions might we investigate? What might you expect to observe? What makes you think that?
    - What does this study tell you about the relationship of environment to behavior? How is this true with other animals? What examples can you give? What inquiries might be set up to test those ideas?

4. By raising questions that call for the examination of value issues related to the topic, for example:

    - How does the earthworm feel about participating in these experiments? How do you know that? Do earthworms have feelings? How do you know that?
    - What is your opinion about experimenting with live animals? Should this be done? Under what circumstances? What, if anything, might lead you to change your ideas? What are some potential consequences of such experimentation? What data do you have to support your ideas?

Creating

When the limits of the investigative play seem just about reached, it might be useful to culminate the inquiries with one or more of the following tasks:

1. Ask the students to work in trios to gather the materials for a "worm farm." They will have to remember to keep the soil moist. A small piece of wood or a rock on the soil surface for the worms to crawl beneath is a good idea. Worms need privacy too! Worms can be fed with greens, cornmeal, or even particles of food from the family table. About once a week, the contents of the farm can be spread on a table and examined closely with a magnifying lens. The pupils may record any changes in the physical characteristics of the worms themselves and describe changes in the soil or in the contents of the farm.
2. Have the pupils work in pairs to draw a picture of the earthworm based on their observations both with the naked eye and with the magnifying lenses.
3. Have the children work in pairs to write a story called "Marvin, My Pet Earthworm."
4. Have the children work in pairs or alone to write a story or a poem about George, the Marsworm.
5. The children may wish to collect data about animal experimentation. Reports may be presented with at least two points of view: benefits to humankind and excesses of animal experimentation.

Activity 56: Eggs

In this center the children work with hen's eggs to observe some of their general characteristics. They are asked to record their observations.

Activity Card

- Use the materials in this center to make some studies of eggs.
- What observations can you make of the outside of eggs?
- What observations can you make of the inside of eggs?
- What observations can be made about texture? size? weight? color? the various parts of eggs? smell? shape?
- What observations can be made about thickness? strength?
- What differences do you find among the eggs in the center? What similarities?
- Try some investigations to see what you can discover. Talk with each other about what you found. Then record your observations.

You may have some additional ideas for conducting inquiries to study eggs. Try your ideas and see what you can discover.

Materials

Several hen's eggs, preferably brown and white (one egg for each pair of students working in the center); bright light; paper or aluminum foil plates; paper towels or newspaper; blunt knife; probing sticks (toothpicks or tongue depressors); magnifying lenses

Thinking Operations Emphasized

Observing and recording; comparing and classifying data; interpreting data; suggesting hypotheses; designing investigations; applying principles; making decisions; evaluating; imagining and creating

Big Ideas

Hens (and many other animals) lay eggs as a means of reproducing their young. The inside of a fertilized hen's egg contains an embryo that develops into a chick.

Notes to the Teacher

- This activity is definitely messy. It is very important, however, that each pair of students be allowed to break their own egg and carefully examine its contents. Do not discard the shells, as there is much to observe about them as well.
- If you are going to extend the activity into the hatching stage, such a move requires some prior consideration. For example, what will happen to the young chicks? Has a home for them been established? Have steps been taken to convey the chicks to that home? Will the chicks be disposed of? If so, how will this be handled? In what ways will children's feelings about this be dealt with? Another reading of the ethical considerations for the care and keeping of live animals, found in the introductory section of this chapter, may be helpful. Some prior research, and perhaps consultation with the high school biology teacher, may also be of use.
- Here are some points that you will want to know:
  - Eggs will require about 21 days to hatch.
  - They must be kept warm (102–104°F) in an incubator.
  - They must be kept moist (sprinkle them with water early in the morning and before leaving school, and keep the incubator water well full).
  - They must be rotated, especially for the first eight or nine days. Turn them over early in the morning, at noon, and upon leaving school.
  - Do not help the chick to escape the shell.
  - About an hour after the chick is hatched, move it to a brooder. (A brooder can be a small box kept warm, but not hot, with a small light bulb close by or directly inside.)
  - Feed the chicks starter mash, but don't handle them too much.

Debriefing

The following examples of questions may elevate levels of thinking about eggs and stimulate additional investigations. They should, however, be used selectively.

- What observations did you make about the shell?
- What hypotheses can you suggest to explain its shape?
- What observations did you make about its thickness? What other observations did you make about the shell?
- What differences did you observe when you examined the shell under bright light? with your magnifier?
- How do you explain the differences in the colors of the shells? What hypotheses can you suggest to explain them?
- What observations did you make about the inside of the egg? What observations did you make about the different parts of the egg?
- What other observations did you make with your magnifying glass?
- In what ways were the eggs alike? How were they different?
- From what part of the egg does the chicken develop? What makes you think that? What data are you using to support your idea?
- What other animals lay eggs? Can you make a list of the animals that lay eggs? How can this list be classified? In what ways might these eggs be similar? What makes you think so?
- What are eggs good for? How do you know that is true?

Extending

When the children seem to have exhausted their initial investigations, you may wish to use one or more of the following ideas to extend the inquiries:

1. By introducing new materials, for example, asking the children to collect other kinds of eggs (quail, duck, goose, turkey, fish, insect) for study and investigative play
2. By introducing new activity cards reflecting the additional materials, for example:

   - Comparing fish eggs and poultry eggs
   - Comparing fertile and infertile eggs

3. By hatching eggs in the classroom
4. By raising more challenging questions in later Debriefing sessions, for example:

   - How do different eggs differ? How are they alike?
   - How are fish eggs like poultry eggs? How are they different?
   - How are insect eggs similar to and different from poultry eggs? fish eggs?
   - Where do eggs come from? How are they formed? How do you know that?
   - What happens in the case of animals that do not lay eggs? How is the embryo cared for?
   - What are some differences between fertilized and unfertilized eggs? What are some similarities?
   - How do chickens hatch? How is this different from other birthing? How do you know that?

5. By raising questions that call for examination of some value issues related to the topic, for example:

Rapunzel said, "I never eat eggs. Eating eggs is the same as murdering baby chickens."

- What are your views on this? Is this true?
- Should we never eat eggs? What data support your opinions?

Creating

When the children have exhausted their interest in investigative play with eggs, opportunities may be created to extend their thinking into a more creative realm, for example:

1. Ask the pupils to work in pairs to draw detailed illustrations of specimen eggs of chickens, fish, insects, and other animals.
2. Ask selected pupils to undertake the care of a baby chick and to observe and record its stages of development.
3. Ask the pupils to write a story describing what it is like to be in a shell and narrating the hatching process.

Activity 57: Colors

In this center the children use paints, dyes, and prisms to study colors. They are asked to record their observations.

Activity Card

> - Use the materials in this center to conduct some investigations with colors.
> - What observations did you make about colors?
> - What observations did you make about how colors change?
> - What observations did you make about how colors mix?
> - Talk with each other about your observations.
> - Then write about what you found.
>
> You may have some other ideas for using the materials in this center. Try them out and see what new discoveries you can make.

Materials

Several prisms; watercolor paints: reds, yellows, blues, whites; food coloring or other dyes; white paper; several transparent containers; eyedroppers, straws, spoons

Thinking Operations Emphasized

Observing and recording; gathering, comparing, and interpreting data; examining assumptions; suggesting hypotheses; applying principles; evaluating; summarizing; designing investigations; making decisions; creating and imagining

Big Ideas

Sunlight is a mixture of many different-colored rays, even though it looks almost white. White light separates into these colors when it goes through a prism.

Notes to the Teacher

- You may want to remind the children that food coloring will stain. It may be a good idea to provide sponges, soap, and paper towels for cleanup, as well as plastic coverings for the table and floors and possibly smocks for the children.

Debriefing

The following types of questions may contribute to pupils' reflection about color. They should, however, be used selectively.

- What observations did you make about colors?
- What observations did you make about how colors change?
- What observations did you make about the colors seen from the prism?
- How are the colors made by the paint different from the colors made by the dyes?
- What observations did you make about the way colors come from the prism? How are the colors from the prism different from the paint colors?
- What investigations did you make with color mixing? What observations did you make about how colors mix?
- Why do you suppose red and yellow together make orange? How do you explain this?

Extending

After the students have had sufficient time to carry out investigative play with the colors, you may wish to extend their inquiries in one or more of the following ways:

1. By adding materials to the center, for example, mirrors, crayons, oil paints, pastels, additional paper of different textures and colors, pieces of fabric of different types and textures, pieces of plastic sheeting
2. By introducing new activity cards that reflect the materials added
3. By raising more challenging questions in later Debriefing sessions, for example:

   - In what ways is the color yellow made by the paint different from the color yellow seen in the prism? How do you explain the differences? What are your ideas?
   - Why do you suppose the prism needs the sun to make color? What are your ideas? How do you explain this?
   - Where do you suppose colors come from? What are your ideas?
   - Why do you suppose a prism disperses colors? What is there about it that allows it to do this? How can you explain this? Why can't mirrors do the same thing? What are your ideas?
   - Why do you suppose you can't see colors in the dark? How do you explain this? What are your ideas?
   - When (student) sees red, does he or she see the same color as (other student)? How do you know this is true? What investigations can you make to help you find out?
   - What relationship does color have to feelings? How do you know that is true? What examples can you give to support your ideas?

4. By raising questions that call for examination of value issues related to the topic, for example:

   Pauline says that every time she wears a yellow dress, bugs come to her. She says that bugs are attracted by the color yellow.

   - Is this true? Do you believe this? What data can you give to support your opinion?

Creating

Some of the following types of more creative activities may be used to culminate the color investigations:

1. Have the children do tie-dying and other textile dying.
2. Have the children collect materials to make natural dyes, for example, onion skins, marigolds, lichen, raspberries, blueberries.[5]
3. Have the children make batik.
4. Have the children write poetry about rainbows.
5. Have the children write stories about colors, for example: "The Boy Who Hated Yellow" or "Why Red Makes Me Mad."

Activity 58: Metals

In this center the children carry out investigative play with a variety of metals in order to make observations about properties of metals. They are asked to record their observations.

Activity Card

> - Use the materials in this center to conduct some investigations with metals.
> - How are these metals alike? How are they different?
> - Make some observations about the differences in strength, hardness, texture, and pliability.
> - Talk with each other about what you have found.
> - Then write about your observations.
>
> You may have some other ideas for conducting investigations with the materials in this center. Try out your ideas and see what discoveries you can make.

Materials

A variety of pieces of different types of metal (for example, copper, tin, brass, lead, steel, aluminum, nickel, cast iron), a variety of types of metal wire (for example, solder, copper, aluminum), hammer, steel wool, bolts, sandpaper, water, nail, screws, staples, candle (or other source of heat), heavy-duty shears, soldering iron

Thinking Operations Emphasized

Observing and recording; collecting, comparing, and classifying; examining assumptions; suggesting hypotheses; designing investigations; applying principles; summarizing; evaluating; making decisions; imagining and creating

Big Ideas

Metals can be described by what they are made of, their color, weight, texture, strength, flexibility. Metals can be changed under certain conditions, such as heating, or combining them. Different metals are suitable for different purposes.

Notes to the Teacher

- Scraps of metal may be acquired through one or more of the following sources (take your "begging bag" along): the high school metalworking shop, a local construction site, a machine shop, an auto-body shop, a building supply outlet.
- Metal products may also be included in this center, for example, aluminum foil, pots and pans and other cooking utensils, toy cars and airplanes, can openers, ball bearings, magnets, coins, springs, marine propeller or shaft, automobile parts, bicycle chain, machine parts.
- If students are to be allowed to use heat (flame or soldering iron) in their investigations, you might wish to enlist the aid of a parent to supervise the activities from a reasonable but attentive distance.

Debriefing

The following types of questions might be introduced during initial Debriefing sessions to promote pupils' reflections about the metal investigations. They should, however, be used selectively.

- What observations were you able to make about the metals in this center?
- In what ways were the metals different? How were they alike?
- In what ways might these metals be classified? What kinds of categories could you set up? Where would each piece of metal belong?
- What observations did you make about the strength of the different metals? What kinds of tests did you carry out to determine strength?
- What observations did you make about the hardness of the metals? What tests did you do to determine hardness?
- What observations did you make about the brittleness of the metals? How did you determine this?
- What do you suppose are some good uses for soft metals? for hard metals? for strong metals? What examples can you give to support your assumptions?

Extending

The investigative play with metals might be extended in one or more of the following ways:

1. By adding new materials to the center, for example, metal tools, children's toys made with metal, other metal cooking utensils, metal garden tools
2. By introducing new activity cards, for example:

   - Conduct some investigations to see how metals may be combined. Record your findings.
   - Conduct some investigations to see how metals can be changed. Record your findings.

3. By raising more challenging questions in later Debriefing sessions, for example:

   - How are metals made? What do you think? What are your ideas?
   - How do you make a (bicycle chain)? What do you think? What are your ideas?
   - Suppose you wanted to combine two different metals. What might happen? How could you do this? What are your ideas?
   - In what ways are metals important in your life? What are some important things you use that are made with metals? What do you suppose they could be made of instead? How would that be better or worse?
   - Can you imagine what life was like long, long ago, before metals were discovered? What are your ideas?

4. By raising questions that call for examination of some value issues related to the topic, for example:

   Sarah's mother has a set of large aluminum pots. She has just read in an article in the newspaper that aluminum pots may give off bits of aluminum in the cooking process, which would then be absorbed in the food that has been cooked in those pots. Mrs. Carlyle is obviously worried. She does not want to harm her family. Yet those pots are very expensive, and she does not have the money to just throw them away and buy a whole new set of pots.

   - What should Mrs. Carlyle do? Where do you stand on this issue?
   - Is it true about aluminum pots? How might you go about gathering information?
   - Is this something that we should just ignore? If it were true, what advice would you give Mrs. Carlyle?

Creating

Here are some examples of additional extending activities that might culminate the investigations in more creative ways:

1. Ask the children to work in pairs. Have them use some of the materials in the center to create a metal sculpture. Ask them to figure out some good ways to join the metal parts.
2. Ask the children to work in pairs. Have them use some of the materials in the center to build a small metal bridge. Then have them build a small wooden bridge from wood scraps. Compare the bridges.
3. Ask the children to work in pairs. Have them use scraps of metal to design a necklace or other jewelry.

Activity 59: Plastic

In this center the children carry out investigative play with a variety of plastic products to make observations about the properties of plastic. They are asked to record their findings.

Activity Card

> - Use the materials in this center to make some observations about plastic.
> - What differences do you see in the different pieces of plastic?
> - Conduct some investigations to find out about the differences in hardness, texture, smoothness, strength, weight, and flexibility.
> - Talk with each other about what you have found.
> - Then write about your findings.
>
> You may have some of your own ideas about investigating with these materials. Try your ideas and see what new discoveries you can make.

Materials

A variety of plastic products: plastic toys, dishes, cups, forks, spoons, jugs, beakers, other utensils; food containers; ballpoint pens; felt-tip pens; plastic baggies; plastic clothing, such as rainwear, boots, jackets; plastic tubing, such as hoses; garden tools, packing cases, storage cases; baby bathtub; buckets; pail; dish drain; comb; toothbrush; baby pants; egg cartons; Styrofoam cups, Styrofoam chips; hammer, string, nails, saw, scales, source of heat, scissors, staples, pieces of wood, heavy-duty rope, weights, sandpaper, glue

Thinking Operations Emphasized

Observing and recording; collecting, comparing, classifying, and interpreting data; examining assumptions; suggesting hypotheses; designing investigations; applying principles; making decisions; evaluating and criticizing; imagining and creating

Big Ideas

Plastics can be described by their different properties, such as color, weight, texture, flexibility, and strength. Most plastic is not biodegradable.

Notes to the Teacher

- Plastics can be found virtually everywhere. One quick tour around the school and your home should yield a more than adequate collection for this center. Children may also be encouraged to bring in samples of plastics from home. However, they should understand that the plastic may be damaged in the inquiry and they should not, therefore, expect to have the materials returned home intact.
- Some precautions about working with plastic:
  — If children are to be using a heat source to conduct their investigations with plastic, you may wish to enlist the aid of a parent to supervise the activities from a reasonable but attentive distance.
  — Make sure there is adequate ventilation; melting plastic may produce toxic fumes.
  — A few plastics (such as celluloid) are flammable; great care should be taken that such materials are not set aflame.

Debriefing

The following types of questions might be raised during Debriefing sessions to promote reflection about the properties of plastics. They should, however, be used selectively.

- What observations did you make about the plastic materials?
- In what ways were the plastic materials alike? How were they different?
- What observations did you make about hardness? stiffness? toughness? strength? smoothness? flexibility? color? how easily the plastic breaks or tears? how much weight it can hold?
- How might these plastic materials be classified? What kinds of categories could be set up? In what category would each piece belong?
- Some plastics break very easily. Others are very tough. How do you account for that? What are your ideas?

Extending

You may wish to extend the investigative play with plastics in one or more of the following ways:

1. By adding new plastic materials to the center
2. By adding new activity cards, for example:

   - Try to find out which plastic container is the best for packaging food. Conduct some investigations and record your findings.
   - Try to find out which plastic container is the most breakable. Conduct some investigations to determine this and record your findings.
   - Try to find out which plastics can hold the most weight. Conduct some investigations to find this out and record your findings.
   - What happens when you stretch plastic? Conduct some investigations to find this out and record your findings.
   - Compare some pieces of plastic with some pieces of metal. How are these materials alike? How are they different? Try to discover as many similarities and differences as you can.
   - What happens to plastic when we are finished using it? Where does it go? How does it get disposed of? Design some investigations to find this out and record your findings.

3. By raising more challenging questions in later Debriefing sessions, for example:

   - What, in your opinion, are some advantages of using plastic? What are some disadvantages? What work did you do in this center that helped you form those opinions?
   - What, in your opinion, are some properties of plastics that make it a valuable material? What work did you do in this center that helped you form that opinion?
   - How do you suppose plastics are made? What do you think?
   - In what ways do you use plastic products in your own life? Think of as many ways as you can.
   - How might these plastic products be classified? In which category would each item fit?
   - Can you imagine a time before plastics were invented? What did we use before we had these plastic products? What are your ideas?
   - How are plastics disposed of? How do you know this? Is this good? What are your opinions about it?
   - Is it better to use a plastic cup or a ceramic cup? What makes you think that is true? What examples can you give to support your ideas?

4. By raising questions that call for examination of some value issues related to the topic, for example:

Plastics are very useful in our lives. They are used to make all kinds of products, from tools to machinery to equipment to toys to office supplies. In many ways, plastics are an improvement over metals. They are cheaper, lighter, and easier to handle. In some instances, they are stronger. Yet all is not roses in the use of plastics. Plastic products are nonbiodegradable—that is, they do not decompose, so they stay with us, in our garbage, virtually forever. Some plastic products produce toxic wastes, which must then be disposed of in our environment.

- What are your views on the use of plastics and the environmental effects of their use? Where do you stand on these issues?

Creating

There are several ways in which the children may culminate their investigative play with plastics. Here are some activities that they might be invited to do:

1. Work with a friend. Design a mobile using only plastic products as weights. For this activity you will need several lengths of ¼-inch doweling or a wire hanger.
2. Work with a friend. Think together to invent a brand-new way of using plastic material.
3. Work with a friend. Design and build a plastic boat that will hold a 5-pound weight and remain afloat.

Activity 60: Garbage

In this center the children examine the contents of a garbage can and make observations about the nature and amount of waste material that is an adjunct to contemporary life. They are asked to record their findings.

Activity Card

- Use the materials in this center to make some studies of garbage.
- What observations can be made about this garbage?
- How could it be classified? Set up some categories and show where each item of garbage would belong.
- Record your findings.

You may have some other ideas for conducting investigations with the materials in this center. Try out your ideas and see what discoveries you can make.

Materials

Garbage (see "Notes to the Teacher)

Thinking Operations Emphasized

Observing and recording; collecting, comparing, classifying, and interpreting data; applying principles; designing investigations; examining assumptions; suggesting hypotheses; evaluating and criticizing; summarizing; making decisions; imagining and creating

Big Ideas

Waste material is a by-product of a highly technological society. Waste material takes up space and adds to pollution. Recycling waste is an important way to conserve resources and reduce pollution.

Notes to the Teacher

- The collection of garbage for this center should be selective. Garbage can be "cleaner" or "messier"—you might want to consider how far you'd like to go on that continuum. But whatever trash is to be studied, it should not contain anything that might be harmful for the children to handle, such as sharp pieces of glass, metals, or toxic materials, or waste matter that might cause other problems, such as hygienic or sanitary waste.
- The classroom garbage can or the school office garbage can might be good starting points.
- Selected garbage brought from home in a large plastic garbage bag may also be used, even though it is likely to cause some smirks from colleagues in the staff room.
- If wet garbage is to be included, you might wish to obtain disposable plastic gloves for the children to wear. These are available, in large-quantity packages, in drug or medical supply stores.
- You would definitely want to provide a supply of newspapers to spread out over the tables on which the garbage is to be studied.

Debriefing

Here are some questions that may advance pupils' thinking about these inquiries. They should, however, be used selectively.

- What observations did you make about this garbage? What observations did you make about the items found?
- In what ways might the items in the garbage be classified? What kinds of categories might be set up?

- If you were a visitor from another planet and had only this garbage to examine, what would it tell you about the people who lived here?
- Where does the smell of garbage come from? How do you explain it?
- What do you know about how garbage is collected? Where it is taken? What happens to it when it is dumped? What are your ideas?

Extending

The inquiries into garbage may be extended in several ways:

1. By introducing other garbage collections into the center and conducting analyses of their contents, for example, from the school office, from the local supermarket, from a nearby factory or business, from a nearby park or playground
2. By introducing new activity cards that reflect the additions to the center
3. By raising more challenging questions about garbage and questions that call for examination of some value issues related to the topic, for example:

   - We generally have some unpleasant feelings about garbage. Where do these come from? What are your ideas?
   - How are these feelings translated into the way we treat garbage in our own homes?
   - How are these feelings translated into the ways we think about the people who collect trash?
   - Where are the garbage dumps in our own community? What kinds of places are garbage dumps? What are your ideas? What examples can you give to support your assumptions?
   - Sometimes there is a lot of garbage littering the street or the playground. Why do you suppose people do this littering? What are your ideas about it?
   - What do you suppose might happen if all the garbage dumps became full? Where might we put the garbage then? What are your ideas?
   - Suppose a new law was passed requiring each family to get rid of its own garbage. What changes would this mean in your life? What kinds of actions might your family take?
   - Some people recycle some of their garbage. How is this done? Why would they do this? What are your ideas about it?
   - Sometimes, as we look at garbage, we see a lot of waste. What are your thoughts about this? What do you suppose this means?

Creating

The studies of trash may be culminated by having the students undertake one or more of the following activities:

1. Work with a friend. Plan an investigation to figure out how much garbage each of you produces in a single day. Record your findings.

2. Work with a friend. Plan an investigation to see what happens to the following types of garbage after a one-month period: an egg shell, a metal can, a plastic food container, a piece of bread, some potato skins, some scraps of paper, a plastic cup. Record your findings.
3. Work with a friend. Organize a program for your classroom that would collect paper for recycling. Plan an advertising campaign to persuade other pupils in the school about the reasons for contributing their trash to the recycling program.
4. Work with a friend. Conduct some inquiries to find out how much food is wasted during a period of one week in the school cafeteria. Think of some good ways to organize the data from your studies.

NOTES

1. American Association for the Advancement of Science, *Benchmarks for Science Literacy* (New York: Oxford, 1993).
2. *Ibid.*, p. xiii.
3. Schools Council Publications, *Minibeasts: A Unit for Teachers* (New York: Macdonald Educational, 1973), pp. 11–12.
4. *Ibid.*, pp. 22–26.
5. John Bird and Ed Catherall, *Fibres and Fabrics* (Milwaukee: Macdonald-Raintree, 1976), pp. 28–30.

Journey into the Unknown

BUYING YOUR TICKET

It is natural for teachers to want to feel safe, protected, and secure in what they do. It is also natural to feel trepidation, anxiety, and distrust when faced with the prospect of undertaking something so new and so very different that the very foundations of well-established teaching practices are likely to crumble and fall. When traditional methods and strategies give way, what lies ahead? What are some potential pitfalls? What bogeymen do we perceive to lie in wait? What prices may we have to pay?

We have worked with enough teachers over the years to know that teachers' concerns about implementing new programs are very real indeed. Teachers have been misled by notorious hustles and scams into adopting programs that claim more than they deliver. Programs have been parachuted into school districts by administrative fiat, and teachers have had neither a voice in the decision making nor adequate professional development with respect to classroom implementation. Programs have begun without adequate attention to identifying and dealing with their far-reaching implications. No wonder teachers are bruised; no wonder they are wary.

Now along come Wassermann and Ivany to say to teachers, "Here is yet another program." Why should you accept it? Why should you buy a ticket for *this* journey into the unknown?

In the first place, we have *not* said that you *should*. We have stated quite explicitly that such a journey is not for every teacher. We have asked you to examine what we have proposed, to look at the theory, the classroom activities, and the suggestions for implementation, and to make a choice. Such a choice, we feel, can only be made by you as you contemplate teaching science, and the choice will rest on your educational beliefs. Before buying your ticket, you must believe that the Play-Debrief-Replay model of teaching science is congruent with what you think should be happening in your classroom. You must share the beliefs about play, about children, about learning, about curriculum, about educational process—and especially about what you hope children will learn in science and in school. We do not try to "sell" you these beliefs; we are educators, not pitchmen (pitchpersons?). We say that if you share such beliefs, then as educators we may help you with their implementation in classroom practice. So the very first question you must put to yourself is whether you share our beliefs. Because effective implementation cannot occur if a teacher's beliefs are incongruent with proposed practice, we urge you to begin with such reflection before embarking on the journey. (See again the beliefs test in Chapter 2.)

Some of you may have already examined your beliefs and have affirmed, "Yes. This is for me. This is what I want in my classroom. But I have some concerns about what might happen if I try this new program." If you are one of these teachers, we urge you to read on.

A journey into the unknown is not just any trip into a tunnel of darkness. The trip may have a clearly set destination, in spite of the fact that we have never actually been there. So consider this trip a journey to successful implementation—a destination that allows you to move to learning goals in science that you deeply value. Yes, there may be hazards on the road. Yes, there may be dangerous grades and curves. Every journey has its rough moments, but we take them nevertheless because they are full of such wonders as to make the few rough moments a minor nuisance. We expect that once you have bought your ticket, you will find such wonders. And to give shape to some of the potential impediments, we have mapped out in the following section what may be some lingering concerns about implementation. We hope that such discussion will diminish the perceived risks and provide you with the additional support you need to get the program under way.

Some of these concerns relate to feelings of lack of personal confidence. Some are concerns about the "adequate covering of the curriculum." Some are about the way external judges—colleagues, administrators, parents—perceive your teaching performance. Some involve simple logistics; some are concerns about individual students. Whichever group they fall into, we hope that by flushing them out and exposing them to the light of intelligent examination, you will have yet further resources and grounding for your safe and productive journey.

PLAY-DEBRIEF-REPLAY: SOME TEACHER CONCERNS

"I don't know enough science. Can I still make it work?"

It's true that if you have been blessed with the background in biology and zoology of Gerald Durrell, the expertise in chemistry of Linus Pauling, and the wisdom in physics of Sir Isaac Newton himself, these would be valuable assets in carrying out the sciencing program. Not possessing such a fount of knowledge, however, does not automatically disqualify you for the job.

If you perceive teaching science as dispensing information about scientific "facts," then surely it would be imperative that you not only be able to dispense such information accurately and coherently but that you are able to answer questions intelligently as well. Such an approach to science teaching is entirely dependent on the teacher's background and knowledge base. In the elementary school, however, information about science presented to pupils too frequently conveys a wrong impression of the world of science, leading to mechanical memorizations of half-truths and the parroting of simplistic notions that supposedly represent scientific principles but are actually too complex for the pupils to comprehend (for example, "The feet turned into fins and it took about 100 years"). Even worse is the "message" being conveyed about science via such an approach—that science is a magic world where all the facts are known, or can be, if only to those strange men and women in white coats. Nowhere is the give-and-take of guessing, trial and error, and tentative ideas seen.

The approach to science teaching that we have advocated ("sciencing") is that of a laboratory. In a laboratory, inquiries are under way for which many answers are as yet unknown. We want to ensure that such unknowns are allowable, both for the teacher and for the students. When questions are raised for which you do not have answers, neither sciencing nor the walls of the school will come crashing to the ground. (Try it, you'll see.) In a laboratory, we may admit that we do not know, and we may then open the search for data. While it may be more convenient to "know the answers" than to have to search for them, the searching is much more in the spirit of science than is the knowing, and it is such openness to searching that the sciencing program seeks to cultivate.

It may not be easy, at first, to admit to students that you "do not know." Teachers may not be enthusiastic about exposing their human vulnerabilities to their pupils. We all want to be thought of as wise and wonderful, to be admired by students, to have their esteem. Yet esteem is probably more effectively won through honest, direct, and open searching. Certainly the very finest role-modeling we can offer is not that of an "all-knowing sage" but rather that of a fallible, open, nondefensive human teacher.

Will you be able to cope with such uncertainties? Will feelings of needing to know all the answers be one of your biggest obstacles? With practice you will become more comfortable in such a stance; in time you may actually grow to prefer and enjoy it. You may gain confidence if you strengthen your belief that you are, at the very least, doing an improved job of representing science to your pupils and that what you perceive to be your weakness is, in fact, your strength.

"Am I covering the curriculum?"

There are several questions implicit in this concern: "Will such an approach to teaching science allow me to cover adequately the body of knowledge assigned to my grade level? And what if all the science content does not get covered? Will my pupils be in deficit with respect to their scientific 'know-how' on year-end assessments?" In these questions lie perhaps the greatest perceived obstacles to implementation, and we want to make our strongest arguments here to provide such reassurance as you may still need.

First, the 60 activities contained in Chapter 4 do not constitute a curriculum for any grade level. They have been included because most scientific concepts in elementary school programs are embedded in these activities. The activities function to provide you with resources to choose from and, more important, to illustrate the type of treatment that *all* science topics for your grade level may undergo.

In that sense, should you be required, for example, to cover the topic of the greenhouse effect in your grade-level science program, the sciencing format should point the way in which such a topic may be "played out." If the need to cover the science curriculum of your grade level is either self-imposed or imposed by administrative fiat, our suggestions should help you put those concerns to rest.

But what about the amount of time required for this approach? Wouldn't such teaching preclude coverage of *all* the content for any grade level? Will the pupils be in deficit on year-end assessments or long-term acquisition of science learning?

Myths die hard in educational practice, and we tend to hold onto them long after research data has taught us otherwise. The press to "cover the curriculum," despite its documented shortcomings, continues to be embraced by teachers as the way to develop students' scientific literacy. In fact, such "covering" generally leads to overwhelming emphasis on didactic presentation of information, leaving students substantially short-changed in concept development and higher-order thinking skills, not to mention the short "mind life" of the acquired information.[1]

We are suggesting the kinds of science teaching that enables pupils to live scientifically knowledgeable and scientifically informed lives. We are advocating teaching practices that allow students to derive meanings from what they do in science. In these suggestions, we are supported by the advice given by leading scientists in *Benchmarks for Science Literacy*: "To ensure the scientific literacy of all students, the curricula must be changed to reduce the sheer amount of material covered."[2] Their proposal emphasizes the reduction of detail "that students are expected to retain" in favor of emphasis on ideas and thinking skills.[3]

It follows that sciencing will surely end up covering the curriculum more richly and intelligently than the "fact shoveling" that passes for science teaching in other programs. We suggest you try omitting some topics while covering others more fully, rather than attempting to cover everything at the expense of the large goals. It is the *results* that count, so don't take our word for it, but see them for yourself.

"The pupils may get the wrong answers. Shouldn't I correct their mistakes?"

The world of science is indeed a journey into the unknown, and that notion is, for many of us, scary. We like certainty. We are more comfortable with answers than we are with questions. We feel more secure with facts than we do with hypotheses. When we have arrived at a "truth," we relax physiologically and psychologically. Whew! Now we *know!* To be searching, questing, putting out tentative answers is often fraught with dissonance. Who likes dissonance?

There are physiological reasons that help to explain these feelings. Searching and inquiring, which are at the heart of sciencing, cause us to be cognitively "in motion." We pump adrenaline, which excites and stimulates us. When we have found answers, the search terminates. We are becalmed.

There are prices to pay as well as profits to reap in both states. For the price of the uncertainty, of journeying into the unknown, we benefit by the thrill of the search and the cognitive stimulation. For the benefit of calm, we pay the price of putting cognitive functioning to rest. We cannot have higher-order thinking without adrenaline. We cannot have a becalmed physiological state and still have the thrill of inquiry. They are mutually incompatible states.

Unhappily for the educative process, we have often chosen the path of calm, the embracing of the "right answers" model in almost all of our curriculum enterprises. School has become a place where right answers rule the day. They are prized out of all proportion to their real value, and schooling has become a means of acquiring as many "right answers" in as many subjects as is humanly possible. Such orientation is not only destructive of higher-order thinking, but it also fosters the hazardous impression that "right answers" are the keys to life worth living. The insidious underbelly of such an orientation, held in extreme, is seen in the dogmatic assertions of adults who see the world through the simpleminded, two-valued orientation of only rights and wrongs, goods and bads. Preposterous "answers" are proposed as solutions to the most complex and far-reaching problems.

In the real world, there are few, if any, right answers. Should I buy a house or stay in the apartment? Is it all right to go back to work and leave the baby at day care? Is eating at McDonald's healthy for you? Was Reagan a good president? How can I make time in my day for all the things that are important in my life? I want to have a baby but my husband is adamantly opposed; how do we deal with such an impasse? Should the judge have ruled in favor of the surrogate or adoptive mother of Baby M?

How do we help pupils to deal with the questions of life if we program them into believing that the profound questions of science have simple answers?

A right-answer orientation in the teaching of science presents other problems as well. As we have said earlier, it gives a false view of what science actually is. The world of science is best exemplified by the tentative answer, the hypothesis. As students learn this, they learn to respect and value the tentative answer, the world of ideas, the toleration of uncertainty, the role that testing plays in the determination of validity. In such a climate, where sciencing is being carried out, there is no problem when students propose "incorrect" answers, since these are to be tentatively held and tested often and will endure only as long as they are useful and not yet disproved or replaced by better ideas.

All this is not to say that a teacher *never* "corrects" a pupil within the context of sciencing. A student may be attempting procedures that are potentially harmful and that need "correction." There are times when the teacher must be very certain and directive. There are times when a pupil will ask for data and the best response is to give it. (Karen: "What's the name of an animal that has a pouch?" Teacher: "Kangaroo is one, Karen. Koalas also have pouches, and there may be others as well.") Yet when a pupil is sciencing—conducting inquiries and thinking—and he or she is asking about strategies, designs, or solutions, about what's right or wrong, good or bad, it is much more fruitful to use questioning strategies that put the ball back into the student's court and encourage the student to seek the ways for himself or herself. (Logan: "How can I find out which of these foods contains more sugar?" Teacher: "You may have to figure out some ways to test for sugar content. Think about it and talk it over with your group. Then tell me what you've come up with.") In such a response, the teacher nurtures hypothesis building and the testing of ideas. Thinking skills and the development of competence in searching for one's own answers are strengthened. Creativity is fostered and appreciated. In the sciencing program, these may be far more productive teaching strategies than "correcting mistakes."

In almost all of our own educational experiences, we have had deep and extensive exposure to "right-versus-wrong" answer programs. So deeply entrenched are these experiences within us that even when we try to behave in ways that allow our own pupils to think for themselves, an almost unconscious force makes us subtly direct pupils' thinking to the "correct" response. Often a teacher may not even be aware that such subtle directing of pupil thinking is taking place.

One of the ways in which you might monitor this behavior in yourself is by asking yourself if you do have specific information or ideas about what the students should be learning from the activity. If you do have a particular product goal in mind, the chances are high that you will fall back to response patterns of leading and directing pupils to those "answers." Growing in your own awareness of such "hidden agendas" is an important step in freeing yourself from such subtle direction.

Learning to allow pupils the time and the space to find their own ways, to find their own answers, and to correct their own mistakes is not an easily acquired teaching behavior. Yet working toward such behavior is much more likely to result in a far more intellectually healthful classroom climate, not to mention the harvests reaped from learning science, than could ever be gained from the narrow parameters of a right-or-wrong approach.

"It will be too noisy (messy, dangerous)."

If you have read this far in this book, it will not come as news to you that our idea of a classroom is definitely not one in which the children are always seated quietly, listening to the teacher talking and carrying out oral and written directive on command. Sciencing, as we are advocating it, will be more noisy, messy, and risky than what occurs in other programs. What's more, we believe that sciencing, like life, should be noisy, messy, and involve some risks. It's the *extent* to which each of these factors operates that you would wish to control, not the factor itself.

Play, which is the heart of sciencing, means children working and inquiring together. There should be some noise and mess—but you, the teacher, must decide how much of this may be acceptable. Noise and mess do not mean that children are unruly, discourteous, or disruptive. Noise and mess are purposeful by-products; they are never allowed to become chaotic and out of control. Keeping children's play within purposeful and productive boundaries is always the job of the good classroom manager (read: teacher), and specific suggestions for doing this were given in Chapter 2. When you are able to see that your sciencing program is exuberant *and* purposeful, you may find yourself more comfortable with the by-products of noise and mess. Noise, after all, comes from children learning together. Mess, after all, can and should be cleaned up in the aftermath.

With respect to danger, we should like to suggest that *in no circumstance* should any teacher allow activities that put a child's life in danger. Here again, it is up to the individual teacher to make certain choices, for only you can know the maturity and capability of the pupils involved and weigh the risks against the potential advantages. Should pupils be allowed to light matches? Should they handle hot liquids? Age and grade are not the best determinants to answer these questions. Your judgment is the best guide.

"Where will I get the science materials and equipment to do the job?"

You will find an extensive materials list in Chapter 2, "coded" to identify some of the possible sources of acquisition. Most of the materials are normally found in school storage rooms housing science equipment. Some of the materials are found in your own kitchen. Some need to be acquired through more imaginative accessing—parents, garage sales, flea markets, the butcher shop. In no way have we asked you to try to find materials that are hard to come by (dinosaur's bones), exotic (unicorn horns), expensive (Rolls-Royce engines), or idiosyncratic to particular geographical areas (Sasquatch footprints). All the materials listed are accessible to most teachers in one way or another. It is true, however, that you will have to go and get them. We cannot offer you any help other than to commiserate that the teacher's life is a hard one and full of extra duties. Only you can decide if yet another duty is worth your effort.

A materials list is also given for each of the 60 sciencing activities. A cursory glance at this section of each activity will quickly reveal not only what you need but also where you are likely to have to go for it and how much effort it will take. On your most burdensome days, it might be wiser to choose sciencing activities for which materials access is simple, saving ones that require more extensive accessing for lighter days.

If you begin collecting materials early in the year and can liberate a small corner of a storage closet for your treasures, you can eventually accumulate and maintain a sufficient supply of materials to last you throughout the year.

"What will the principal say?"

For many teachers, the specter of the principal as an uninvited classroom guest, shocked speechless by children moving about the room and . . . *talking!* (gasp!) . . . to each other, is unnerving enough to put them off trying anything new for a lifetime. Though we hate to admit it, we know there are such folk out there, occupying administrative positions and collecting large "educational leadership" salaries, who actually impede educational progress. There are, lamentably, principals whose primary concerns are quiet, clean, orderly classrooms where no one talks except the teacher and who still cling to archaic notions that such classroom environments foster healthful learning. If your principal is one of these, there is very little anyone can offer you in terms of advice, for the sciencing program is entirely antithetical to beliefs that generate such behaviors. We can only offer condolences, for in such a school climate, with such obstacles to face, professional growth and curriculum development are the enemy. All forces operate to maintain the status quo, and sciencing is not a program that would either be acceptable or be valued.

Nevertheless, there is a large group of school administrators whose very *raison d'être* is to promote healthful professional growth and curriculum development, administrators who are dedicated to children's learning and wish to be part of the growing movement to foster and nurture pupils' thinking skills. If your principal stands in this group, he or she wants to know certain things, for example: Are your pupils learning science in this program? Are they working purposefully and productively together? Are they learning to be responsible? Are they loving science? Are they learning problem-solving skills? Are their thinking skills improving? We think that all teachers should be able to demonstrate successfully to their school administrators that these learning gains are indeed occurring, and in doing so any potential question about methodology should be adequately addressed. It is more than likely that to show such learning gains in science may net you not only your principal's tacit approval but his or her explicit regard as well.

"What will the parents say?"

Most parents, like most good school administrators, want the very best for their children. Most parents want to know: Is my child learning? Is he or she happy at school? When parents see that their children are happy and learning, parents are usually content. Where the evidence is abundant, parents are usually delighted.

The Play-Debrief-Replay model of sciencing ought to satisfy and delight parents in several ways. It should clearly demonstrate their child's increasing familiarity with science, with respect to both knowledge and conceptual understanding. It should clearly reveal their child's enthusiasm for the subject. It should clearly demonstrate their child's increased capability as a thinker and as a responsible, cooperative learner. When such learning goals can be adequately demonstrated to parents, it seems reasonable that these very same parents will be among your strongest allies.

Some teachers who are getting ready to launch a new program think it a good idea to invite the parents in for an after-school tea. During this session the new program is described in a clearly articulated statement. Perhaps charts are made to give some visual punch to the oral presentation. Learning goals are also spelled out. "This program will help your child to become a better thinker, problem solver, cooperative learner, inquirer. This program will increase your child's understanding of scientific principles. This program will enable your child to become more responsible, more self-initiating, more independent" (see especially "Reporting to Parents" in Chapter 2). Faced with such important learning considerations, parents may be helped to understand how Play-Debrief-Replay may more successfully bring such goals into realization. When the parents understand, truly understand, the learning goals sought and how the means you are using to bring about these goals work, they are not very likely to criticize the program; instead, they will become its chief supporters.

"The custodian will object. I have to have my chairs in rows so that he may do the sweeping."

We have, from time to time, heard about the custodian who rules the school, the person whose standards of acceptable and unacceptable furniture arrangement set the stage for the kind of curriculum the teacher may carry out. Here again, we cannot offer advice on changing this person's behavior. We can only say that when the custodian's rules are dictating what a teacher may or may not do in that teacher's classroom, the school is in very big trouble.

"What about the child who . . .?"

In almost every in-service session we give to teachers there is a question raised about "that certain child who . . ." Variations on the theme include the child who behaves badly, who takes a much longer time to learn, who cannot concentrate, who is aggressive, who hurts other children and destroys property, who doesn't listen—the list goes on forever. There are many such children in many classrooms, and their needs are great. These are the children who are always a source of much pain to teachers and over whom teachers anguish and spend sleepless nights. In virtually every classroom there is at least "one child who . . ."

The Play-Debrief-Replay model of sciencing offers no panaceas for all those "children who . . ." The model promises no magic cures, no tricks to bring socially unacceptable behaviors into line. We can't even say to teachers that this model offers a quick route to success. Actually, quite the contrary is more likely to be the case; that is, it is a hard route to success. But the success is sweet.

In any program that respects the dignity of each pupil, in any program in which pupils are listened to and cared about, in any program that attends to and respects children's ideas, we can expect positive changes in children's behavior. The data for such claims exist in abundance in the literature on child growth and development, and these data are incontrovertible. No one claims that such changes come about overnight or that they are easily won. Behavioral change—especially in children operating out of grave social-emotional deficits—comes about only after much long-term, consistent application of the right conditions. But it does come, and when changes occur, they are likely to endure. Such claims cannot be made by the behaviorists or any other group that would seek to circumvent the long-term process by short-term "cures."

What do teachers do in the interim? How do teachers keep from going under, maintain balance, and keep the program alive in the face of children who manifest such behavioral symptoms? How do teachers cope until the signs of change can be seen?

Here's where we fail you. We do not know how. We only know that if you are able to "stick it out" and to apply the strategies advocated with consistency, changes will occur. This is an incomplete answer, and we wish we could offer more. As former classroom teachers ourselves, we are well aware of the toll such children take on the minds and hearts of teachers. Yet if we will not be there to help them, who will?

"Does sciencing always have to involve experiences with manipulative materials? Are there times when other types of experiences may be appropriate?"

No teacher is unaware of the role that experience plays in learning. We can have experiences of many kinds, and each one will contribute to our learning in its own special way. However, as most teachers realize, the quality of an experience is fundamentally connected to the quality of the learning. For example, one is not very likely to learn much about mollusks from experiencing Fred Cipher's delivery of the world's most boring lecture on the subject. From such an experience, one is more likely to learn indifference than anything remotely significant about this species of invertebrates. Yet a lecture on the same subject delivered by that charismatic zoologist Stephen Jay Gould would almost certainly result in a "better" experience and consequently a different kind of learning.

It has been said that experience is the best teacher, and we may learn from the

experiences of books, newspapers, television, theater, and film, as well as from the experience of lecture, group discussions, and debate. Experiences derived from reading, from viewing, and from listening may all be valuable, but it is the extent to which the learner *engages* in the experience that contributes substantively to a higher-quality result. That is why a boring lecture fails us while an exciting one "turns us on." In the case of the former, we retreat rather than engage. In the case of the latter, we engage with interest and enthusiasm. The same is true for experiences with other media— books, plays, films, discussions; they may contribute substantively to our overall learning only to the extent that we engage. Adrenaline must pump in order for the learning to "take effect."

That is why experience's reputation as the best teacher almost always refers to the experience of life. To spend two weeks in Venice is a far more engaging experience than seeing a film about Venice. Reading about Venice in a travel brochure is a less engaging experience than seeing a film. Each experience generates less adrenaline; each experience is therefore less substantive and offers less in terms of learning opportunity to the learner. If all your options were open, how would *you* choose to learn about Venice?

We have stressed the advantages of experience with manipulative materials as a way of promoting conceptual understanding in and enthusiasm for science. We have seen unmistakable evidence that suggests that when pupils have such primary, hands-on, real-life experiences, the learning that results is substantive. Playing with materials is very much like going to Venice. You are there, right in the thick of it. You are not learning secondhand or thirdhand, from someone else's experiences. (Is there anything more boring than listening to a friend tell at length about *her* experiences in Venice? Does it not lose a lot in the translation?) If hands-on primary experiences with manipulative materials produce such good results, we think they should be used whenever possible.

But it is not always possible to go to Venice. Sometimes we must settle for a different quality experience, acknowledging that it is second best. We may look at beautiful photographs, a film travelog, a travel book. Such experiences may also engage us and offer us much potential for learning and knowing.

In providing sciencing opportunities, we may not be lucky enough to get to see whales firsthand, to experience their beauty, their grace, their intelligence, their size, from real-life experience. But that does not mean we should not turn to second-best experiences—photographs, films, books—in our studies. We may not have a Museum of Natural History a subway ride away to experience the real-life adventure of gazing on the skeletal structure of a dinosaur. But we may study these incredible animals through secondary experiences. Being able to visit the seashore is a much more valuable experience than reading about it, but if books and films and photographs are all we can gather about the seashore in classrooms in Colorado or Nebraska, we must make as much of these second-best experiences as we can. Second best need not mean second rate, so how the experience is offered becomes an equally crucial factor in generating the kind of learning experience that will engage students.

Studying about whales, for example, can occur from "playing with ideas" substituting for actual real-life experience. Playing with ideas rather than with manipulatives also calls for students' active engagement in the learning experience. In organizing playing-with-ideas experiences, the same model is followed. The children play and are cognitively engaged, but they do so with pictures, diagrams, articles, and a variety of other audiovisual media. Instead of manipulating manually, they manipulate ideas. But in these "minds-on" tasks they must be actively engaged with the ideas in order for results to be effective.

In a playing-with-ideas experience, the teacher might ask that observations be made from photos of whales. Comparisons of whales and other animals might be asked for. Students might imagine what a whale's life is like. They could be asked to generate hypotheses about the intelligence of whales. They might be asked to reflect on whether we should bother to "save the whales" and why this species has value. Many thinking operations might be used to promote students' inquiry about whales, and it is understood that in such play students are sharing ideas and thoughts and recording their ideas from their examination of the audiovisual media. Thus play with manipulatives is translated into play with ideas and becomes a substitute, an alternative to the option of real-life experience.

Playing with ideas can offer great opportunities for students, but several caveats should be noted in its use:

1. Students must have the opportunity to engage in active, cognitive play with the ideas. This is more productively done in cooperative learning groups similar to those used in manipulative play.
2. The audiovisual materials (photos, slides, diagrams, reports, etc.) should be accompanied by some requirement to *think* at higher cognitive levels. Thinking opportunities must be included for playing with ideas to be an effective learning experience. (See Chapter 3 for more specific help with this.)
3. Debriefing the playing-with-ideas activity follows, in much the same fashion as in the original model.
4. Replay may consist of other opportunities to examine the materials with the same thinking focus and/or by extending the invitation to think into deeper and more substantive inquiries. The format of each of the sciencing activities should give ample clues as to how this can be done.
5. Playing with ideas is probably more effectively carried out with more mature students. A primary teacher would probably wish to give many, many opportunities with manipulatives before moving pupils into playing-with-ideas experiences.
6. Finally, playing with ideas should never be allowed to deteriorate into the "third-best" approach, that of lecturing to or telling students everything you think they ought to know about whales. Sitting and listening requires the least amount of engaging and higher-order thinking, so care must be taken lest "third best" becomes third rate.

"Most of my students are computer literate. Can technology be used to support the Play-Debrief-Replay model of teaching science?"

While we remain unabashedly committed to real-world, hands-on experience as fundamental to learning elementary science, technology can play an important role in furthering certain kinds of scientific inquiries, even in the Play-Debrief-Replay model. Recent developments in computer-assisted learning show real promise, particularly in the promotion of collaborative learning. Virtual classrooms have been constructed on the World Wide Web (www) and on other local learning networks, in which students from many classrooms, even across the continent, are brought together with teachers and with scientists, facilitating collaborative inquiry.

Think of an on-line notebook that can be accessed from school computers. In it, students can make comments, record observations, ask questions, and carry out other ways of gathering scientific data. Other members of the learning network—fellow students, teachers, or experts—can insert their own comments to create an ongoing dialogue. For example, inquiries on a topic or in a learning center such as "Pond Life" can include field trips that are debriefed on the Internet. Unusual specimens could be described by a pupil who might pose questions of indentification, with comments from a teacher or expert that would promote the next phase of inquiry.

Several working examples of such collaborative, multimedia networks already exist. Arguably, the leading current example of groupware technology is CSILE, developed at the Ontario Institute for Studies in Education by Bereiter and Scardamalia, and now commercialized by Apple Computer.[4] CSILE has been used successfully at all educational levels, from first grade to university. Another example of group interactive learning environments, CoVis Collaborabory Notebook is being used at the secondary-school level.[5] CoVis can actually be visited on its own www page at: http://www.covis.nwu.edu

Multimedia systems, using CD-roms, also provide ways of enhancing work in science that are compatible with this instructional model. For example, tools such as *Hypercard* and *Amazing Animation* produced by the Apple Multimedia Learning System provide students with opportunities to combine digital video with text, graphics, animations, and sounds of their own making, allowing them to create multimedia productions that reflect their understanding of any topic. After investigative play with materials, and extensive debriefing, such a system can be used as a follow-up in replay situations and will allow for demonstration of understanding of scientific principles and concepts. While these systems are more appropriate for the upper-intermediate grades, there is no doubt that, even as we write, software is being produced for younger children as well.

CONCLUSION

Mary D. has been running her sciencing program for her grade 3 class since January. It is mid-June and she is taking stock of where she has been, what she has done, and what she has seen occur in the responses of her students. She tells us that it takes until the third round at Play with the materials before the pupils really "take off" with their inquiries. She has observed that cooperative learning has become the norm and that pupils behave more responsibly and with greater independence. She has noticed considerably more language development, both in quantity and quality. (Fancy that! When pupils are allowed to talk with each other more, they become more skilled in their language usage. Why didn't we think of that before?) Children's writing skills are also noticeably improved, since they are asked to record their observations after every sciencing session. Writing "just flows." Children say they have made "lots of new friends" in this class, and Mary says "it's so much more fun for the kids."

"It's a great way to end the year," says Mary. "Laughing."

NOTES

1. American Association for the Advancement of Science, *Science for All Americans* (New York: Oxford, 1990).
2. American Association for the Advancement of Science, *Science for All Americans Summary* (New York: Oxford, 1989), p. 10.
3. *Ibid.*, p. 5.
4. Marlene Scardamalia & Carl Berieter, "Computer Support for Knowledge-Building Communities," *The Journal of the Learning Sciences*, 3(3), pp. 265–283.
5. Daniel Edelson & Kevin O'Neill, "The CoVis Collaboratory Notebook: Supporting Collaborative Scientific Enquiry," in *Proceedings of the 1994 National Educational Computing Conference* (Boston, MA: ISTE, 1994).

APPENDIX
Profiles of
Thinking-Related
Behaviors

Introduction to the Behavioral Profiles

A student's ability to think does not come about automatically. While we all have the "technical cognitive equipment" to learn these skills, thinking capabilities need to be developed over time through repeated practice and experience.

A student who has had insufficient experience in practicing the skills of higher-order thinking will reveal this limitation in certain specific patterns of behavior. Each of these behavior patterns reveals how the student has been impaired and is consequently unable to function cognitively in effective and productive ways.

The thinking-related behaviors included in this instrument come from the original research of Louis E. Raths, whose work on thinking theory is fully described in the text *Teaching for Thinking: Theory, Strategies and Activities for the Classroom.*

This instrument identifies eight behavioral profiles that are related to a student's lack of skill in higher-order thinking tasks. Properly used, the instrument should be helpful in identifying those students who are having difficulty with higher-order thinking processes, and should provide the teacher with data for directing classroom instruction.

Directions for Rating

Each profile identifies a type of behavioral pattern that is seen when a pupil's thinking capabilities have been insufficiently developed. Some students may exhibit one pattern in the extreme. Some pupils may exhibit two or more patterns in the extreme. Some pupils may exhibit one or more of these behaviors in a less acute way.

Using your class list, check each pupil against each of the behavioral descriptions. Decide if, in your best professional opinion, that student manifests the behavioral pattern (a) to a very great extent, (b) from time to time, (c) or rarely. Rate "to a very great extent" as 3, "from time to time" as 1, and "rarely" as 0. When you have rated each child, fill in the rating numbers on the Class Rating List on page 315.

1. The Profile of the Very Impulsive Student

These are children who typically act without thinking. When a problem or an activity is introduced, these children leap into action first. They don't seem to have a plan; nor have they considered alternatives. Their mode of operation is *doing*—and sitting down to think things out does not seem to be their strong suit.

Name of Pupil	To a Very Great Extent	From Time to Time	Rarely

Teacher's notes:

2. The Profile of the Overly Dependent Child

These are children who typically want help with practically everything they do. They find it hard to begin work without asking for help in getting started. Once they have begun, they request help again. Often these children say "I'm stuck," "What shall I do now," or "I don't know what I'm supposed to do." This insistent calling on you for help is a strong characteristic of the inability of these children to carry out tasks on their own. When your help is not available, they may just sit and do nothing until you can give it.

Name of Pupil	To a Very Great Extent	From Time to Time	Rarely

Teacher's notes:

3. The Profile of the Dogmatic Student

These are children who seem to have all the answers and are unyielding in their opinions that they are right. They reject discrepant data; their minds are made up and they stick to those positions regardless of the facts. We generally think of them as intemperate, unreasonable, and unyielding. "Don't confuse me with the facts; my mind is made up" is the basis on which they mainly operate.

Name of Pupil	To a Very Great Extent	From Time to Time	Rarely

Teacher's notes:

4. Profile of the Rigid, In-a-Rut Student

These are children who typically want to stick to doing things in the same old ways. They don't like new or different ways of doing things. The fact that a problem or task is new and calls for new procedures doesn't make a difference to them; these children try to force old methods onto new problems. When these don't work, they complain that the problem is at fault.

These children are most comfortable when carrying out routines. They learn lessons and formulas, but they have great difficulty in applying the principles they have learned to new situations.

Name of Pupil	To a Very Great Extent	From Time to Time	Rarely

Teacher's notes:

5. Profile of the Student Who Misses the Meaning

These are children who typically don't understand. They miss the point—of a lesson, an assignment, a story, a joke. They often say, "I don't get it." We think of them as children who don't listen and don't pay attention. Actually, they are not able to interpret data intelligently and to "sort out" cognitively what is happening. It is as if their ability to process data cognitively has been seriously impaired.

Name of Pupil	To a Very Great Extent	From Time to Time	Rarely

Teacher's notes:

6. Profile of the Student Who Cannot Connect Means with Ends

The outstanding characteristic of these children is their tendency to use means that are inconsistent with or inappropriate to the ends they seek to achieve. It is not that they don't have any ideas. These children have ideas about what they want to do, but the paths that they take to arrive at those goals may be silly, illogical, impractical, or even irrational. There seems to be an absence of cognitive awareness in choosing these paths. Their choices do not reveal a great deal of thinking about the connections between means and ends, but rather suggest an indiscriminate and random selection of means. Perhaps that accounts for the fact that these children's goals are seldom realized.

Name of Pupil	To a Very Great Extent	From Time to Time	Rarely

Teacher's notes:

7. Profile of the Underconfident Student

These are children who typically lack confidence in expressing their thoughts. During class or group discussions, they rarely volunteer information—not because they have nothing to say, but because they are fearful about exposing what they think to public scrutiny. At the end of a class, they might say privately to the teacher that they did have an idea, but were concerned about how it might be received by the group. Underconfident children are not necessarily shy; rather, they lack confidence in their ability to think and to expose their thoughts to possible criticism.

Name of Pupil	To a Very Great Extent	From Time to Time	Rarely

Teacher's notes:

8. Profile of the Antiintellectual Student

These are children who typically scorn thinking as a preferred mode of operation. They believe that action is more important and that thinking is for "eggheads." Classmates who they see as intellectually superior are held in contempt. When asked to do some thinking, these children reject the process. "It's the teacher's job to tell us what to do" is their position. These children see their function as *acting* rather than reflecting. They make strong value judgments about people who think and their judgments are clearly negative.

Name of Pupil	To a Very Great Extent	From Time to Time	Rarely

Teacher's notes:

CLASS RATING LIST

Name of Student	Behavioral Pattern(s) Exhibited	Rating

Index ———————————————————————

ABOUT THE AUTHORS

Selma Wassermann is a Professor in the Faculty of Education at Simon Fraser University, Vancouver, Canada. A recipient of the Excellence in Teaching Award at Simon Fraser Univcersity, she has published widely and is in much demand as a leader of teaching-for-thinking seminars and for case study teaching throughout the United States and Canada.

J. W. George Ivany is currently President of the University of Saskatchewan, Canada. Formerly he was a faculty member and Head of the Department of Science Education at Teachers College, Columbia University, and Dean of Education at Simon Fraser University in British Columbia. His interests include studies in elementary science education, especially with respect to encouraging young women into science and technology studies from an early age.